On the Scope and Truth of Theology

ON THE SCOPE
AND TRUTH OF
THEOLOGY

Theology as
Symbolic Engagement

ROBERT CUMMINGS NEVILLE

t&t clark

NEW YORK • LONDON

T & T Clark International, 80 Maiden Lane, Suite 704, New York, NY 10038
T & T Clark International, The Tower Building, 11 York Road, London SE1 7NX
T & T Clark International is a Continuum imprint.

Cover design: Ralph M. Chisholm

Library of Congress Cataloging-in-Publication Data

Neville, Robert C.
  On the scope and truth of theology : theology as symbolic engagement / Robert Cummings Neville.
      p. cm.
  Includes bibliographical references and index.
  ISBN 0-567-02722-8 (hardcover) — ISBN 0-567-02732-5 (pbk.)
  1. Theology. I. Title.
  BR118.N48 2006
  230.01—dc22

2006002261

Printed in the United States of America

06 07 08 09 10   10 9 8 7 6 5 4 3 2 1

For the members of
the Comparative Religious Ideas Project
1995–1999

CONTENTS

CHAPTER 6

CHAPTER 7

CHAPTER 8

Preface

The following pages lay out a particular project for theology conceived as symbolic engagement, inviting thinkers to join it. The project is self-conscious about its historical location, appropriate for our time and place, difficult to imagine in previous centuries, surely to be outdated in years hence, and not appropriate for many people now who think about theological topics. At the present moment, no functional theological public exists in which the project would be at home. Nevertheless, the pursuit of the project can help build such a public. In a strict sense, the project can never be completed, only continued or abandoned, because it aims to be indefinitely self-correcting.

A commitment to the ideal of truth in theology directs the aim at indefinite self-correction. Because of this commitment, the project involves deliberate efforts to make theology vulnerable to correction, requiring theology in each tradition to be open to learning from other traditions and from the arts, sciences, and practical disciplines. Yet there are many functions of theology as commonly practiced for which the ideal of truth is subordinated to other concerns. For instance, theology sometimes is most concerned to order a community, or to inspire difficult action in resistance or change, or to provide religious identity in an ambiguous or confusing situation. In these contexts, vulnerability to correction might be counterproductive. Theological wisdom might consist in cutting off criticisms from outside a given tradition or habit of thought. In tight times, the maintenance of a community against the distractions of the world might require turning inward and stopping the ears, rather than reaching out for correction. Theologies oriented around these concerns are not likely to be sympathetic to the project at hand that puts the pursuit of truth above all the rest, even though they acknowledge the importance of truth. So it should be said at the outset that the project proposed here is one among others, all appealing for legitimacy in one context or other. The last two chapters of this book will provide some justifications for this contextual pluralism in theology. These justifications will come, however, from conclusions about how best to approach the truth; other theological projects make their own justifications.

On the one hand, the argument here is *about* theology and takes place on a meta-level. On the other hand, the argument is tied to some first-order theological hypotheses, many of which appear for explicit consideration but others of which operate while not analyzed here. Part of the project's historical location is just this logical intermingling of first- and second-order claims. No theological project in any time or place could have it differently: first-order theological claims naturally lead to reflection on themselves, and second-order proposals operate within first-order frames of reference. The second-order proposals here reflect the plausibility conditions of our time, a point to which chapter 7 will return. The special virtue I claim for the project here is that it includes procedures for correcting the biases of both the first- and second-order hypotheses as they become evident.

The hallmark of this entire project is its effort to show theology to be hypothetical and to make it vulnerable to correction, a characteristic theme of classic pragmatism. If a theological claim is mistaken or misleading, this should be brought to attention as efficiently as possible. Therefore, theological claims should be formed for vulnerability, admitting that sometimes we cannot imagine, for the moment, how certain claims could be mistaken, partial, or misleading. Those claims that are most vulnerable, and yet are sustained and steadied through as many critical tests as can be devised, including criticism from all sides of a global public, have the greatest rational warrant. They can be supposed to be true until some new reason to doubt them is found. Good theology hunts up reasons to doubt in order to reinforce its preciously vulnerable ideas. The claim that theology is hypothetical is surprisingly complicated and will be discussed at many points in the chapters to follow. Some preliminary remarks here, however, might be helpful.

Some theologians, such as Wolfhart Pannenberg, can say that their whole religious tradition is a grand hypothesis, but to be probated only in the eschaton. Nothing much hangs on this sense of hypothesis, except perhaps a comely sense of modesty, because theology before the eschaton can be as authoritarian as it likes. Pannenberg himself is careful to relate his theology to philosophy and the sciences, though not much to other religions.

Theology as symbolic engagement seeks to make itself vulnerable to correction in a more moderate short run than Pannenberg's approach to theology as hypothesis.

A more cautious approach than Pannenberg's to religious traditions as hypotheses would be to say that theology can work confessionally within a tradition, solid in its commitment, yet understanding that the tradition itself is aimed to develop and test the best hypotheses. Much, though not all, of the current "science and religion" discussion is of this sort, with the "religion" in question being a fairly conservative form of Christian theology and its hypothetical character being efforts to express theological claims in ways congenial to science. The drawback to this approach is that it is unlikely to look closely and sympathetically at other religions and secular cultures that might present critical arguments for assessing its own theological suppositions and that might have dimensions of religious truth simply missing from its home tradition.[1] Not much is gained by treating a whole tradition as a hypothetical project if its internal parts are not put in a position to learn from the outside. Theology as symbolic engagement seeks to be vulnerable through interaction with as many domains of reality that might correct it.

On the other hand, individual theological assertions need not be treated as so immediately hypothetical that each one needs to be tested on the spot. Rather, theological assertions hang together in arguments and theories, and it is often the whole, or large chunks of the whole, that can be turned to a vulnerable testing. Chapters 5–8 will detail some of the natural points of contact for assessing the vulnerable truth of theology.

The specific language of hypothesis in this project comes from Charles S. Peirce's claim that all thought is fallible. That it is fallible does not mean that it is all false, nor does it mean that it should not largely be taken for granted. Its fallibility, rather, consists in the fact that any given part of theological thinking is subject to being proved false or misguided as new evidence or perspectives for criticism are found. One of the most important tasks in theology is to devise ways of testing, correcting, or affirming claims that we had been unable to question before. This book will argue that "system" in theology is not merely correlating assertions, but rather building perspectives from which we can render the various parts of theology vulnerable for assessment.

The language of hypothesis here has much obvious resonance with modern science. Two qualifications of this resonance should be pointed out, however. First, theologians who are rightly irritated by a kind of

---

1. See the discussion of the Divine Action Project in chap. 5.

Enlightenment skepticism about inherited theological ideas are likely to think the emphasis on "testing hypotheses" is too negative. Rather, there should be an equal emphasis on the work of creative imagination in forming hypotheses in the first place. This creative emphasis is surely important in science as well as in theology, particularly in light of the general distinction between "normal science," which works within established paradigms and scientific programs, and "revolutionary science," which presents new paradigms and programs that in the long run replace the old ones without falsifying them from within, so to speak.[2] In religion, imagination runs from the formulation of revelations and primal witnesses to the construction of elaborate theological systems. The creativity involved in this should not be underestimated, nor hamstrung by premature testing. In many respects, testing theological hypotheses is not as difficult as imagining and formulating them in the first place.

Second, theology in the sense of this project is like philosophy rather than science in that it calls for steady examination of assumptions, premises, and principles as well as the formulation and probation of hypotheses following from them. In this, theology as symbolic engagement is a bit like "permanently revolutionary science." The examination of assumptions is difficult, however, and even the most vulnerable hypothetical theology goes for long stretches simply assuming its assumptions. Yet if it is properly systematic, theology will come around eventually to working backward with carefully cultivated vulnerability.

This volume has systematic connections with others. I conceive it as the first of four volumes of a systematic theology, called *Theology as Symbolic Engagement*, drawing upon world religions and the arts, critical practices, and sciences that have something to contribute. This volume introduces the general conception of theology as symbolic engagement. The second volume is to deal with ultimacy as such, the third with the religious dimensions of human predicaments, and the fourth with how to live religiously in the face of ultimacy. The present volume also relates to some of my previous work in which I have developed at length points that are only reviewed here. Rather than citing my previous work in every relevant instance, I will have a longish footnote at the beginning of major discussions that explains where and how I have dealt with the topic in more detail.

---

2. The distinction was made famous by Thomas Kuhn and, although much critical, sophisticated discussion has flowed from his work, it has been established as a good working distinction. See also the work of Stephen Toulmin and Van Harvey.

I can indicate the particularity of theology as symbolic engagement in a prefatory way with a personal reflection on a near theological neighbor and friend, Stanley Hauerwas. His Gifford Lectures, *With the Grain of the Universe: The Church's Witness and Natural Theology*, is a magisterial presentation of a conception of theology apparently in almost diametrical opposition to my own. This opposition exists despite the facts that we are of the same country, about the same age, and have shared much of the same paideia. We came to maturity in the American theological wars of the neo-orthodox Barthians with the differently neo-orthodox Tillichians.

With the Grain of the Universe studies three major thinkers (Gifford lecturers) of the twentieth century: William James, Reinhold Niebuhr, and Karl Barth. My own philosophic roots are in pragmatism, more Peirce and Dewey than James, but in the same league. Hauerwas reads Niebuhr as a liberal Protestant anxious to reconstruct classical Christian ideas for a late-modern world (in opposition to an older liberal Protestantism that abandoned them). My own theological program is similar, though I was influenced in this more by Paul Tillich than by Niebuhr; Hauerwas associates Tillich and Niebuhr.[3] The great hero of Hauerwas's account is Karl Barth, whom I came to know through our common teachers Hans Frei and George Lindbeck.

The opposition between Hauerwas's theology and my own does not consist in my defending James and Niebuhr, whom he attacks, and criticizing his hero Barth, although I am more sympathetic than he to the two Americans and less sympathetic to Barth. The opposition consists rather in serious differences over (1) theological method (witness in his case, inquiry in mine); (2) the theological public (speaking from and for the Christian community with an invitation to others in his case, making a case to a global public in mine); and (3) resources for Christian theology (mainly the Bible and its interpretive witnesses for him, the Bible and tradition among a broad array of learned discourses for me, including the theologies of other religions, the sciences, the imaginative arts, and normative disciplines such as the law). The result of these differences is that theology for Hauerwas is the assertion and interpretation of *Christian identity*, subject to the limitations of whatever is supposed to define Christian identity (his European orientation regarding identity is a curiosity from the perspectives

---

3. *With the Grain of the Universe: The Church's Witness and Natural Theology*, p. 138. Hauerwas does not draw out the association, and surely there are many differences between Tillich and Niebuhr. Hauerwas wants to emphasize the American character of Niebuhr in continuity with William James, whereas Tillich was thoroughly European. Nevertheless, in America, Tillich was taken up enthusiastically within the Methodist theological world as the philosophical idealism of Boston Personalism gradually collapsed. Tillich's intellectual mysticism dovetailed neatly with Personalism's intellectual pietism.

of emerging African and Asian Christianity). Theology for me is the search for *truth* in theological matters in respect to which Christian identity has been growing, if not changing, since the inception of the Christian movement. Hauerwas's theological project is excellent for those for whom a steady Christian identity is a great need, and it is pragmatically extremely useful when Christians need to stand for something in the face of opposition; my theological project can get in the way of firm action if applied at the wrong time, and it is unnerving to those needing a steady identity. Theology as symbolic engagement, however, is far more sensitive to sorting the better from the worse theological claims, to encouraging learning that might show up one's limitations, to cultivating intellectual curiosity, daring, and humility, and to worshipping the ultimate with understanding and love of truth; Hauerwas's theology is impatient with these things.

Those differences acknowledged in the irenic interest of the "coincidence of opposites," I should say that Hauerwas's bullish Christian theology is in accord with mine insofar as its principal topic is God. We agree that concerns for the human condition and how to live in the world with proper "spirituality" should be controlled by the theology of God. We are in further agreement that the "cash value" of theology, to use James's phrase, is in how we live, including ethical actions about the great issues of the day. I am nearly always in agreement with Hauerwas's pacifism; this is to say, pacifism is nearly always (but not entirely always) right.

Nevertheless, the reasons for my theological oppositions to Hauerwas are the following, stated here in bullet form and developed in repeated buckshot discussions in the chapters of this book.

- Because any theological witness needs interpretation, and interpretations need to cope with arbitrariness, witness cannot be viewed as the infallible beginning of theology but at best as an orienting stimulus and tentative conclusion. Hence, theology is inquiry primarily, and witness only as interpreted. This is compatible with the valid point that theology sometimes takes place within the practice of a community that is itself continuously based on, and expressive of, witness. Bringing theology to that practice puts a humbling spotlight on the fallibility of the community's understanding of its witness.

- Because the function of reason, as Whitehead said in his book by that name, is to guide life, and it guides life better the more it understands what is true, the function of theology as rational reflection about ultimate matters is to guide life, especially the religious life. Theology is an ultimately practical discipline, both in its goals and in its tests. While there might be immediate practical needs that justify abandoning the search for truth in favor of acting now on the basis of what one believes, in the not-so-long run it will be more practical to keep pressing for truth rather than practicing theology in ways that subvert inquiry. Theology as symbolic engagement claims that the loving pursuit of truth is the most practical approach to the details of living before the ultimate.

- Because theology aims primarily to be true, it needs to be vulnerable to correction by anyone who has a point to make, and therefore must be global and "omni-disciplinary" in its public. Although the connection between proper vulnerability to correction and the constitution of a public is complex, its consequence for theological orientation is great. Hauerwas and people in his line can use the argument that a Christian theologian who disagrees with them is not really a Christian because he or she does not conform to their canon of orthodox Christian identity. They can in fact leave the merits of their opponent's case untouched, delegitimating rather than refuting it. Hauerwas's objections to James and Niebuhr are of this sort. I could never argue that way. I would have to make a case for why another theologian is wrong: if the case fails, then Christian identity should be altered to include that position and I should abandon my previous opposition. Christian identity, I argue, should follow the truth rather than substitute self-proclamation of some identity for criteria of truth.

- Because the importance of truth is so great for salvation and related religious ends, theology needs to learn from whatever sources are available. Hence, it should attend to many that go beyond the Christian Bible. From my perspective, therefore, Hauerwas's program of narrowing down on Christian witness looks like one more defensive reaction to the collapse of Christendom rather than the creative reassertion of Christian theology he believes it to be. Theology, if it were truly confident, would move into a global public. Christianity will be transformed by this move, as it has so often before been transformed by similar moves.

- Indeed, theology as symbolic engagement should be open to theologians from any religious tradition or community, not only Christians. The matter of "belonging" to a religious tradition while engaging in theology that takes one outside that tradition is very complex and will be discussed below. Obviously, religious traditions change from their theological encounters with conditions new to them. The invitation to theologians from other traditions to engage in theology with a Christian such as myself needs to be seen as a particular, non-neutral theological proposal, whose merits need to be assessed. Nevertheless, an important element of theology as symbolic engagement is that each tradition, Christianity in Hauerwas's and my cases, needs to learn from the fact that it is an "other religion" from the standpoint of those others. To learn that kind of thing requires the development of some elements of language not native to any of the traditions that arises from their dialogue. The importance of this dialogue is a counterweight to the emphasis on witness that appears in most other religions as well as in Christianity.

- Stated starkly, my opposition to Hauerwas's theological program is to affirm a naturalistic philosophical theology in contrast to his witness-supernaturalism.[4] In contrast to his seemingly confident assumptions about Christian identity, I believe that such identity is vulnerable to inquiry and should be stated in definitive theological form at the end of inquiry, which of course never ends finally. In contrast to his view that theology is the work of Christian intellectuals, I say that theology is the work of people interested in the topic. Christian life comes from putting on Christ and then attempting to understand what those garments are. Not all Christians need to be serious theologians. For Christian theologians, theology is somewhat independent of the insistently lived Christian life that has to make do with unfinished theology, even though the long-run criteria for judging a theology lie in living it out.

Christian theology has been systematically difficult from the beginning. On the one hand, it rightly moves with an impulse to witness to the people, events, and faith that initiated and subsequently quickened the Christian movement. Witness is not easy or innocent, as the Greek word for it, "martyr," indicates. Jesus, then Stephen, James, Peter, Paul, and other apostles,

---

4. These phrases will be defined in detail in what follows. Insofar as they are defined by affinities, my naturalistic philosophical theology arises from the "mediating" theological tradition of the nineteenth century and is much influenced by classical pragmatism, especially that of Peirce and Dewey. Contrary to many naturalists, I do not reject supernatural symbols as long as they are "broken," as Tillich called symbols that are shown to be not literally true; indeed, part of my project is to rehabilitate those symbols for contemporary life. Hauerwas's "witness-supernaturalism" comes from Barth's theory of revelation that employs supernatural symbols without "breaking" them or seeking a "second naivete."

and then centuries of other martyrs witnessed to the faith in a bewildering variety of trying circumstances. The lives (and deaths) of these witnesses lie at the center of the formation of Christian practices and communities, not the only determining factors, to be sure, but central ones. Christian theology moves with an impulse to reflect on, to understand, and to draw out the implications of these witnesses, witnessing itself in the process. Stanley Hauerwas's *With the Grain of the Universe* is a magnificent expression of this theological move.

On the other hand, Christian theology also moves with an impulse to know the truth come what may. Whereas the impulse to witness is drawn to stories, the impulse to truth can be suspicious of the bias in stories and is drawn instead to larger contexts, theoretical constructions, and philosophical debate as ways to be vulnerable to correction. Whereas the impulse to witness seeks a public that accepts the witness, the impulse to truth seeks a potentially universal public that can appreciate and correct the daring and steadiness of theological positions that come from unfettered imagination and cumulative corrections. Paul Tillich, Karl Rahner, and perhaps John Zizioulis are recent virtuosi at this theological impulse.

The two impulses are not mutually exclusive. In fact, each requires the other in various ways. Nevertheless, they are extremely difficult to reconcile, and too often ritualized patterns of mutual rejection harden the discourse. Theologians in the thrall of the impulse to witness seem mesmerized by the question of religious identity and often jump to dismiss those who disagree with them as not Christians. Dismissal is not theological refutation but rather delegitimation, and its success depends on power. The influence in America of the witness-oriented theologian Karl Barth during the last half of the twentieth century has been to delegitimate more liberal theologians, often driving them from seminaries into religious studies departments. The pattern of rejection for theologians in the thrall of truth has been to reduce the witnesses and objects of witness to instances of larger theoretical categories in the social sciences and philosophy. If Christians have their martyrs, so do Jews, Muslims, Buddhists, Hindus, Confucians, neo-pagans, and shamans. The religiously compelling character of the witness is muted, lost, or even ridiculed. The development of religious studies departments in which religious witness and practice are "explained" sometimes has given rise to downright hostility and contempt toward religion, not that liberal Christian or Jewish theologians in those departments often go that far. Given the great difficulty of theology, it ought to be imperative to integrate these two impulses and inoculate them against their too-typical extremes. The four loci of theological truth introduced in chapter 1 provide a scheme for attempting that integration.

The more vital impulse, better in the long run, is plainly to claim that Christianity bears theological truth and argue to show what this is, how, and why. Jews, Muslims, Buddhists, Hindus, Confucians, and Daoists can do the same with regard to their theological traditions. Once the discussion reaches a working global public, theology is no longer Christian theology, or Buddhist or Islamic theology, just theology inclusive of all these. This global discussion can consider what truth is revealed in the Christian witness, the Buddha's dharma, and the revelations to Muhammad. This is the better strategy, I shall argue, for purifying and vivifying the Christian witness in saving ways, as it would do also for the witnesses of the other faiths.

My strategy cannot work, however, if the primary Christian witness (or the witnesses of other faiths) is merely subsumed into higher categories as species under genera. That subsuming move loses the power of the witness, its imaginative ground and the genius of its fundamental symbols, to move people to faith and practice. No martyr would die for an instance of the category of avatar. Essential to the program I recommend, therefore, is to treat the primary symbols of the faith in a way that makes them preach, and also to provide an account of how the symbols do that. Theology without the witness cannot get at the truth of the elementary theological topics—God, the human condition, and how to live in light of ultimacy. It can have some truth about the nature of religion, perhaps, but not about the ultimate topics. Normative theology cannot address the question of truth without the witnesses. These should not be construed positivistically; the witnesses cannot be expressed truthfully without the other levels of theological intentionality, including subsuming theories. All this illustrates the point that theology is very complicated, which is not new news. Theology as symbolic engagement is a project to sort this out.

This volume is dedicated to the members of the Comparative Religious Ideas Project who met collaboratively for four years, representing diverse disciplines and religious traditions, to discuss and write about the human condition, ultimate realities, and religious truth, rediscussing and rewriting until all the arguments we could think of were made and embraced in response.[5] Peter L. Berger and John H. Berthrong were my co-directors of the project, and Wesley J. Wildman was the recorder and my co-author for much of the publication; we four were "generalists" representing sociology

5. The publications reporting the results of the Comparative Religious Ideas Project are *The Human Condition*, *Ultimate Realities*, and *Religious Truth*, listed in the bibliography under my name as editor.

of knowledge, history of religions, theology, and philosophy. The specialists in the religious traditions compared were Francis X. Clooney, S.J. (Hinduism), Malcolm David Eckel (Buddhism), Paula Fredriksen (Christianity), S. Nomanul Haq (Islam), Livia Kohn (Chinese religion), and Anthony J. Saldarini (Judaism). Graduate students were essential participants in the collaboration, aiding the specialists and participating in the discussions, sometimes functioning as authors. They included Christopher Allen, Joseph Kanofsky, James E. Miller, Hugh Nicholson, Tina Shepardson, Celeste Sullivan, and John J. Thatamanil. Susan Only was the project administrator, and Mark Grear Mann and Raymond Bouchard helped bring the project's volumes to publication. Graduate students also helped prepare bibliographies for the publications, including Marylu Bunting, John Darling, Greg Farr, Andrew Irvine, He Xiang, Matt McLaughlin, David McMahon, Glenn Messer, and Kirk Wulf. The project benefited from distinguished outside advisors who met with us from time to time, commenting on the collaboration. These included Anne Birdwhistell, Jose Cabezon, Julia Ching, Jordan Pearlson, Arvind Sharma, Jonathan Z. Smith, Max Stackhouse, Tu Weiming, and Lee Yearley. I learned different things from each of these people, and together they contributed to a truly remarkable collaborative comparative project that I take to be a foretaste of a genuine global theological public.

Because this book draws upon everything I have written over a long career, its intellectual debts are too numerous to mention with any thoroughness. I have already alluded to my teachers, Hans Frei and George Lindbeck, to whom I am grateful; George Lindbeck has remained my teacher and conversation partner to this day. Thanks also to other teachers, including Robert S. Brumbaugh, Richard Bernstein, Rulon Welles, F. S. C. Northrop, Brand Blanshard, Paul Weiss, and most especially John E. Smith, who set my intellectual orientation for life. William Wiebenga, Carl Vaught, and Stephen Erickson were fellow graduate students and many of the positions developed in this book were first expressed in our conversations. One learns more from students than one teaches them, and I am especially indebted to Elizabeth M. Kraus, Steve Odin, Warren Frisina, Lawrence Cahoone, Elizabeth Baeten, James E. Miller, and John J. Thatamanil. Jay Schulkin began as a student and has been a deep friend in intellectual as well as comradely ways for thirty years. The American Theological Society, the Boston Theological Institute, and the New Haven Theological Discussion Group have discussed central ideas of this volume, and the current text is greatly indebted to those discussions. A penultimate draft of the volume was read, with very helpful comments, by Nathaniel Barrett, John Berthrong, Brandon Daniel-Hughes, Peter Heltzel, Kirk Wegter-McNelly, and Amos Yong; I am deeply grateful for their help. Wesley J. Wildman is the friend and intellectual partner most associated with the topic of this book. He read the manuscript with extraordinary care and critical rigor and offered systematic comments on nearly every page that affected its whole tone. Some of my debt to him is evident in the discussions of his work in the text. Often I have taken his felicitous suggestions for word changes or points to be developed without explicit credit. He reminded me again and again that I simplify opponents' arguments to the point of caricature, which is exactly what theology of symbolic engagement with an open public is not supposed to do. On four points of profound disagreement he has forced me to greater clarity. First, he takes Kant's critique of metaphysics more seriously than I do (though Wildman himself practices metaphysics in the sense I defend), and so I have spelled out my grounds for rejecting that critique. Second, he believes that the negative effects of science result from scientism, not real science, and I have had to spell out repeatedly that I believe that it is real science that lies behind the cultural project of making scientific knowing paradigmatic for all objective knowing, even if scientists qua scientists do not push that cultural project. Third, he insists on the legitimacy of many theological projects that are hostile to making themselves vulnerable to correction as theology as symbolic engagement urges. They subordinate the purpose of seeking the truth in theological matters to purposes of articulating and defending religious identity or seeking and maintaining social cohesion. I accept these as sometimes legitimate purposes in the short run, but have had to argue repeatedly that they are dangerous in the long run if not subjected to the vulnerability of truthseeking. Fourth, Wildman objects to my claim that the problem of the one and the many is essential to metaphysics and is the avenue for dealing with intelligibility per se. He argues instead that the problem of the one and the many can be limited to local instances, with local interpretations of intelligibility; therefore, a metaphysical system that privileges some other basic principle or concern and fails to deal with the problem of the one and the many is legitimate for him, and the issue is a matter of choice. I have had to argue in return that the intelligibility of saying there are local manifestations of the problem of the one and the many supposes a more generic framing of the problem at the metaphysical level. This manuscript is greatly improved over its previous version by his detailed arguments. We discover what we really think, and why, in these careful arguments, and have come to be patient with each other's impatiences.

The text and footnotes of this book cite books and articles by titles. The full publication information is given in the bibliography.

Milton, Massachusetts
March 2005

CHAPTER 1

Approaches to Theology

—⁓ℳ⁓—

Theology is reflection on ultimacy or ultimate matters, embracing things that are ultimate and the ultimate dimensions of things that are not. We will see the value of this vague definition in the long argument to follow that makes its elements specific and displays why theology is so interesting, exciting, compelling, and urgent. Theology discerns, articulates, systematizes, and guides practice with regard to what is ultimately important and valuable. At least, theology has always attempted to do this and is called to do so now.

In this book I lay out and defend the complex hypothesis that theology as reflection on ultimacy is best understood as *symbolic engagement*. The conception of theology as symbolic engagement shows how theology can be normative, that is, true or false about ultimate matters, and not merely descriptive of what people believe about them. The general thesis of the "symbolic engagement hypothesis" is that reflection on ultimate matters takes place by means of symbols through which ultimacy is engaged and thereby interpreted.

According to the hypothesis, interpretation in general engages reality by symbols in at least four modes of symbolic engagement. The analysis of the four modes of symbolic engagement in theological topics constitutes the argument structure of this book. To use shorthand labels for very complex matters, the four modes of symbolic engagement are (1) imagination, (2) critical assertion, (3) dialectical systematic theorizing, and (4) practical reason or symbolic interpretations guiding religious and other practice. Interpretations in each of these modes allow being true or false, and interpretations in the second, third, and fourth modes can assess the claims to truth. Theology as reflection on ultimate matters is concerned with the truth of symbolic engagements in all modes, and critical theological concerns for truth are raised in the modes of assertion, system, and practical reason.

Any given theological interpretation might involve one or more of the modes of symbolic engagement, blending them in various ways. Nevertheless, as I will sketch out in chapter 2 and detail subsequently, a predominant emphasis of each of these modes defines a specialized locus of theological reflection. Each locus has its own concerns, norms, and kinds of truth. To thinkers neglecting a view of the whole, each might seem to define a self-standing kind of theology. These loci of theology, to state the matter in a preliminary way, include: (1) primary revelations and witnesses, in which imagination is predominant; (2) articulated teachings, doctrines, and claims typically associated with theology, including the cases made for them, in which critical assertion is predominant; (3) systematic theologies, worldviews, and theories of religion adumbrated by scientists and secular scholars as well as religious thinkers, in which theoretical systematizing is predominant; and (4) symbolically directed spiritual exercises, liturgies, communal practices, personal lives, ritualized wisdom, and informed leadership as these are shaped by and in turn test all the others, in which practical reason is predominant. Theology as symbolic engagement interprets ultimate matters in all of these loci, and in their interconnections.

Whereas most religious thinkers want their claims to be *true* in some sense, vast disagreement exists across cultures about the *scope* of theology. Is theology almost exclusively reflection on scripture, as many Vedantist and Protestant Reformation theologians say? Does it include the evolution of traditions, authoritative pronouncements of officials or religious bodies, appeals to firsthand experience, reflections from other religions, intellectual tools from the secular world, insights from the arts, literature, and sciences? What are its genres and modes of thought?

The question of truth in theology is directly related to the question of scope. The scope of theology consists of all the things from which it might learn: its resources, including all those positions that might give it correction. In the long run, the scope of theology determines the public to which theology is accountable in some sense or other. The conception of a theological public is a central topic for the general hypothesis about symbolic engagement. The conception has three nested elements. The first, the "audience element," is that a theology's public consists of those it intends to address, with the institutionalized language that makes that address possible; this element will be discussed in the last section of this chapter. The second or "dialogue element" is that theology's public consists of all those religions, disciplines, and points of view that might be resources and corrections for theology. In this sense, theology has many publics, connections with which are made by various languages resulting from many dialogues. Chapters 5 and 6 explore this element. The third or "assessment element" is that theology's public consists of all of social, intellectual, and spiritual life that collectively tests a theology. In this sense, a theology is tested by the living of it, and the public to which theology is accountable for testing is the whole of human civilization as this can be interpreted as probating theology. Chapter 8 makes this assessment point. The fourth or "practical element" is that theology's public consists of all of life that needs to be guided by theology, for which theology is a certain practical reason relative to ultimate matters. The contours of the practical element of the public have to do with how intelligence can be brought to ultimacy in human life. Chapter 7 argues this case. The argument shall be that only insofar as theology is practically embodied in life as its reflective guide in ultimate matters can theology be tested in a public with an assessment element. Audience, dialogues, assessment, and practical elements are obviously intertwined in theology's public. I shall argue that, in the end, the audience of theology is not a limited community but the whole of life that it might guide and by which it is assessed. Each element provides a sense in which theology is accountable to its public. The scope of theology is directly relevant to the dialogical element of the public, because it consists of all those things from which theology might learn and be corrected.

Theology needs to make its case in each and all of the loci. For some thinkers, a case might be little more than citing scriptural warrant, or historical precedent, or consensus of a community. For most theologians from any tradition, however, the scope of theology is a complicated network of diverse appeals, of reflections on reflections, of methodological considerations, and of philosophical considerations about the nature of theology itself. To make a successful case for its truth, a theology needs to address to the extent feasible all elements within its scope in appropriate ways. Its public, to which it is accountable both for making its case dialogically and in assessing ways, and for offering practical guidance, is as complicated as the whole of its scope.

This book argues that theology cannot make a stable case for its truth unless its scope includes a global public of all religious traditions with which it might interact, and these as brought into dialogue with secular

thought. Moreover, theology needs to learn from the expressions of ultimate matters in the arts and imaginative literature, the natural and social
sciences, and practical normative disciplines such as law and economics.
For theology in the long run needs to be vulnerable to anything that might
correct its biases, errors, or omissions concerning ultimate matters. Not to
be so vulnerable is to have a shaky case for truth. Practical emergency might
justify postponement of vulnerability, but only on the supposition that
whether it is true in the relevant respects does not matter as much as the
emergency. Most emergencies require truth. These remarks outline the
hypothesis for considering theology as symbolic engagement. The next
chapter will begin its positive defense.

Our current intellectual situation requires preliminary orientation,
however, because theology is no innocent discipline. Many modernist
thinkers among us, including people in the humanistic disciplines as well
as in the social and natural sciences, are skeptical of theology as such. They
doubt that there is anything ultimate to serve as its subject matter and suspect theology to be just the ideology of religious organizations that ration-
alizes their claims to power. Many postmodernist thinkers agree with the
modernists in this.[1] So theology from the outside cannot be taken for
granted as a discipline with proper critical rigor and legitimacy.[2]

As a preliminary orientation, therefore, this chapter will introduce the
project of theology as symbolic engagement by examining four orienting
considerations about theology in general. First, it will discuss the nature of
"ultimacy" and its cognates, the concept at the heart of the definition of
theology's subject matter above. This discussion will be only of an orienting nature because ultimacy is the topic of the entire next projected volume
of *Theology as Symbolic Engagement*. Second, the chapter will make some
remarks about the history of the term "theology" and its cognates, especially in relation to philosophy. An argument will be made that it can be
expanded from its particular history in Western, mainly Christian thought
to be the collective term for reflection on ultimacy in all traditions.

---

1. Modernism and postmodernism are notions to which reference will be made in this book but
without a thorough analysis. See the intriguing study by the geographer David Harvey in his *The
Condition of Postmodernity*. For my analysis, see *The Highroad around Modernism*. For background, see
Malcolm Bradbury and James McFarlane's *Modernism* and Lawrence E. Cahoone's *From Modernism
to Postmodernism*. See also Cahoone's insightful *The Dilemma of Modernity: Philosophy, Culture, and
Anti-Culture*.
2. Early in the nineteenth century, Friedrich Schleiermacher had attempted to give theology in
three forms—philosophical, historical, and practical—scientific places in the modern university. See his
Brief Outline on the Study of Theology. He was one of the founders of the University of Berlin in 1810,
was dean of the theology faculty, and then was appointed rector of the university in 1815. See Gary
Dorrien's discussion of Scheiermacher as a *university* theologian in his *The Word as True Myth*, pp. 16ff.

Perhaps a majority of self-identified professional theologians in our own contemporary American situation, however, object to an easy transition from theology within and for a community to theology that embraces many traditions. For these theologians, theology is primarily the explication of the revelation on which their religious communities are founded, including the explication of personal and communal religious identities based on that revelation. Little need exists, from this point of view, to consider theologies arising from other revelations. The third point of this chapter, then, is to examine this position as a preliminary to theology as symbolic engagement, which does make theology among different religions essential. The fourth point of discussion, in sum, is to discuss different genres of theology as addressing different publics, from the internal public of a theologian's religious community to larger publics.

Ultimacy

The philosophical approach to identifying theology has already been broached in the references to ultimacy. What is ultimacy, ultimate matters, ultimate realities, or the ultimate? "Ultimacy" is a kind of logical placeholder in much of the argument of this book for the subject matter or topic of theology. "Ultimacy" is a term that can be used to step back from specific conceptions of God and include alternatives to monotheistic ideas, such as Brahman, the Dao, Principle (in the Neo-Confucian sense), the One, or Non-being. All these are symbolized as ontological realities of one sort or another (actually, most are said not to be "sorts" of reality) and they are taken to be more basic than all other kinds of reality. The other kinds presuppose the ultimate ones, but not the other way around. In penetrating through to the last conceivable reality that does not presuppose anything beyond it, the ultimate realities are in the last place. The major religious traditions have different models of how their ultimate or ultimates relate to everything else.

This ontological side is only half the story of ultimacy, however. Some religions, for instance, most forms of Buddhism, argue that there are *no* "ultimate realities." In fact, the belief that anything in reality is ultimate is a snare and delusion that binds the believer to suffering, according to both Theravada and Mahayana Buddhism. Yet release from the ignorance and bondage causing suffering is ultimately important. The religious quest is ultimately important. So important is the religious quest that bodhisattvas, in the Mahayana traditions, postpone their own full release from suffering until all other sentient beings have attained enlightenment. In addition to ontological ultimate realities, then, we need to talk about what might be called anthropological ultimates: ultimate purposes, quests, or tasks.[3]

The theological conception of ultimacy, both ontological and anthropological, was introduced systematically by Paul Tillich, following Max Weber. In attempting to find ways to connect the ancient world in which he found the kerygma of Christianity to the late modernity of his time, Tillich devised a series of bridging categories that in fact are fruitful beginnings for a globally public comparative language. These all have to do with ultimacy. "Ultimate concern" was his guiding phrase for what might be called the anthropological side of religion, its quests.

> Ultimate concern is the abstract translation of the great commandment: "The Lord, our God, the Lord is one; and you shall love the Lord your God with all your heart, and with all your soul and with all your mind, and with all your strength." [Mark 12:29, RSV] The religious concern is ultimate; it excludes all other concerns from ultimate significance; it makes them preliminary. The ultimate concern is unconditional, independent of any conditions of character, desire, or circumstance. The unconditional concern is total: no part of ourselves or of our world is excluded from it; there is no "place" to flee from it. The total concern is infinite: no moment of relaxation and rest is possible in the face of a religious concern which is ultimate, unconditional, total, and infinite.[4]

This characterization could apply to the Buddhist quest as well as to Christian concern, indeed, to a kind of concern that characterizes the ideal practice of most if not all religions.

On the ontological side, as Tillich put it, ultimacy names the most fundamental realities, symbolized as God in the West Asian traditions. Tillich explored at length the Christian tradition's various candidates for the ontological ultimate and connected his discussions with the mystical as well as with kerygmatic traditions. For Tillich, the anthropological and ontological sides of ultimacy were always connected. That is, nothing is worth being the object of ultimate concern unless it is in fact ontologically ultimate, and the criticism of false ontological candidates is the critique of idolatry.

---

3. This point about the distinction between ontological ultimacy and anthropological ultimacy derives from long deliberations of the Cross-Cultural Religious Ideas Project, as laid out in its volume *Ultimate Realities*, ed. Neville. In particular, see chaps. 6, "Cooking the Last Fruit of Nihilism: Buddhist Approaches to Ultimate Reality," by M. David Eckel with John J. Thatamanil, and 7, "Comparative Conclusions about Ultimate Realities," by Wesley J. Wildman and Robert Cummings Neville.

4. Tillich, *Systematic Theology*, vol. 1, pp. 11–12. See the "Introduction" to that volume for his more complete discussion of ultimacy.

The point of Tillich's discussion was to define the subject matter of theology. Theology has two formal criteria, he argued. The first is that the *"object of theology is what concerns us ultimately. Only those propositions are theological which deal with their object in so far as it can become a matter of ultimate concern for us."*[5] This means that any dimension of life that has ultimacy about it is part of the subject matter of theology. The second formal criterion for the subject matter of theology is this: *"Our ultimate concern is that which determines our being or not-being. Only those statements are theological which deal with their object in so far as it can become a matter of being or not-being for us."*[6] Tillich's existential philosophy gave him a particular interpretation of "that which determines our being or not-being." Theology as symbolic engagement casts a wider net than his existentialism, as will become clear.

The working hypothesis of theology as symbolic engagement is that the topic of theology is ultimacy, either in ontological realities or in the anthropological ultimate; any dimension of human life that has ultimate significance, either regarding ontological realities or an ultimate concern, is to that extent a theological topic.

Tillich argued that the material criteria for theology come from historical religious revelations. For him as a Christian theologian, the central revelation was the New Being in Jesus the Christ.[7] Theology as symbolic engagement generalizes this point to say that the symbols in various religious traditions that have engaged the ultimate or ultimacy in human life, and have done so truly in their contexts, are revelatory in those contexts. The purpose of theology of symbolic engagement is to determine whether and how those symbols engage ultimate matters, and then to articulate the truth and error in those engagements. Ultimacy can be engaged in the four loci of theology listed above and, within each locus, according to the four modes of symbolic engagement.

"Theology" in History

Historically, theology can be identified as a specific tradition of thought within Western culture. "Theology" in its current usage among many Christian theologians is sometimes defined as reflection faithful to and under the authority of religious bodies, in contrast to philosophy, sometimes

---

5. Ibid., p. 12; italics Tillich's.
6. Ibid., p. 14; italics Tillich's.
7. Ibid., pp. 47–66.

descried as "secular humanism."[8] The Protestant Reformation advocated a special kind of theology couched in biblical language, in accord with its principle of *sola scriptura*, and this branch of biblically based church theology continues to this day.[9] Parallel with this, some European and American traditions of philosophy have prided themselves on separation from religious authority. Freedom of philosophic thought is believed by some to be incompatible with intellectual religious faithfulness or "faith seeking understanding."[10] Both sides in this forced distinction are incapable of sustaining themselves except in extreme cases. Even the most "faithful" theology is susceptible to arguments that undermine authority, and no philosophy is as truly without a presupposed "religious" context as some anti-theological Enlightenment philosophers thought. "Mediating theologians" knew this long before postmodern thinkers made the case.[11] The issues have to do with examining the authorities and their contexts, which falls among the roles of theology as critical reflection on ultimate realities and their bearing on human life.

Whether theology is primarily a Christian mode of thought can be given a decisive historical answer: No. *Theologia* was the word used in the ancient Greek world, by Plato and Aristotle, for instance, for the study of gods. The Greek pantheon was a development from the earlier proto-Aryan pantheon that unfolded in roughly parallel ways in the Indus Valley and Iran as well as in Italy. Those cultures also had inquiries into their gods. By the time of the rise of Christianity, theology had come to include comparative studies of different pantheons, with suggestive correlations from one

---

8. The classical way of putting this opposition between theology and philosophy is to ask: What has Jerusalem to do with Athens? For a theory of the relation of theology to philosophy, with a discussion of outstanding examples of several types, see Hans Frei's *Types of Christian Theology*. For a careful defense of Christian theology as biblical over against philosophy, see Royce Gruenler's *The Inexhaustible God: Biblical Faith and the Challenge of Process Theism*; process theology is almost wholly philosophical, and Gruenler takes this seriously.

9. Contemporary Protestant evangelicalism does this, with striking parallels in Islamic fundamentalism. For a careful statement by an evangelical theologian, see vol. 1 of Donald G. Bloesch's *Essentials of Evangelical Theology*. For another more classically pietist position, see Stanley Grenz's *Theology for the Community of God*. For the tortured story of biblical inerrancy in American evangelicalism, see Gary Dorrien's *The Remaking of Evangelical Theology*.

10. Immanuel Kant proclaimed the independence of philosophy from all authority in his essay "What Is Enlightenment?" He also made room for nontheological religion in *Religion within the Limits of Reason Alone*.

11. Friedrich Schleiermacher was the grandfather of mediating theologians, and his strategies worked, with adaptations, for Sri Aurobindo in South Asia and Fung Yulan in East Asia; see his *On Religion: Speeches to Its Cultured Despisers* as well as his classic *The Christian Faith*. For a focus on Christian mediating theologians and Christology, their central issue, see part 1 of Wesley J. Wildman's *Fidelity with Plausibility*. For the Barthian criticism of mediating theology on the points at hand, see Gary Dorrien's *The Barthian Revolt in Modern Theology*. For mediating theologians in America, see Dorrien's magnificent two volumes (so far published) on *The Making of American Liberal Theology*.

to another and some understanding of the overlay of one culture's pantheon on another's. Early Christians took up the term "theology" in this
sense, explaining and justifying their conceptions of the God of Abraham,
Isaac, and Jacob, the divinity of Jesus, and the Holy Spirit, to people of other
religions as well as to themselves. Christian theology began as comparative
and apologetic.[12]

The most common early Christian term for the internal reflections of its
communal self-understanding and practical guidance was "philosophy,"
not "theology."[13] Christianity was "a philosophical way" in competition
with other "philosophical schools" such as the Stoic, Pythagorean, and
Epicurean, organized into living communities with disciplines, special
teachings, and often rituals. This usage lasted at least through Augustine's
time.[14] Theology, meanwhile, continued to have its comparative and apologetic connotations through the medieval period during which it developed
detailed scholastic forms of argument. Whereas revealed theology appealed
to the authority of revelatory sources (which could be compared and
argued about, as between Jews, Christians, and Muslims), natural theology
was open public discourse that was conceived in the world of competing
Abrahamic religions in Europe, North Africa, and Asia Minor. By the time
of the European Middle Ages, the boundaries between philosophy and natural theology were not clear, and philosophy itself lost many of its associa-
tions with schools of religious practice.

Since the European Reformation and Roman Catholic Counter-
Reformation, the term "theology" and its cognates have been much more
closely associated with inquiry within and for the sake of the Christian
community, marked by the authorities over which Protestants and
Catholics disagreed. The roots of this are more ancient, lying in the "faith
seeking understanding" conception in Anselm and earlier in Augustine.[15] In
the period of European modernity, intellectual contact between European

---

12. St. Paul, for instance, compared emerging Christianity with other forms of Second Temple
Judaism and also, in at least one instance, with pagan religion (Acts 17). The extant writings of Justin
Martyr, born 114 CE, are nearly all both comparative and apologetic.

13. For an interesting though not unbiased discussion of philosophy and theology in the ancient
world, see Wolfhart Pannenberg's *Systematic Theology*, vol. 1, chap. 1.

14. Indeed, there were two different though overlapping forms of Christian organization, the
"catholic" organization of the episcopacy with parish congregations and the "academic" organization of
schools with great teachers, such as Origen, and communities of disciples. Athanasius attempted to sup-
press the latter in favor of the former, and his efforts eventually were successful. See Rowan Williams's
Arius, pp. 82–91, and more especially David Brakke's *Athanasius and Asceticism*, pp. 58–79.

15. See Karl Barth's brilliant little book *Anselm: Fides Quaerens Intellectum*, and contrast it with
Charles Hartshorne's title essay in *The Logic of Perfection and Other Essays in Neoclassical Metaphysics*.
Whereas the former argues that reason finds itself in faith, the latter argues that when reason finds its
true self, faith follows along. See Hartshorne's discussion of Barth's book, pp. 111–16.

Christianity and Islam diminished greatly. As early as Luther's virulent anti-Judaism, barely distinguished from anti-Semitism, Judaism ceased to be respected as a dialogue partner by Christians and its thought was not taken seriously as theology.[16] With some striking exceptions, such as Matteo Ricci's attempt to find Confucian parallels to Christian ideas, the colonial encounter of European Christianity with defeated peoples did not encourage theology to look beyond the boundaries of Christian intellect.[17]

One effect of modernity was to sharpen the distinction for Christian thinkers between accepted theological beliefs and the authorities that justified them. Enlightenment thought severely criticized what it took to be superstition. Some, like John Locke, attempted to reconstruct Christianity without superstition.[18] Others, like David Hume, rejected Christianity as cognitively viable because of its superstition.[19] Many Christian thinkers attempted to defend Christianity and its beliefs, now known as its theology, over against philosophy, which was skeptical.[20] Barely known in the ancient world and handled as neatly complementary in the European Middle Ages, the distinction between philosophy and theology became an antagonism for many thinkers in the late modern period. Some thinkers defend theology as the grammar or underlying logic of the belief system of a community, usually a Christian community, and some of these fear philosophy to be the explicit undermining of the authority of a community to which people have pledged their faith.[21] Some philosophers in turn regard theology as the defense of supernaturalism, superstition, or putatively invulnerable absolutism, and reject its claim to any public legitimacy.[22]

Although Enlightenment European thinking often contrasted philosophy and theology, it was not consistent in this contrast. The Jewish philosopher Spinoza, for instance, called his political work the *Tractatus Theologico-Politicus*

---

16. See Heiko Oberman's *The Roots of Anti-Semitism: In the Age of Renaissance and Reformation*.
17. See John D. Young's *Confucianism and Christianity: The First Encounter*.
18. See Locke's *The Reasonableness of Christianity*.
19. See Hume's *Dialogues concerning Natural Religion*.
20. This was true of most Protestant and Roman Catholic Scholasticism of the seventeenth and eighteenth centuries, as well as Protestant pietism.
21. That theology is the description of the underlying grammar of a religious cultural-linguistic community is George Lindbeck's theory in *The Nature of Doctrine*. See also Hans Frei's *Types of Christian Theology*, chap. 3. Chapter 4 of Frei's book is an intriguing catalogue of different possible relations between philosophy and theology in the recent scene. Lindbeck and Frei argue that theology is closer to sociology than to philosophy, and their view will be discussed in connection with the social sciences below; their argument for this, however, is neither theological nor sociological but philosophic, as they both admit. Their general approach is the "Yale School" discussed below.
22. See John E. Smith's insightful essays "Christianity and Philosophy" and "The Present Status of Natural Theology" in *Reason and God*, chaps. 7 and 8, respectively. See also his important interpretation of Charles Peirce's views on religion and theology in "Religion and Theology in Peirce," chap. 4 of the same volume.

because it dealt with God and religion in society, among other topics. Other modern philosophers such as Descartes, Hobbes, Locke, Leibniz, Kant, and Hegel had important and influential theories of God that have been called theologies, following the ancient use. Whitehead's process theology in the twentieth century has been influential among Christian and non-Christian thinkers. Thus, "theology" retains a wide range of meanings and is not limited to Christian church theology or some religious community's authority except in the writings of certain authors.

The theology arising from the great philosopher-scientists of modernity is closely connected with their sense of nature. The rise of modern science, especially physics and astronomy, had a profound impact on Christian and Jewish theology in Europe, stimulating thinkers such as Descartes, Spinoza, Newton, Leibniz, and later Whitehead, to develop new conceptions of God. For them, the interesting parts of theology were the ways by which it grew under the tutelage of the new science. Although none of these thinkers cut themselves off from the scriptural traditions in theology, because of the movement in which they were such originals, the European tradition came to identify one strand of theology as "natural theology." This had ancient roots in classical Platonism and Aristotelianism, and medieval roots in the distinction between theology dependent on supernatural grace and revelation, on the one hand, and theology as it could be known by reason alone, on the other.

Natural theology in the Enlightenment often found itself tending toward Deism, with which it is often now associated. Deism is only one model of scientific-oriented theology, however. Each of the thinkers mentioned conceived God to be involved in a causal network with the rest of reality, often as ontological creator of everything else, although sometimes with other kinds of causal relations to things, as in Whitehead's process theology. Because of the causal networks, even when God's causation is conceived to be quite different from other things' causation, God and the world are conceived to be in a kind of unified causal nexus, the whole of which can be conceived as nature.

"Natural theology" is not the same as "naturalistic theology" or "theological naturalism." "Natural theology" deals with what can be known of ultimacy from nature alone, prescinding from what Schleiermacher called "positive religion." "Theological naturalism," by contrast, can embrace positive religion even while its metaphysics of ultimacy is structured around unified nexuses of cosmological and ontological causation. Theology as symbolic engagement is naturalistic in its metaphysics while focusing intensely on the symbols of positive religion.

The causally defined naturalistic theologies of modernity were extremely various, reflecting the original genius of so many of those modern scientist-theologian-philosophers. Spinoza construed God as the infinite substance of which the things of the world that science studies are modes. "Nature natured" is the determinate world of science; "nature naturing" is that very same world construed as God being Godself. Leibniz conceived God to be one infinite monad among an infinity of finite monads, all reflecting one another by streams of perceptions inbuilt in each and coordinated by a preestablished harmony. Whitehead adopted Leibniz's model but claimed that the monads actually exert causal influence, not mere reflective influence, on one another, so that God is an actual entity interacting with other actual entities through time, though not in an ontologically causal manner as creator. Thus Whitehead did not have to adopt Leibniz' view of preestablished harmony. Hegel said that his theology was like Spinoza's except that the static divine substance of Spinoza was reconceived as dynamic subject, othering and reuniting itself. Hegel's contemporary Schelling developed Spinoza somewhat differently, giving rise to the "Ground of Being" theologies of which Tillich's is the best known. All of these theologies are metaphysical "naturalisms" in the sense of defining God within some kind of a causal nexus with the rest of reality, where the causation can be understood in some compatible relation with what science knows.

The general term "theology," including supernatural as well as natural theologies, does have a particularly biased history associated with Christianity and the West, which in turn has been overly influential in framing scholarly discussions of world religions. Moreover, the very root of the word refers to gods: not all religions focus on gods, especially not the monotheistic God of surviving West Asian religions. Thinkers sympathetic to other religions legitimately worry about monotheistic assumptions imported with the use of the word to cover intellectual inquiry more generally.[23] There would be parallel worries about any other word coming from other religious traditions, however, because they all bear the particularity of their historical biases.

What is needed, therefore, to describe reflection on ultimacy in any culture is a word that does have a particular history, as "theology" does, but that can deliberately be made vague so that it can encompass religions with alternative histories and register their intellectual reflections without bias.

---

23. See, for instance, Rita M. Gross's discussion of the use of the term for Buddhism, indeed, feminist Buddhism, in *Soaring and Settling: Buddhist Perspectives on Contemporary Social and Religious Issues*, pp. 155–70. Despite misgivings like mine, she too settles for the term "theology."

A notion is vague (in a technical sense that will be developed later in connection with comparative theology) when it can entertain mutually conflicting or contradictory specifications. As a vague term, "theology" allows that different theologies might not be compatible at all, and makes the question of whether they are compatible an empirical question.

Critically to purify the meaning of a word so that it can function vaguely beyond the usages of its past is itself a particular historical move. That the use of the word "theology" to describe reflection on the ultimate is historically determined entails that it is subject to criticism when it fails properly to be embracing. That the word can be re-construed in a broad, embracing way, however, means that it can register the highly particular and even contradictory thought-forms in different religions that are different ways of specifying the vague notion of matters bearing upon ultimacy.

The historical approach to identifying theology thus is to understand its particular history in the West and its potential to be made vague enough to bring the reflections on ultimacy in the other traditions of the world under one umbrella for discussion. Precisely because of its vagueness, theology can entertain debates among positions that otherwise would not see one another as proper dialogue partners. Theology as symbolic engagement needs to be able to register diverse theological programs under its vague categories.

Revelation and Religious Identity

Probably a majority of professional theologians in America and Europe today, Jewish as well as Christian, do not share this project's sense of responsibility to engage theology across traditions and religions. Although they recognize that interfaith dialogue is courteous, practically helpful for building understanding, and intellectually satisfying, it carries little obligation for them. The most typical view of theology is that it is the work of explicating a particular revelation and formulating the identities that believers in the revelation should have as individuals and communities, identities that are forged in relation to the contingencies of existence. While usually admitting that other religions have their own founding revelations, these theologians take their own to be authoritative. Their job, as they construe it, is to interpret their revelation for their community of believers, perhaps in all the theological loci mentioned above: primary witnesses, doctrinal claims, theological systems, and theologically directed practice. In times of stress, the consideration of alternatives can be a distraction.

Revelation or primary witness is a common element in all the Axial Age religions, and chapter 3 will discuss some of its varieties and characters.

Revelation has played many roles in different traditions at different times. In our time, however, it has come to dominate the self-consciousness of Christian theology because of the extraordinary theology of Karl Barth. Although other religious traditions have not had towering theological figures such as Barth in the twentieth century, segments of Judaism, Islam, Hinduism, Buddhism, and Chinese religions have had somewhat analogous dynamics with regard to revelation. The result is that a great many of our contemporary theologians think of theology as the explication of revelation and its significance for religious life.

Karl Barth's impact on mid-twentieth-century Protestant theology in America was enormous. For one thing, he worked brilliantly against the Nazis, as many of his German theological compatriots much admired by Americans did not do. For another thing, both the liberal and fundamentalist conservative theologies that had prevailed before World War II were at loose ends, and Barth provided an audacious new orientation. He proclaimed that Christianity is simply based on the divine revelation of God in Christ, which is told in the story of Christian redemption. Then he went on to tell that story in many beautifully elaborated volumes.

Locating the center of theology in that story, he dismissed the nineteenth-century liberal Christian need to get at the real revelatory Jesus through historical means. With the same strategy, he dismissed as well the fundamentalist need to get the revelatory material in a literal reading of the Bible. Barth's telling of the story was so compelling that many people believed it like believing a novel. And because the revelation was in the form of a story, he could leave out or marginalize all the things that did not fit into the story, such as other religions, non-narrative or metaphysical forms of Christian theology, and even other tellings of the story than his idiosyncratic Calvinist version. People became "Barthians" by buying into his story and that story provided an identity for Christians as Christians. The story itself was taken to be *the* revelation. Stanley Hauerwas says, "Jesus is the story that forms the church," and I do not believe he means the obscurely known *historical* Jesus.[24] He means Barth's Jesus (as reworked with John Howard Yoder's version of the story in Hauerwas's case).[25] Barth's story is the revelatory witness par excellence.

---

24. In *A Community of Character*, p. 12. I owe this reference to Peter Heltzel.
25. See Jeffrey Stout's *Democracy and Tradition*, chaps. 6 and 7, for a fine discussion of the influence of Yoder on Hauerwas's theology, with special attention paid to ethics. Stout's book in general, although it is mainly about political virtue and argument (including the place of religion in politics), addresses many of the questions of plausibility addressed in the present volume and finds inspiration from a similar pragmatism.

The logic of the revelatory definition of theology is clear. However many competing revelations might exist, theologians in a tradition can always say that the given deposit of faith in their own revelatory tradition *might* be true. Of course, inconsistencies need to be worked out. Nevertheless, the positive core of the revelatory witness might be *the* true revelation and the others all mistaken or complementary, whether one's own belief be Barth's biblical story of creation and Christian redemption, a Jewish witness in the Torah, the Muslim witness in the Qur'an, the Hindu witnesses in the Vedas, and so forth down to the local revelations of new religions. An individual's or community's own belief in its particular revelatory witness gives it authority for those who believe. In Christianity, the slogan "faith seeking understanding" has been taken to construe this primary commitment to the revelatory witness that then goes on to define theology as what is limited to its theoretical and practical explication. Alternatively, that slogan also has been taken to mean a primary commitment to a religion's way of life with a much looser connection to the religion's revelatory witnesses or any interpretation of them. In our time of emphasis on authority grounded in revelation, the latter sense of "faith seeking understanding" has not been popular.

What accounts for commitment to a particular positive revelatory witness, since there are so many competing alternatives? The most obvious answer is that most people are born into a religious tradition and acculturated to take it as the fundamental way of seeing the world, including that religion's interpretation of ultimate matters based on its primary witnesses. Since religion is so much a part of culture, religious specificity is part of cultural specificity. The culture of modernity, however, has been very difficult for the religious authorities of the Axial Age religions—Hinduism, Buddhism, Confucianism, Daoism, Judaism, Christianity, and Islam (and their variants). Christianity and Judaism have been coping with these difficulties since the beginning of the modern era. Islam is only just beginning to do so. Marxist modernism was very critical of Chinese religions, and the religions of South and Southeast Asia have been "modernized" by Western colonialism. All those religions are now attempting to find "postmodern" forms that evade the critical difficulties of modernism for traditional authority, often by citing rather local authorities. In Europe and North America, much of the authority of Christendom collapsed in the mid-twentieth century, and being born into those cultures did not automatically guarantee religious faith with a search for understanding.

In light of the collapse of Christendom, the fideism of Barth's revelatory theology was especially attractive. It was beautiful and had great aesthetic appeal. Moreover, it defined a practical identity of resistance for Christianity over against the Nazis and then against other forms of oppression. Most important, however, precisely because there was no culturally semiautomatic plausibility to a Christian (or Jewish) way of life, the act of faith in committing oneself to the revelation and its consequences constituted an existential self-definition. In a cultural world of no obvious ultimate meaning, people create meaning by commitment. The more paradoxical one's revelatory witness, the stronger and more virtuous one's commitment. The more absurd the exclusive particularity of one's commitment, the more existentially self-definitive it is. The Kierkegaardian themes of paradox and absurdity were hallmarks of mid-twentieth-century fideistic theology.

Nevertheless, the arbitrariness of fideism in Barth and other theologians has given rise to an uneasy conscience. Barth said, in effect, that Christianity is just the truth, not a religion in a cultural sense, and all other religions are just cultural artifacts. This is difficult to maintain in serious dialogues with theologians from other traditions: it involves an unreligious form of disrespect for others. It is also difficult to maintain when the study of religions by so many disciplines shows that Christianity (or any other religion) is indeed a religion much like others, as has resulted from the burgeoning of religious studies in the last third of the twentieth century. Furthermore, the phenomenal growth of travel and cultural pluralism in Europe and North America have made it simply odd to affirm that one's own religion is the true revelation and way of life in the midst of so many alternatives when there is no argument besides one's commitment for that superiority. When a positive religious culture is powerful, persuasive, and taken for granted, to believe in its revelatory witnesses and their consequences does not seem arbitrary from within the culture, however arbitrary it might seem to people outside that culture. But when the positive culture is relativized, the arbitrariness of fideism seems both attractive and repellent.

In light of this bad conscience, some Christian theologians have moved from proclaiming the immediacy of the Christian revelatory witness to a higher-level philosophical theory of the appropriateness of revelatory commitments for specific religious communities. Hans Frei and George Lindbeck developed what has become known as the "Yale School" of theology, whose cardinal principle is that Christian theology is the expression of the deep grammar of the cultural-linguistic system of the Christian community.[26] Frei and Lindbeck began as enthusiasts for Karl Barth's story of

---

26. The founding books of this school are Lindbeck's *The Nature of Doctrine* and Frei's *Types of Christian Theology*. See also Frei's *The Eclipse of Biblical Narrative*.

Christianity but appreciated that it was simply arbitrary, however beautiful, in comparison with other stories of Christianity and in comparison with other religions' theologies. Writing as *philosophers*, they claimed that Christian theologies, and by extension the theologies of other religious communities, are to be construed as the deep grammars of cultural-linguistic communities. The tools of theological analysis therefore are more akin to the social sciences that can ferret out the nature of that deep grammar and its effects on structuring the communities than they are to philosophical or biblical forms of theology that try to appeal to normative truth beyond the communities in question. Theology is normative for people within those communities only in the sense that they aim to be loyal to the deep principles of their community; for these theologians, "faith" is commitment to the community and its way of life as normatively structured by its deep grammar.

The Yale School is widely appreciated for its articulation of the roles of theological principles within religious communities, and the subtleties of distinguishing between the *de facto* principles exhibited in religious behavior and the *normative* principles to which a community's behavior aims to conform. Confessional theologians also widely appreciate the Yale School as a trumping tool for theological debate with representatives of other religious or secular communities: you have your community with its theology and we have ours—they are not normatively competitive. The only normative element in theology, as mentioned, is faithfulness to the deep theological grammar of one's own community. Hence, Barth's arbitrariness is justified according to the Yale School.

One downside of the Yale School is that the notion of integral cultural-linguistic communities defined by deep theological grammar is factually mistaken. Religious communities constantly interact, overlap, and modify one another. Theological debate within a given community is often about whether to change the fundamental theological grammar because of something learned from some other community or theologian. One need not agree with Wilfrid Cantwell Smith that there is a thorough interfusion of influences among the world religions to note that the notion of relatively isolated cultural-linguistic religious communities is a fiction.[27]

A more grievous criticism is that nearly everyone who affirms a theology wants it to be at least a little non-arbitrary. Admitting that theological rhetoric is historical, contextual, and socially constructed, its inner intentionality is to refer to its ostensible topic, not merely to the way people in a particular community talk about that topic. The cultural-linguistic theory seems to cut away any meaning to reference beyond a community's grammar

---

27. See Cantwell Smith's *Towards a World Theology.*

to what realities might be represented within the grammar. When Jews say that God is both just and merciful, they do not mean only that Jews always say that and should organize their lives around that claim. They mean that God really is just and merciful, however inadequate those notions are to express the divine nature.

Of course there might not be any realities of the sort referred to in theological language; that was Feuerbach's position in claiming that theology is mere human projection. This is not the position of the Yale School. One could claim that there are, or might be, such realities to which reference simply cannot be made. This seems to be the implication, though surely not the intent, of the Yale School. An argument will be made in this book that there are indeed such ultimate realities and that they can be known, however bounded that knowledge is by context. The great contribution of the Yale School is to elaborate the contextuality of theological language, and its limitation is that its theory of contextuality prevents reference beyond that.[28] Theology as symbolic engagement urges that the context itself, with its grammar, be taken as symbolic of that which is not bounded by the context.

The Radical Orthodoxy of John Milbank and his colleagues comes to conclusions superficially similar to the Yale School. Milbank notes that classical Christianity has been subjected to deep skepticism by the social sciences of modernity—Marx, Durkheim, Weber, and others.[29] He gives postmodernist arguments to show that these social sciences, which he calls "secular theory," themselves have an arbitrary base. If classical Christianity's critics are arbitrary, then classical Christianity, although just as arbitrary, can be reaffirmed by those who want to. This is something like Frei and Lindbeck's claim that theologies, as well as their critics, are functions of discrete and noncompetitive communities. Whereas the Yale School is concerned to cordon off apparently competing theologies from other religions, Radical Orthodoxy is concerned to cordon off its kind of Christianity from other kinds and also from its secular modernizing critics—while criticizing them all from its own perspective. For the Yale School, Reformation theology is the preferred type of Christianity, whereas for Radical Orthodoxy,

---

28. Richard Lints distinguishes the Yale School as postliberalism from David Tracy's approach, which he calls moderate postmodernism (a label he assigns to my work, too). Moderate postmodernism rejects the Enlightenment view of objectivity in knowledge, but retains the Enlightenment loyalty to rationality as public discourse. Postliberalism of Lindbeck's sort rejects the Enlightenment view of rationality as public discourse in favor of the nonpublic intertextuality of thought within a particular cultural-linguistic community. Hence, for postliberalism, no way exists to refer the "text" beyond itself. See Lints's "The Postpositivist Choice: Tracy or Lindbeck?"

29. See Milbank's *Theology and Social Theory: Beyond Secular Reason* and *The World Made Strange: Theology, Language, Culture.*

the preferred type is a kind of Thomistic Anglicanism. In addition to a general embrace of arbitrariness in both its positive theological affirmations and its critiques of other theologies, Radical Orthodoxy extends the rights of arbitrary affirmation to many of its readings of modern culture. Like Barth's theology, Radical Orthodoxy's great attractive power lies in the aesthetic quality of the case it makes.

The Yale School, Radical Orthodoxy, conservative evangelicalism within Christianity, and fundamentalist movements in most of the world's religions have developed into what can be called "identity theology."[30] Identity theology says in effect that theology is less committed to honest and vulnerable inquiry into truth than it is to conveying an identity upon those who profess it. Negatively, those who disagree with one's theology are to be denied the identity of belonging to one's religion, although they of course are free to have some different religious identity. Identity theology reflects the attempt to find normative theology by means of social identification. Convinced members of a religious community or school can say, "As an X, I believe. . . ." This is a sociological report rather than a theological claim about the truth of the belief(s). Perhaps the most common attraction of identity theology, however, is for those whose theological convictions are shaky. For them, identification with a community or school that supplies a theology with its grammar or creed gives instant theological identity. The normative theological elements of that identity then consist only in coming to understand the implications of that theological identity.

The severe limitation of identity theologies, however popular they are these days, is that they are arbitrary, with all the drawbacks of arbitrariness discussed above. To be sure, any theology has a history and thus is somewhat arbitrary in origin because alternative histories approach the common topics in other ways. Complicated matters of taste and instinct shape each theology. Nevertheless, theologians who construe their work to be to engage their putative ultimate objects, rather than to sort social identities with built-in theologies, make their arbitrariness vulnerable to correction. By contrast, identity theologies, once the identity is chosen and elaborated, are stuck with the errors that particular identity bears with no built-in method of correction. An invulnerable theology bears its errors until it is changed by chance or circumstance. Theology as symbolic engagement guarantees at least the possibility of vulnerability by its explication of the realistic interaction of religious realities and interpreters in the symbolic engagement.

---

30. The preface above mentioned this in its contrast between Stanley Hauerwas's theology and theology as symbolic engagement.

These critical remarks about identity theology proceed from a primary commitment to theology as truth-seeking. Identity theology is important on its own, irrespective of truth-seeking, because religious identity itself is important. Although religious identity should be as true and valid as possible, sometimes its articulation and defense require the suppression of vulnerability for the sake of loyalty and faithfulness. Aside from concerns for theological truth, religious identity often is important for social coherence, playing the role of civil religion. This is illustrated well in many immigrant cultures, where the continuity of religious identity allows for social coherence through serious dislocations. The other side of the point is that religious identity supports the cohesion of racist, sexist, and totalitarian societies, which demand identity theologies to justify themselves. In these latter cases, identity theologies would be well advised to make themselves vulnerable to correction in the short run as well as the long.

Theology's Publics

David Tracy, the distinguished Roman Catholic theologian at the University of Chicago, defines theology in relation to three publics.[31] *Systematic Theology* for him has as its public a church community and aims to render in clear and consistent form the basic beliefs of that community. At first glance, the conception of the public for systematic theology is the same as the Yale School's definition of theology as limited by the beliefs of a particular community. Tracy has in mind, however, a much larger conception of religious community, such as the whole of Roman Catholicism, or the whole of Christianity. Systematic theology in his sense draws on the history of doctrine and the understanding of the intellectual contexts in which the doctrines arose and developed. It also draws on biblical and liturgical studies as well as the philosophies that influence church doctrine. The aim of systematic theology in his sense is to make the richness of a church tradition available to its current thinkers as they systematically integrate a comprehensive belief system for contemporary life. Systematic theology has direct input into catechesis. The main public for systematic theology is the church.

Tracy distinguishes systematic theology from *fundamental theology*. Fundamental theology is what Roman Catholics call the kind of radical philosophical thinking that Protestants call "philosophy of religion" or "philosophical theology."[32] Its intended public is the entire academy or the

---

31. See his *The Analogical Imagination*, chaps. 1–2.
32. Karl Rahner understands "fundamental theology" as the philosophic underpinnings of faith, but argues for a close interweaving of that with dogmatic theology, his word for systematic theology. See the Introduction to his *Foundations of Christian Faith*.

world of intellectuals who sustain or question the philosophy supposed in systematic theology. Fundamental theology learns not only from philosophy, irrespective of religious commitment, but also from the sciences, the arts, and, especially in Tracy's case, from cultural studies, and is responsible to those disciplines as within its public. Even though in our time philosophy is far behind theology in having a cross-cultural comparative public, the philosophy in fundamental theology requires comparison all the way through. Whereas Christian systematic theology can presuppose monotheism, for instance, fundamental theology needs to set monotheism beside the paradigms of Buddhism, Hinduism, Chinese religions, shamanism, and a reviving polytheistic paganism, to debate their merits.[33]

In a rough sense, Tracy's systematic theology and fundamental theology are aimed at theology departments and religious studies departments respectively, in the American academic scene, with the former serving as the academic arm of particular church constituencies. Yet the distinction is hard to maintain intellectually, as Tracy well knows. The philosophy in systematic theology nearly always draws a larger academic public into the discussion, even when the agenda of systematic theology is church theology in a narrow sense. Systematicians of the twentieth century who aim at a church audience, such as Karl Barth and Robert Jensen, still enter philosophical debates that carry them beyond the church public. Other great systematic theologies of that century, Karl Rahner's and Paul Tillich's, are all frequently classified as fundamental or philosophical theologies.

Tracy's third kind of theology is *practical theology*, by which he means theology aimed at social change and at ecclesiastical order and practice. Liberation theologies of many kinds are defined by this public, not by the church or academic publics, and are to be judged by practical criteria. Tracy would include also the arts of ministry and formation of practical religious life that Schleiermacher identified as practical theology.[34] The impact of Tracy's discussion of practical theology is to call attention to the fact that criteria for good practical theology do not necessarily include the concerns for consistency and faithfulness to tradition associated with the church public of systematic theology, nor the far-reaching critical debates of speculative philosophy involved in fundamental theology. In fact, the concerns of systematic and fundamental theology are often perceived by liberation theologians as inhibitive or even prohibitive of effective practical change and management. In the long run, however, in contrast to Tracy, theology as symbolic engagement argues that the practice of life is the widest public

---

33. For sophisticated contemporary retrievals of classical paganism, see the works of Pierre Hadot and Christos C. Evangeliou.

34. See Schleiermacher's *A Brief Outline on the Study of Theology*.

within which theologies of all sorts of lesser publics are to be judged. All the concerns of the publics of systematic and fundamental theology, in Tracy's senses, find their ultimate context for truthfulness within practical theology conceived with its proper scope. They are not true because they are practical: they are true because in practice they say what is good and right in their objects.

Another approach to characterizing theology through publics is offered by Rowan Williams, now archbishop of Canterbury. Most people know theology as a genre of thinking, or several genres, and the differences in genres are constituted by differences in publics. Rowan Williams nicely distinguishes three: the celebratory, the communicative, and the critical.[35]

Celebratory theology works with the language and symbols of worship, hymnody, preaching, and suchlike, and aims with aesthetic sensibilities to "evoke a fullness of vision." This theology finds its natural home in religious communities and private religious practice. The reflective elements in symbolic religious practices often are formed to teach the appropriate modes of symbolic engagement to novices and youths. Of course, just living in a community that punctuates time by the festivals of a yearly cycle, that has architecture, art, and music expressive of the symbols, folklore and commonsense expectations shaped by religious symbols, and whose patterns of life are assumed to be ways of living in light of considerations of ultimacy, is to exercise and celebrate life before the ultimate. This is how to live properly engaging the ultimate according to the community's religious culture, and is not always intended to be explicitly pedagogical. Yet living in a symbolically shaped social life has a transformative effect on the soul. The symbol-shaped life is that culture's path of maturation regarding ultimate matters, and so cultural life itself can be conceived as pedagogical. Celebratory theology draws heavily on the locus of primary witness and revelation and other elementary constructions of religious imagination.

Reflection in celebratory theology can be exquisitely subtle. Nearly all religious traditions have institutions for the training of subtle religious virtuosi. Perhaps the oldest on record are the institutions organized by the guru-disciple relation in Vedic India. Analogies of the guru-disciple relation appear in nearly all religions and are continuous with the production of written records in the literary religions, and hence with the academy.[36]

35. See his *On Christian Theology*, pp. xiii ff. Williams has in mind Christian theologies, though his classification works well with other traditions as well. What he calls "celebratory theology" is sometimes called "doxological theology" by other theologians.

36. These analogies are drawn out from a Christian perspective by M. Thomas Thangaraj in his *The Crucified Guru: An Experiment in Cross-Cultural Christology*.

Much theology in theological seminaries is celebratory in Williams's sense. Celebratory reflection, however, is to be found in just about every temple or place of worship, including the family home in Confucianism and Judaism, where decisions have to be made about how to order devotions.

Not all celebratory theology is sophisticated in an academic sense. Nevertheless, it is reflective and therefore theological. That everyone has a theology or philosophy of life, whether they know it or not, is a truism in Western societies. Celebratory theology does not have to be self-consciously abstract in order to involve critical thinking in the embracing of symbols, meditating on their meaning, using them differentially to engage the ultimate issues of life such as birth, sickness, coming of age, marriage, and death, and working out their implications for new situations. Where deliberately secular cultures attend to ultimate matters, for instance, *denying* "transcendence," they too have celebratory theology, celebrating perhaps freedom, creative integrity, mental and physical health, and material security and comforts.[37]

Communicative theology in Williams's sense does not abandon the primary symbols of the communities' practice but attempts to enrich understanding by expressing the tradition's points in new languages or "intellectual idioms"; for example, as the ancient Christian theologians took on Greek categories and some twentieth-century Christians gave Marxist expression to their theology. Williams writes:

> The assumption is that this or that intellectual idiom not only offers a way into fruitful conversation with the current environment but also that the unfamiliar idiom may uncover aspects of the deposit of belief hitherto unexamined. In fact, it involves a considerable act of trust in the theological tradition, a confidence that the fundamental categories of belief are robust enough to survive the drastic experience of immersion in other ways of constructing and construing the world.[38]

Communicative theology is evidenced in all the historical examples of one tradition learning from and taking on some of the thought-forms of another. In China, for instance, Confucian and Daoist sources employed one another's texts and characters in ancient times, and then both were influenced by the massive influx of Buddhism in the later Han Dynasty. Buddhism in turn evolved significantly in China from its Indian roots to

---

37. On this point, see the works of Harvey Cox, *The Secular City* and *Religion in the Secular City*.
38. *On Christian Theology*, p. xix.

native Chinese modes of thought. Neo-Confucianism in the Song Dynasty was explicit in the adoption of Buddhist and Daoist vocabularies to reconstitute the Confucian tradition. The "six orthodox schools" of Hinduism formulated themselves as recoveries of the Vedic tradition in opposition to Buddhism, which in turn developed in dialogue with Hindu critics. Islam adopted much of the language of Neoplatonism. Judaism split over the extent to which Hellenistic thought-forms should be employed, and extended itself to the mystical language of Cabbala. Just about any religion that aims to be relevant to the late-modern world with its science, global economics, Internet communications, and the interweaving of different cultures, needs to engage in communicative theology.[39]

The *critical style of theology*, according to Williams, arises at the crisis points where it is not clear what the real continuities of truth are among the various idioms, for instance, sacred and secular language, and where the tensions inherent in theology come to the surface, as in the apophatic moments. Critical theology asks fundamental questions, as in the thought of Hegel, Schleiermacher, Hick, Frei, Lindbeck, David Kelsey, Don Cupitt, Mark C. Taylor, Maurice Wiles, and Gordon Kaufman (William's list), to name only Christian ones, and can respond conservatively or radically, Williams points out. Even when radical critical theologies work themselves "out" of their communities, they still are theologies that define themselves as coming from the community. Williams notes that the public of celebratory theology can be imagined as a believing one, whereas the public of communicative theology must be assumed to have less of a commitment to the language and symbols of belief. It also sees merit in language that is not part of the tradition. Critical theology, he says, should not be constrained by conventional piety when examining celebratory or communicative theology. Regardless of the breadth of the publics associated with his three styles of theology—Williams does not go so far as to affirm a global public and all three senses of theology are "Christian utterance" for him—the boundaries among them are fluid, as bespeaks the living and indeed apophatic character of theological utterance.[40]

With regard to the questions of truth, all the ways of conceiving separate publics for different kinds or genres of theology find their boundaries breached as they need to make themselves vulnerable to correction. Both

39. Karl Barth would insist that the adoption of an alien language is treacherous for Christian theology, which always needs to assert its own authority over the adoption procedure. Chapter 2 will discuss this point in more detail, because theology of symbolic engagement does not privilege any one language over another except in terms of its subtlety.

40. *On Christian Theology*, p. xvi. But see pp. 93–106 for a discussion of Christianity and other religions.

Tracy and Williams had Christian theologies in mind, but for both, the move to fundamental or communicative, not to say critical, theologies involves cross-cultural and religious comparisons. Moreover, both know that major dialogue partners for any kind of theology in the late-modern period are secular humanism and science. Therefore, theology, even when it explicitly attempts to limit itself to a particular religious or academic community, tacitly reaches out to a global public inclusive of anyone with an interest in the outcome of the theological discussion. The problem, of course, is that the language for such a global theological public does not yet exist. The language of global comparison is in the process of development. Yet there is much more to the global theological discussion than comparative theology.

The most often cited public for theology, that which employs most theologians in the United States, is the religious community, Christian, Jewish, Muslim, and other. In a broad sense, these are ecclesial publics. In America, theology is most often taken to mean the kind of thinking that a religious community does for itself. Karl Barth begins his *Church Dogmatics*, "As a theological discipline, dogmatics is the scientific test to which the Christian Church puts herself regarding the language about God which is peculiar to her. . . . Dogmatics is a theological discipline. But theology is a function of the Church."[41] Tillich begins his *Systematic Theology*, "Theology, as a function of the Christian church, must serve the needs of the church."[42]

Specific religious communities often have a high stake in formulating their theologies well and probating them by whatever tests might reveal their weaknesses and improve their claims to truth and importance. Whereas religious communities require some kind of commitment to their traditions as celebrated, most also want them extended into relevance for the late-modern world. Moreover, thoughtful people in religious communities usually are sensitive to many reasons to doubt traditional visions, and are committed at some level of intentionality to setting aside such arbitrary biases as they feel to find out the truth of their interests on relatively neutral ground. This leads them to seek out resources beyond their communities, and to gain access to those resources a common public needs to be achieved, because they would not want to be the last to know they are in error.

Paul Tillich began his monumental *Systematic Theology* about fifty years ago.[43] At that time it was plausible, even required in the Protestant Christian circles to which he belonged, to construe systematic theology as

---

41. *Church Dogmatics*, vol. 1, part 1: *The Doctrine of the Word of God*, p. 1.
42. *Systematic Theology*, vol. 1, p. 3.
43. Volume 1 was published in 1951, vol. 2 in 1957, and vol. 3 in 1963.

the expression of Christian truth to the contemporary Christian situation. Like his great contemporary Karl Barth, Tillich believed there is a Christian truth or kerygma that needs to be correlated with the issues contemporary with the theologian.[44] He differed from Barth in the greater extent to which he addressed questions raised outside the Christian church by secular culture. For Tillich, the public for theology was the Christian community and perhaps its "cultured despisers," to use Schleiermacher's phrase.[45]

Our own situation for systematic theology a mere half century later is so different as scarcely to be believed. The theological public needs to include thinkers from all religious traditions who can acknowledge and address one another's perspectives, traditions, claims, and arguments. This book will argue that the theological public includes the arts, normative disciplines, and sciences that bear upon ultimate matters. To make a case for a theological claim today involves making it to this vastly expanded public.

In one very important sense, to speak of Christian theology or Buddhist theology, Hindu theology or Islamic theology, is a misnomer. A theology steadies its truth claims to the extent that it can make its case in a global public that includes all the resources for correction as well as all those persons and institutions for which practical theological guidance is relevant. In the long run, there is just theology. But three other important senses should be noted in which one still must speak of theologies as identified by specific traditions.

One is that any theologian always has a specific cultural background, even if syncretistic; honesty requires putting this forward. To speak in the first person, I am a Methodist, Protestant, American Christian who left Missouri for Boston and who is a self-identified Confucian. This complex background shapes the present project. What it means most specifically is that my sense for the subtleties of theology, the uses of symbol and metaphor, the ways in which theology itself not only expresses a religious life but importantly arises out of religious practices, comes from the forms of my Christian background, and to some extent from Confucianism. I hunt for analogies in other religions.

A second is that many theologians feel special responsibilities to speak to and for particular religious communities while at the same time developing theological views that are probated within the larger global public. On the one hand, this involves embracing the symbols, scriptures, traditions,

---

44. Compare their similar statements, for instance, in Barth's *Dogmatics in Outline*, chap. 1, "The Task," and in Tillich's *Systematic Theology*, vol. 1, "Introduction," parts A and B.

45. The reference is to Schleiermacher's *On Religion: Speeches to Its Cultured Despisers*.

and practices of one's religious community. On the other hand, it means comparing them to their parallels (or important failures of parallel) in other communities, relating them to the imagination of the present day in comparison with the imaginative base within which they arose, reconciling them with what is known and accepted in the rest of contemporary life, and engaging them in relevant critical ways with our situation. In such an enterprise, questions of truth and falsity, relevance and obfuscation, practical probity and moral impoverishment, are constant themes. All this requires a reconstruction or reinterpretation of the symbols and other older forms so that the contemporary religious community might be vital. This reconstruction has taken place in all periods, even those that pretend to be returns to the "originals." Sometimes the reconstructions have involved allowing some symbols, doctrines, or practices to be rejected or sink into oblivion, while elevating others to a prominence never enjoyed anciently. Many religious traditions now, for instance, are embracing the feminist revolution with radical changes in symbols and practices. At the same time, they search their traditional storehouses for evidence that women's perspective have already received classic expression. Most theologians are concerned in this sense to give vitality to religion in their time, working closely with the historical communal symbols, scriptures, and practices of their tradition.

A third reason for treating theologies as specific to traditions is that abstract theological ideas usually presuppose a deep background of particular concrete religious symbolism, often developed through centuries of religious practice and honed by practical as well as intellectual controversies. Put the other way around, unless theological ideas can identify themselves with the deep texture of some extensive religious practice, even if in negative critical ways, they are likely to be symbolically shallow, irrelevant in their interpretation, and incapable of referring in such a way as to engage people with their ultimate objects. A theology of symbolic engagement therefore needs communally committed theology. In a global theological public, the ideas discussed come from many different traditions of thought and practice, including secular communities. But if ideas come from no such tradition, or from no concrete encounters among such traditions, they are likely to be worthless. Therefore, the global theological conversation needs to be grounded in concrete traditions of religious, artistic, normative, and scientific life as these have developed and are currently changing.

All this leads to the point that the present theological project comes out of a Christian background. That it "comes out" means it is no longer Christian in the sense that Barth's and Tillich's were, namely, without curious resources for argument in the global public. Christian theology is changed and transformed in this work and in the movement of which this work is a part; critics need to ask whether the transformation is legitimate. On the other hand, the results of this theology in a global public should be able to be returned to a specifically Christian context so that it can function as theology for Christians. It should be a Christian theology in this sense. At the same time, thinkers from other religious traditions also should be able to engage this theology and return with it to their own traditions. So its themes need to be able to express truths in Buddhist, Hindu, Daoist, Confucian, Jewish, Muslim, and other traditions of religious practice and thought. Its major claims need to be able to be represented as Buddhist theology, and so forth. The obvious limitation to this point is that the global discussion might broach topics and ideas that simply are not represented in a given tradition, and so cannot be translated back to the traditional theology without the addition of material new to that tradition.

Perhaps more important than the traditional identifications of theology as symbolic engagement is that it participates in the development of a new global theological community whose members "come out" of different traditions but whose inquiries into theological truth engage one another as their primary public. Extraordinary theological debates across competing religious traditions have taken place before; for example, that between Buddhists and Hindus in the sixth through ninth centuries and between Jews, Christians, and Muslims in the twelfth and thirteenth centuries. The difference now is an emerging sense that a grasp on theological truth requires that the public include all religious traditions, that the absence of any impoverishes the discussion. This in turn rests on emerging conceptions of what religious traditions are and how they carry truth, all of which will be discussed in the chapters to follow.

My thesis is: The point of a theological public is to provide a community of critical imagination and discourse to which a theology is responsible for making its cases and in which it can prove itself. A theology is vulnerable to its public. For this reason, the conception of a global public is extraordinarily important as the testing ground for theology.

CHAPTER 2

Theology as Symbolic Engagement

Theology as symbolic engagement rests on two principal hypotheses. One is that *signs engage us with reality; without signs, we are causally implicated in reality but cannot engage it. Religious signs, or symbols, are necessary for engaging religious realities; and the existence of religious signs makes engaging religious realities possible.* The second is that the *signs that do engage can be true or false in the engaging interpretations.* Thus, two thematic questions pervade theology as symbolic engagement: engagement and truth.

The first question is whether putatively religious symbols in fact engage the people who live by them with their real objects. One of the chief complaints about religion in modernity is that classical symbols have lost their meaningfulness.[1] This surely is true for many people in social classes that experience elite modern education, although the great burgeoning of traditional religion around the world indicates that the classic symbols still are meaningful, indeed, existentially gripping, for many.[2] "Meaningfulness"

---

1. This complaint was popularized by John A. T. Robinson in his *Honest to God*. See also Don Cupitt's *The Long Legged Fly* and *Life Lines*. The general point lies behind liberal theology's moves in the nineteenth and twentieth centuries to deconstruct the classical symbols because they are meaningless in modern culture, starting perhaps with Schleiermacher's *On Religion* and culminating with Bultmann's program.

2. On the question of whether we live in an age when traditional symbols have become outmoded, see Peter Berger's *A Far Glory*, which notes that many people around the world and in America are finding the traditional symbols to be very gripping, and that the differences between those who find themselves in those symbols and those who do not are to be explained largely in terms of social class differences having to do with income, occupation, and education.

here means symbols' power to engage. Without engagement, the play of symbols is merely play—a game for those who like to toy with symbols. A related complaint, made by existentialists, among others, is that we have no effective symbols for engaging what we vaguely feel to be real and pressing. The classical religious symbols are now impotent for engagement, they say, and the latest symbols imagined by artists and those with a literary imagination work only for special classes.[3] A chief theme of empirical inquiry within theology as symbolic engagement is whether and under what circumstances this or that symbol engages.

The second thematic question is that of the truth of symbols that do engage. Given our consumerist society that heralds anything that works, and given the situation in which traditional religious symbols commonly do not engage people or "work" among some classes of people, engagement by itself might seem the goal of theology. But that is not so. Events of the last century have shown that religious symbols can be used to effect powerful engagements that shape what Tillich called "ultimate concerns" and still be false or, in worst-case scenarios, "demonic."[4] The interpretation of an engaging symbol is demonic when the infinite passion and commitment of an ultimate concern is directed at what is really a finite and proximate, indeed parochial, object. Tillich's example was the Nazi ideology that made a religion of blood and soil out of "Aryan" parochial ethnic self-interest. Interpretations with engaging symbols need not be demonic to be simply wrong. Problems of theodicy, for instance, make some symbols of God as a moral agent problematic and others not.[5] Whether, for instance, Brahman is to be conceived as the cause solely of the physical aspects of the world or also of the formal or teleological aspects is a complicated question of truth to which classical Vedantic theologians believed there were several wrong answers. Whereas only engaging symbols can be true or false in interpretations, that they are engaging does not by itself determine whether they are true or false. Truth is a separate though related issue. The main themes of theology as symbolic engagement are engagement *and* truth.

Theology as symbolic engagement conceives its task to be the analysis of how religious symbols engage, if they do, and whether they do so truly. The first two sections of this chapter will explore engagement and truth

---

3. See the complicated discussion in Frank Burch Brown's *Religious Aesthetics: A Theological Study of Making and Meaning*.

4. See the discussions of the demonic throughout Tillich's *The Courage to Be*. See also his *Theology of Culture*, chaps. 3–6.

5. See Wesley J. Wildman's discussion of divine agency theories in his excellent review article, "The Divine Action Project: 1988–2003," where he concludes that all of the theories of divine action represented in that remarkable project stumble on the issues of theodicy.

respectively. The third will elaborate the distinctions and connections among the four modes of symbolic engagement introduced in chapter 1. The fourth will integrate these discussions with a preliminary map of how theological truth is contextualized. The mode of argument here and in subsequent chapters is the laying out of a complex hypothesis about theology as symbolic engagement and situating this hypothesis among other approaches, which also should be considered to be hypotheses. This mode of argument does not involve a dialectical defense of the symbolic engagement hypothesis by refuting all alternatives, although that is one kind of case to be made for it.

Engagement

Interpretation is the act of taking a sign to stand for an object in a certain respect.[6] An interpretive act engages the object by means of the sign. Although some interpretive acts might seem to be purely mental, even the most abstract are implicated in interpretive networks that engage the interpreter's environment.[7] The best image for interpretation is John Dewey's notion of the interpreter as an organism in an environment.[8] An organism discriminates what is important in its environment and behaves accordingly. It ingests foods and avoids poisons, it pursues its purposes, however rudimentary or sophisticated, and it protects itself from dangers. Each discrimination is an interpretation, and the interpretations network together to engage the organism through time in a complex, shifting environment. Millions of interpretations are taking place through a brief passage of time in a complicated organism such as a human being.

Consider someone driving a car along a busy, winding road. Each second, the driver is interpreting visual, auditory, kinesthetic, and sometimes olfactory data. When the driver was first learning to drive, he or she consciously had to identify the relevant signs, noting what to look for in driving down the street, how to tell what other drivers are doing, how to signal

---

6. This sentence is a kind of slogan defining the heart of Charles Peirce's semiotic theory, which will be discussed in the next section. Religious signs are usually called "symbols," and so will usually be called that in this book. A special distinction between sign and symbol will be made shortly.

7. For those interested in Western philosophical epistemology, this position rejects the dominant tradition of representational knowledge. The background for this rejection in the West is in the pragmatic tradition, and in world philosophy, the strongest and most elaborate alternative to representational theories of knowledge is in Confucianism and Daoism. For a splendid new study of this, see Warren Frisina's *The Unity of Knowledge and Action: Toward a Nonrepresentational Theory of Knowledge*. Frisina treats, among others, the Confucian Wang Yangming. For the Daoist side, see the writings of Chad Hansen.

8. Of Dewey's many works, see, for instance, *Human Nature and Conduct* and *Experience and Nature*. For a fine interpretation, see John E. Smith's *Purpose and Thought: The Meaning of Pragmatism*.

turns, what traffic noise means, how to feel acceleration, deceleration, the feel of tipping as turns are taken at various speeds, the smell of burning brakes, and so forth. This can be a terrifying experience for an absolute novice who does not know what to look for and to whom everything is happening at once. An experienced driver, however, has so internalized the requisite signs and the patterns of interactions among the interpretations employing them that driving seems automatic or unconscious unless a crisis arises. Even in a crisis, a good driver often responds before much conscious analysis takes place and only afterward feels the stress of a wildly beating heart and an adrenalin pump. The signs for driving are culturally conveyed (as in a drivers' education class) and are learned relatively easily by people brought up in a culture with paved streets, cars, traffic signs, and habits of correlating high speeds with distances crossed. A native from the Amazon jungle who had never been out of the forest would have a far harder time learning to drive, just as an urban dweller would have a hard time recognizing what not to step on in the jungle.

Human organisms interpret their environment in rudimentary as well as in sophisticated ways. A baby learns to take the feelings of the pull of gravity as signs to be interpreted with muscular movements in order to walk, first learning to stand still upright and then to toddle. Perhaps much of these first movements is hardwired into physical responses. Nevertheless, different cultures stand in different ways. Traditional Chinese, for instance, stand with their feet rather parallel, whereas Western Europeans stand with their toes angled out. The Chinese walk with their toes coming down almost simultaneously with their heels, like a shuffle when exaggerated, whereas Westerners flick their feet out to put the heel down and rock forward onto the toes, like the goose step when exaggerated. These are culturally learned differences in styles of standing and walking, which means that each culture's particular system of signs for movement is being taught to its infants. Perhaps even the ways parents initially help their babies to stand is culturally signified. Following the Confucian analysis, we should understand culturally signified or sign-shaped behavior to be ritual.[9] Rituals teach signs for rudimentary motion, styles of eating, eye contact, and a host of other

---

9. The Confucian conception of ritual was an ancient and very rich approach to what we now understand as semiotics. Confucius himself taught ritual as the way to improve society. See Herbert Fingarette's classic analysis, *Confucius—The Secular as Sacred*, for a discussion of the balance between ritual and the learning of humaneness. The ancient thinker who most seriously developed ritual theory was Xunzi, who said that nature gives us broad, underdetermined ranges of physical and mental activity, and these can be exercised only when we learn specific conventional rituals that give them relevant determination. See his chap. 19 in vol. 3 of the Knoblock edition; see also Edward Machle's *Nature and Heaven in the Xunzi*. See my analysis of ritual in *Normative Cultures*, chap. 7.

behaviors of which people frequently are unaware. The most important ritual is language, which opens up vast new levels of conscious and unconscious interpretive behavior. Communication takes place through body language, grimace, and gesture, but it attains sophistication and flexibility when it uses words as signs, words whose semiotic code has a grammar.

The image of an organism in an environment illustrates two aspects of interpretation. First is the environment, with its features that can be discriminated with relevant signs when interpreted. Second is the set of purposes within the organism that guide its approach to the environment, from the baby's impulse to stand and walk to the diplomat's desire to communicate peaceful intentions to nervous barbarians.[10] Although some purposes might be purely physiological, most are themselves learned through the acquisition of a culture's semiotic system. Or perhaps it is better to say that raw physical impulses, highly underdetermined in themselves, are shaped by culture into determined purposes.

The adaptive value of evolving signs and semiotically rich cultures is obvious from an evolutionary standpoint. The better the organism can discriminate what is important to it in the environment, the more it flourishes. Moreover, as signs become more complex, they open ways to new activities and richer senses of flourishing, thereby helping to evolve more complex organisms, or organisms adaptive to new niches in the environment. With the origin of language and an easy capacity to think about counterfactuals, complex human societies with social roles and cultural ambitions are possible. A crude pragmatism might well apply to simple organisms that need signs to discriminate only what is important to their survival and reproduction. The crude value in the environment is nothing more than what is important for the organism's survival and reproduction. With the development of civilized signs, however, people ask not merely what is important for them in a crude pragmatic sense, but also what is worthwhile in the environment irrespective of them. What is there in the environment that is in the organism's interest to learn to discriminate, even when it has no crude pragmatic importance? Although organisms might be born with biological purposes, higher organisms can ask what higher purposes are worth having. Then the notion of purpose is transformed from self-serving to aiming to engage what is valuable on a higher scale. After self-serving needs are met more or less, human cultures redefine the self as that whose fulfillment consists in engaging reality's most fundamental and

---

10. On purpose, see John E. Smith's *Purpose and Thought*.

subtle values as discernable by the most imaginative and creative inquiring minds. This is part of civilized culture.

All signs function within interpretations to engage interpreters with their environing realities, so that they can stand and walk, drive cars, and pursue the good, the true, and the beautiful. Some though not all of those signs function with special reference to the semiotic systems that give them meaning, referring to those systems as well as referring to the objects interpreted. So, for instance, a person might put his or her hands together upon seeing another person; for people in East Asian cultures, this is a special sign of greeting, whereas for a Westerner it might be a kind of defensive gesture, or even just a way of maintaining balance in the surprise of the encounter. When the sign bears the meaning of a greeting, it can be called a symbol, for that meaning gives prominence to the conventions of a culture. When a person makes the sign of the cross, most Westerners would take that to be a symbolic gesture of a Christian, whereas the Amazon native might take it to be only a nervous tick. In the former case, it is a symbol; in the latter, a barely meaningful sign. Who is right depends on the intent of the person making the gesture.

Without appropriate discriminating signs, the realities of the environment cannot be discerned relative to intentions and purposes. The baby would not know what muscles to use to toddle if it had no kinesthetic signs for gravity; the driver could not negotiate the road without the driving signs; the diplomat could not negotiate peace without the language of diplomacy. Signs are necessary to make engagement possible. Without them, the environment supports or batters organisms but cannot be engaged by any discriminating response of the organism.

Religious symbols are the ones that allow people to engage ultimate matters. Without religious symbols, people could not engage the ultimate realities, ultimate projects, and ultimate dimensions of the parts and whole of experience. Perhaps people would feel their loss, as when they know they are missing something and do not have the means to say what that is. They might feel that proximate matters are being treated too seriously, or that they are speechless in the face of what does not fit the signs and symbols of ordinary life. Most religious symbols have a brokenness to them that indicates a kind of ultimate speechlessness; we shall return to this apophatic character of religious symbols later, though not without first exploring the positive functions of engagement with ultimacy. Without religious symbols, people would simply not be able to engage ultimacy, or at least not engage it well. Poets and prophets invent or "discover" symbols by means of which ultimate matters can be engaged, and yet people also believe that their symbols are never fully adequate.

Truth

Engagement is only half the story for a theology of symbolic engagement. The other half is truth. Suppose that a symbol engages its interpreter with its object: does it do so truly?

Symbols by themselves are neither true nor false. They are true or false only when functioning within an interpretive act that engages the interpreted object. Strictly speaking, it is the interpretation that is true or false, and it is true or false because of the way it takes a symbol or sign to stand for the object in some respect.

The nature of truth is a vexed question in philosophy as well as in theology. In a vague common sense, an interpretation is true when what it says of reality is what reality really is. Modern Western philosophy calls this truth *correspondence*. Correspondence, however, might suggest too much of the modern Western conception of mind as a mirror of nature, to use Richard Rorty's felicitous phrase.[11] The correspondence sought for truth should not be that of a proposition or mental entity to some objective reality. An interpretation, engaging reality as it does, includes its object within itself, not as something external to be mirrored. The question of truth is whether the interpretation determines the interpreter's experience to correspond to the object so that the interpreter can relate to the object appropriately. In the Western tradition since Aristotle, the common assumption has been that it is the *form* of the object to which *form* in the mind should correspond. Surely there is form in the object and form in the interpretive experience. Yet is seems clear from the discussion of engagement that the better hypothesis is that it is the *value* in the object for the interpreter that should correspond to what the interpreter thinks is valuable. There might also be a correspondence of form, as when a taxi driver has a mental map of the city. But the correspondence of value or importance might take a very different form in the interpreter's experience from what it has in the object. In order to make sense of this, it is necessary to introduce the theory of interpretation that will be elaborated in chapter 4.[12]

---

11. See Rorty's *Philosophy and the Mirror of Nature*. See also Warren Frisina's *The Unity of Knowledge and Action*, which thoroughly refutes Rorty's own position in favor of one similar to that defended in this book.

12. The theory that truth in correspondence is the carryover of value rather than form is the chief thesis elaborated in my *Recovery of the Measure*, especially chaps. 1–4 that discuss this claim in relation to classical and contemporary philosophical alternatives. The discussion of Aristotle (and Tarsky) on the carryover of form versus value is on pp. 67–70. The theory that truth is the carryover of value depends on a philosophy of nature that reveals how value is a trait of natural things, rather than mere projections. This is the main topic of chaps. 5–12. The general theory of truth here summarizes the more extensive discussion in my trilogy, *Axiology of Thinking*. The point of the *Axiology* is to show that

The theory of interpretation employed here, namely, that symbols engage us with reality, religious symbols with religious realities, arises out of American pragmatism, especially the work of Charles S. Peirce, John Dewey, and George Herbert Mead. Peirce was the original genius.[13] He conceived all of knowing (and much else) to be interpretation.

An *interpretation*, for Peirce, is the taking of a sign to stand for an object in some respect.[14] Here is an irreducible triadic relation with three components: the object, the sign, and the taking of the sign to stand for the object in some respect (the actual interpretation). When the "taking" is objectified, that is, made the object of a subsequent interpretation, Peirce called it an *interpretant*. If a person (interpreter) says "God is awesome," God is the object, the symbol "awesomeness" (with its network of other defining symbols) is the sign, and the locution "God is awesome" is the interpretant. Insofar as the person *thinks* God is awesome, the interpretant is the whole of the person's experience that is determined by that thinking interpretation. Though convenient for describing experience, propositional language (explicit locutions) is a radically biased abstraction from the concrete interpretation made: religious transformations are in the concrete.

---

all thinking is valuational in specified senses. Its first volume, *The Reconstruction of Thinking*, develops a theory of imagination from sources such as Kant's "A Deduction" (which he subsequently rejected) in the *Critique of Pure Reason*. The second volume, *Recovery of the Measure*, develops at length the theory of interpretation summarized in the present book and provides a philosophical cosmology justifying its claim that interpretation is a natural extension of biological and social human life. The *Axiology*'s third volume, *Normative Cultures*, presents a theory of theoretical knowledge aimed to be vulnerable for correction of bias and marginalization, and then argues that all knowledge is most comprehensively integrated in practical reason: knowing is for the sake of guiding life; practical reason is supported with a theory of ritual and community. My *The Truth of Broken Symbols* elaborates the theory of how religious symbols can engage the ultimate, which is not an object in any ordinary sense; *Symbols of Jesus* and *Boston Confucianism* detail how symbols from the past might find new relevance in the present. The issue of personification in symbols of God is discussed in *Religion in Late Modernity*.

13. Peirce's *Collected Papers* contain relevant discussions for semiotics and metaphysics throughout, especially vols. 1, 2, 5, and 6. I have cited a number of the most important in chap. 1 of *The Highroad around Modernism*, which is a summary interpretation of Peirce. For good commentaries see Douglas Anderson's *Strands of a System: The Philosophy of Charles S. Peirce*, Vincent Colapietro's *Peirce's Approach to the Self: A Semiotic Perspective on Human Subjectivity*, Robert Corrington's *An Introduction to C. S. Peirce: Philosopher, Semiotician, and Ecstatic Naturalist*, and Michael Raposa's *Peirce's Philosophy of Religion*. Hermann Deuser has collected Peirce's writings on religion and translated them into German in *Charles Sanders Peirce: Religionsphilosophische Schriften*, which is the only collection in any language of the religious writings.

14. The most influential statement of Peirce's theory of interpretation is in two early published articles, "Questions concerning Certain Faculties Claimed for Man" and "Consequences of Four Incapacities," in *The Collected Papers of Charles Sanders Peirce*, vol. 5, paragraphs 213–317; the standard way to cite this is CP 5.213–317, a convention that will be followed in the notes here. These two essays are in most collections of his works. The sentence footnoted here is a paraphrase of the following from CP 2.228: "A sign, or *representamen*, is something which stands to somebody for something in some respect or capacity. It addresses somebody, that is, creates in the mind of that person an equivalent sign, or perhaps a more developed sign. That sign which it creates I call the *interpretant* of the first sign. The sign stands for something, its *object*. It stands for that object, not in all respects, but in reference to a sort of idea, which I have sometimes called the ground of the representamen." Italics all in Peirce.

The pragmatic semiotic theory never lets us forget that interpretations are acts made by concrete interpreters in real contexts. To objectify the interpretive act as a logical interpretant runs the risk of saying, as is common in European semiotics, that semiotics is an affair of codes of signs, logical relations of syntax and semantics. Pragmatic semiotics by contrast insists that acts of interpretation engage real objects by means of the discriminations articulated in the semiotic systems.[15] An act of interpretation might get its object very wrong, thinking, for instance, that it is *God* as defined by some theology when in fact the actual object engaged is some projected human aspiration (Feuerbach). But the engagement is real in an act of interpretation. The object, however it might be misconstrued by the interpreting signs, is real on its own account.

The pragmatic logic of interpretation specifies three fields of study: the signs involved, the reference of the signs to the objects, and the purposes and contexts of the acts of interpretation.[16] Much has been said in theology, and will be said here later, about systems of religious signs or symbols, and also about the contexts and purposes of religious and theological interpretations. Theology as symbolic engagement shares the emphasis on reference with many other approaches to theology.

Peirce distinguished three kinds of reference, although he should have said these were three modes of reference that might jointly be present in the reference of any actual interpretation.[17] *Iconic* reference is to objects as being *like* what the sign says, often in a one-to-one mapping relation like the taxi driver's mental image of the city's streets. *Indexical* reference is a pointing to objects to establish a kind of causal relation between the objects and the interpreters. On the one hand, just as pointing gets the interpreter to turn to look in a new direction, indexical reference in interpretation involves some transformation of the interpreter.[18] On the other hand, just as pointing picks out the objects against a background, so indexical reference identifies objects in a far more complex way than would be involved with simple iconic relations. Peirce called the third kind of reference *symbolic*, by which he meant the reference defined internally within a semiotic system by conventions; such defining networks of symbols will be discussed in what

---

15. Peirce sometimes confuses this point by speaking of everything in reality as a sign. He means by this that anything at all can be taken to be a sign of something else. Postmodern semioticians, however, can construe that to mean that everything is only a mental sign, not an engagement with external real things. Dewey never was misleading on this point.

16. See Peirce, CP 2.227–380.

17. See Peirce, CP 2.274–308.

18. Plato in the *Republic* said that true education is not pouring knowledge into an empty cognitive container but rather the turning of the head (mind) so as to see what it had as yet missed.

follows. Because of special uses of the term *symbol* in religion, as discussed above, his third kind of reference is better called *conventional*.

Most if not all theological references involve all three kinds of reference. Any theological reference made in language has to be conventional at least to the extent of its language. Because indexical reference is what establishes cognitive causal engagement, engaging references are at least indexical, although the indexical causality might be complicated and indirect. Because much theology, though much less than theologians commonly believe, attempts to *describe* its ultimate objects, much theology is iconic as well as conventional and indexical.

Indexical reference is particularly important in theology because religious symbols are involved so much with the transformation of the interpreter so that ultimate matters can be engaged. People live with symbols for many years in reflection, meditation, and rituals, so that their souls are transformed in ways that can register the real value in the symbol's objects. Ordinary lives are ill equipped to let what is important in divine matters be carried across. People are not ready for religious truth until the symbols have done their work (and sometimes not even then), just as they cannot hear in music what an educated musician hears.

Perhaps even more important is the complexity within reference of identifying the religious object, of picking it out from its background. How do we identify the ultimate among so many proximate things? Indexical pointing to God is not a spatial indication. The indirectness of religious language is largely a function of the requirements of indexical reference for identifying the ultimate as a logical "object" to be interpreted with the symbols at hand. The complexity of indexical theological language is such that an interpretation that contains a thousand interpretations of interpretations adds up to a peculiar finger pointing. Ultimate matters, of course, are never absent; but they cannot be noticed until we have the interpretations with indexical reference that can orient us to them.

The result of this emphasis on indexical reference is that theology as symbolic engagement does not have to say that divine matters are "like" what the symbols say. The "rock of my salvation" is not a topic for geology. Typically, the "rock of my salvation" indicates a profound depth or power in the ultimate such that, if I orient myself to it, I am not threatened by influences that would disconnect me from the ultimate ground. God the "Lord" is not a political figure. Typically, referring to God as Lord indicates an acceptance of the divine agenda (however that might be interpreted) as having priority over one's personal agenda. The fact God is addressed in personal terms does not mean that God is referred to iconically as a person.

It typically indicates rather that people orient themselves to the ultimate in ways similar to the way they do to human persons. Insofar as symbols such as these refer indexically, the question of truth is whether, in the acts of interpretation employing them, they actually carry across from the object into the interpreter what is valuable or important in the respects in which they refer to God.

Peirce's idea of indexical reference is far more complicated and powerful than he realized in his brief discussions of causality and pointing. In the chapters to follow, layer after layer of definition and significance for indexical reference will be unfolded as the details of the semiotic theory are worked out. Chapter 4 contains an extended discussion. Indexical reference is a core idea in theology as symbolic engagement because it explicates the causal ground of engagement. Moreover, it motivates the Platonic conclusion of this volume, namely, that a theological system not only has its accountability and tests in public practical life shaped by the system, but also that the truth of theology consists in people practically bearing in their lives the value the theology carries over. Theology is not wholly true merely as *thought*, but as thoughtfully *lived*. Subsequent chapters will lay out the ways by which indexical reference, among other things, leads to these conclusions.

For theology to explicate the meaning of an interpretation with iconic, indexical, and conventional reference thus requires it to specify the respect in which the symbols stand for the object in the interpretation at hand. Theology as symbolic engagement has as two of its chief tasks the specification of the respects in which ancient founding symbols of the traditions interpreted their objects and the specification of the conditions under which those or other symbols might interpret those objects today.

As mentioned, whether an interpretation is true depends on whether it carries over what is valuable or important in the object into the interpreter in the respects in which its signs stand for the object. The notion of *carryover* is unusual in a philosophical climate framed by Fregean metaphors for intentionality. The "carryover" imagery actually goes back to Aristotle, however, for whom truth is the carryover of the form of the thing known into the mind of the knowers. The material component of the objects known was not carried over, and the material reality of the knowers constituted the matrix, for Aristotle, within which the formality of the known resides. The difference in the present hypothesis from Aristotle consists in the claim that what is carried over is the value or importance rather than the form. Actually, the form that bears the value in the interpreter might be very different from the form that bears the value in the object. The important thing from a pragmatic perspective is that the interpreter gets what is important or valuable in the object.

Behind the Aristotelian theory of carryover of form lies the alternative Platonic theory that the Form of the Good mediates objects and knowers, and that "forms" in the Platonic sense are not simply patterns but rather those patterns that gather the *important* elements in the object. Courage, justice, beauty, friendship, and other topics for which the early and middle Platonic dialogues sought "forms" are all normative notions. The arguments always have to do with how to pattern the togetherness of the features that the people agree ought to be in the "virtues." A more detailed account of value needs to be given than Plato gave. Nevertheless, he was right, over against Aristotle, that the carryover is of what is valuable in knowledge. This point obviously accords with the pragmatic tradition that regards interpretation as acquiring access to what is important to know and then acting upon that.

The carryover of value in interpretation defines truth. It does not constitute the criteria by which we can tell whether an interpretation is true, a topic that will dominate the rest of this book.

Modes of Symbolic Engagement

The complexity of theology as symbolic engagement rests primarily on its recognition of the four modes of symbolic engagement mentioned in the previous chapter, each of which has its sense of theological truth. The four can be labeled (1) imagination, (2) critical assertion, (3) dialectically systematized theory, and (4) practical reason as guiding practice.[19] Roughly, these can be correlated with the theological loci mentioned at the beginning of chapter 1. Thus, the symbolic function of imagination is most prominent in primary revelations and witnesses. Assertion is most prominent in articulated teachings, doctrines, and claims usually associated with

---

19. These four modes reflect roughly the four levels of Plato's Divided Line (in *Republic* 6.509d–511e): images (*eikasia*); commonsense belief guiding action in the concrete changing world (*pistis*); theorizing or knowledge of formal structures (*dianoia*); and dialectical integration of knowledge moving up to first presuppositions (*noesis*). Unlike Plato in the *Republic* passage, but following his development elsewhere (e.g., *The Parmenides*, see Robert S. Brumbaugh's *Plato on the One*) of the hypothetico-deductive method for knowing concrete changing things, I take the third level to employ forms (symbols within interpretants) to interpret the concrete world of the second level. My own three-volume work, *Axiology of Thinking*, makes a related use of Plato's Divided Line, distinguishing four kinds or families of valuational thinking: imagination, interpretation, theorizing, and practical reason or the pursuit of responsibility. Readers who compare the present work with the *Axiology* will note a change in terminology. In the present work, I substitute "assertion" for "interpretation." The reason is a recognition that all four families of thinking involve interpretation that putatively carries across value into the interpreter; imagination is not an exception, even though it is not critical or assertoric.

theology. Theorizing and dialectical synthesis is most prominent in systematic religious theologies, worldviews, and theories of religion adumbrated
by scientists and secular scholars as well as by religious thinkers. Practical
reason is most prominent in symbolically directed spiritual exercises, liturgies, communal practices, and personal lives as these are shaped by and in
turn test all the others. These correlations are only rough, however, as noted
earlier. Imagination is not limited to primal witnesses, but occurs also in
the formation of doctrine, the construction of systems, and the guidance of
life by theological ideas. Thomas Aquinas's hitting upon the idea of Act of
Esse to refocus the entire Aristotelian philosophical theology was every bit
as imaginative as St. Paul's hitting upon the ideas of paschal and atonement
sacrifices to interpret Jesus. Similarly, assertion is involved in primary revelation, systematic thinking, and practical theology; there is system in the
background of imaginative primal symbols, the construction of doctrines,
and practical life; and the practical embodiment of ideas, both for guidance
and for the testing of the ideas, is involved in primary revelations and witnesses, doctrine, and system. Yet the correlated predominance is important.

The inner logic of symbolic engagement depends on the philosophical
characteristics of these modes of engagement—imagination, assertion, theory, and practical rational life—that this section shall begin to explain. The
distinctions among these notions and the senses of theological truth
involved provide a framework for sorting theological disputes and projects
having to do with revelation, doctrine, systematic theory, and religious
practice as the theological loci mentioned at the beginning of chapter 1.
After a brief introduction here, chapter 3 will deal at length with imagination and primal revelation and witness. Chapter 4 will deal with interpretation and the testing of doctrine. Chapters 5 and 6 will elaborate issues of
theological systematic theorizing, and chapters 7 and 8 will deal with practical reason and religious life, especially as religious life relates to the culture
in which theology in all modes is tested.

The Truth of Theological Symbols in Imagination

Imagination in the most general philosophical sense is the capacity to synthesize elements into images, the elementary building blocks of experience.
Imagination has great variety and many dimensions. For Kant, it was the
basic thinking activity that underlies both intuition and reason. In the
human organism, imagination is the synthesis of all sorts of causal influences into images that have some semiotic shape, marking the transition
from merely organic mechanical responses to experiential responses.
Imagination might have some pre-cultural biological origination, yet its

products, the images, are cultural. The ways human beings see space and feel time differ from culture to culture; so do the ways they move and engage in elementary interactions such as eye contact. The more images are codified into semiotic systems, the more cultures take on definite characters and differences from one another.

The sources of imagination have been viewed in many ways. The European romantics viewed imagination as arising from a deeper penetration of the soul into nature than was allowed to be expressed in instrumental, technological, or even scientific thinking. Many religious cultures take certain kinds of imaginative works to be directly inspired by divinity. Some people take highly inventive imagination to be the work of genius. From a biological perspective, whatever other sources of imagination might be, at least it is an evolved human capacity to allow for more effective coping.

Images, the products of imagination, are the terms by which human beings articulate the world they experience. These include articulations of spatiotemporal extensions, ways of distinguishing foreground and background, temporal processes, causal connections, objects that are isolable from backgrounds, as well as social roles and relations, goals, purposes, emotions, and all forms of thinking as objects of intentionality. Without images, people would not be able to respond to the world at all symbolically, but only in terms of the mechanisms of pushes and pulls, and the chemical reactions of biology.

The truth of symbols in imagination, therefore, is whether they pick up on what is important in reality. Importance is first of all pragmatic—being able to distinguish those things in the environment necessary for food, safety, sociality, and so forth. To the extent that people are interested in more than their own survival and comfort, they take interest in what is valuable on its own in the environment, and can do so only when they have the images that allow them to notice it. The imaginative truth of symbols is different from assertoric truth. Imaginative truth is not assertive; it does not take the form of an interpretation that says something is as the symbol says. Imaginative truth is only an image or symbol's capacity for articulating something worth appreciating and discriminating in human experience as this is presupposed in interpretations. Most of the time we do not think of imaginative symbols as true except insofar as we use them to interpret reality.[20] But we often are in situations in which we are conscious of not having

---

20. In my earlier work, I often spoke as if imagination could not be true because images cannot be false unless interpretively asserted of something. Now I think that imagination itself can be said to be true in the sense specified in the text, namely, that imaginative elements are assumed in background interpretations that surround more assertive interpretations.

the terms to articulate something we feel to be important and real. That is when we long for the inventive minds, the poets, artists, and imaginative writers, to give us the images that let us say, "Yes, that's it!"[21] Symbols, even limited to their imaginative construction, are true in the sense that they allow something valuable or important to be carried over into experience.

Religious and theological symbols are the building blocks of religious life and its intellectual theology. They can be viewed as revelatory in the basic sense that they reveal what cannot be appreciated without them. Most if not all religious symbols, even the most concrete, are synthesized out of antecedent materials. The atonement symbols applied to Jesus in Paul's theology, for instance, synthesize the Levitical atonement imagery of the scapegoat who bears away the sins of the people with the Passover sacrifice imagery of Exodus that protects people from death; however, neither of these Israelite symbolic traditions had been applied to a single man such as Jesus before the early Christian movement. As with atonement symbols for Jesus, so with the symbols of him as Messiah, cosmic Christ, Son of the Father descended from heaven, Alpha and Omega, redeemer of the world, founder of the Christian movement, and all the rest. The Christian symbols include not only these early biblically and liturgically charged symbols, but also the evolving traditional symbols articulating ways of life, those constructed in complicated theologies and philosophical commentaries on how religion relates to the rest of life.

So it is with most or all of the world's religions—layers on layers of symbols constitute the terms by which people take the world, including the ultimate. Without adequate symbols, no deliberate organization of religious life or theological assertions are possible. What cannot be symbolized cannot be engaged so that what is important might be carried over into experience.

Theology focused prominently in the imaginative mode is prophetic and a matter of witness, the framing of core texts and motifs of religious life. In the practical life of religions, it is theology in what Williams calls the "celebratory" mode, even though it might also ascend to the critical interpretive mode that Williams describes as "communicative."

Theological Truth as Critical Assertions

Whereas the myriad interpretations constituting practices might have become unconscious as part of the background of intentional life (like the

---

21. On imaginative art in music relative to religion, see Jeremy S. Begbie's *Theology, Music and Time*. A broader approach to the imaginative contributions to religion in art is found in Frank Burch Brown's *Religious Aesthetics*.

lessons of driver's education that have become unconscious habits), assertions that are conscious are explicit about what's what. However they select
their objects out of the background of other interpretations, and however
their symbols are defined within semiotic codes with other symbols in syn-
tactical and semantic relations, explicit acts of assertion take their objects to
be important, as their symbols say.

What those symbols express within the assertions might be right or
wrong. To make an assertion in this sense is to make an implicit claim that
a satisfactory case can be made for its truth, which is the significance of calling assertion "critical."[22] Where the assertion does not make an implicit
claim, it takes on something of the form of a question—Is this symbol right
for its object?—rather than the form of an assertion, the active determination of something, or the exhibition of some feature of the object.
Assertions can also be in the subjunctive mood rather than the declarative,
which means that the case for them is subject to unspecified conditions.

Theology itself becomes explicit when it makes judgments about theological topics with a claim that in fact these assertions do carry over what
is important or valuable. Theological claims are hedged around by the
cases that have been or might be made for them. There are many kinds of
cases—conformity to scripture, liturgy, creed, official teaching, rational
simplicity, refutation of alternatives, coherence with other well-justified
beliefs or with a theological position, and so forth. Theology as symbolic
engagement, with its commitment to a global public, entertains more
kinds of cases for theological claims than most theological programs do.
In fact, it is inadequate on its own terms if it leaves out any practically possible kind of adjudication.

The truth of theological claims tested for carryover is to be understood
in the ways that follow from the theory of truth as carryover. The truth lies
in whether the theological claim in fact carries over what is important or
valuable in its object in the respect in which its interpretive symbols stand
for the object. An assertion affirmed to be true is one for which it is affirmed

---

22. The language of "making a case" in theology I take from Van A. Harvey's *The Historian and the
Believer*. That language is preferable to "proving" or "justifying" a doctrine because both of those terms
suggest that there is a method or rule of inference for validating a theological claim. On the contrary,
all potential methods or rules of inference themselves are to be evaluated in making the claim. "To make
a case" is to argue in whatever ways might be relevant to evaluate an assertion as a hypothesis. I follow
Charles Peirce in distinguishing an argument from what he calls an argumentation. An argument is any
line of thought or plot that comes to a conclusion; an argumentation is an argument that does so by
following a logical rule. Because in theology the issues are so close to the very premises of rational
thought, the premises themselves are among the things being evaluated; argumentations are rarely successful. Arguments, however, cases made, can deal with whatever comes up to evaluate the hypothesis.

that a case can be made. The interesting aspects of this level of truth, to be sure, are identifying the cases that can be made and the criteria for testing whether what is important has in fact been carried over in the right respect.

Many academic theologians would identify theology almost wholly with this sense of making assertive claims that are tested or are supposed positively testable for whether they are true. Theological doctrines and systems operate at this level of truth. So do the claims in commentarial traditions such as the Talmud and the Buddhist and Hindu scholastic commentaries. Interpretations of scripture and expositions of basic religious teachings are at this level. When theology asks explicitly whether the practices of individuals or a community are rightly shaped by the symbols of the faith, it is making assertions of this sort, aimed to be true. In general, the kinds of theology that take place at this level of truth can all be called *inquiry* in one sense or another because of the cases required or supposed to be made.

The Truth of Theorizing as Dialectically Synthesized

The third level of theological truth is the specific kind of inquiry that attempts to articulate the connections of all the other levels of theological truth with the theologies of all religions and with whatever can be learned from the arts, normative practices, and the many sciences about religious topics. The establishment of such connections in so many areas on so many levels requires the construction of systematic connecting categories, and these too need to be treated as hypotheses to be probated as carefully as possible.

Theological synthesis cannot be taken very far without metaphysics. Although metaphysics as a philosophical discipline is currently unpopular in Western philosophy, it is the ancient and still current attempt to articulate categories that are vague enough to apply in all contexts and are capable of registering and connecting the breadth and depth of experience across cultures and all disciplines of inquiry. A metaphysical account of the ultimate should be vague enough to entertain conflicting accounts of ultimate realities, such as Brahman in Advaita Vedanta, the Dao in Chinese thought, and the monotheistic ideas of God. A metaphysical account of creation should be vague enough to allow that either the big bang or steady state theory might be true. A metaphysical account of the person should allow that the Freudian and Skinnerian theories might each be true, though they conflict with one another. Like all else in thought, a metaphysics is an hypothesis vulnerable to correction for its consistency, coherence, adequacy to experience, and applicability to everything.[23] One of the chief functions of metaphysics is to provide "models" of the real that can give an underlying stability to the metaphors so important in religion, especially those that are the primal imaginative building blocks of theological traditions.

Few individual theologians have attempted such a dialectical system. Perhaps Thomas Aquinas and George Hegel are the only outstanding examples in Western Christianity. Moses Maimonides did something of the sort in medieval Judaism. Ibn Sina might be considered an example as well, combining while distinguishing theology from philosophy in Islam and relating it to the science and literature of his day. Whereas few individual theologians have developed explicit dialectical systems, theological cultures have done this frequently, as for instance the Neoplatonic and Aristotelian theological movements in the Christian, Jewish, and Muslim Middle Ages; the great theological systems of Madhyamika and Yogacara Buddhism; those of Advaita Vedanta; and the Daoshwei movement in Neo-Confucianism.

Theology as symbolic engagement is a program precisely because it cannot encompass all the kinds of expertise required for a dialectical system today with a truly global public. Nevertheless, for the reasons given earlier, it is not enough just to make some cases for theological claims. The truth of theological claims can be ascertained only by looking into all the cases that might possibly be made, which is to say, by being wholly public to all modes of inquiry concerned with theological topics, namely, with the ultimate and how that bears upon cosmic processes and human life. Or to put the point another way, even though all theological claims are hypothetical, those made without benefit of being interpreted within a dialectical system are more tentative than they need be. A dialectical system is the ground for proper vulnerability, and anything less than systematic has not asked all the potentially corrective questions.

The Theological Truth as Practical Reason Guiding Practice

The practices of a religious community are mostly those of the surrounding community. We find the special symbols of the religion, however, in rituals of family and sometimes community life, shaping the rituals and the

---

23. These four criteria are those Whitehead cited in the famous opening chapter of *Process and Reality*. That work demonstrated, according to the principle that *esse* proves *posse*, that metaphysics in this hypothetical sense is possible. Whitehead's own metaphysics has severe limitations for theology, as argued in my *Creativity and God*; nevertheless, he reestablished the endeavor after many people had thought that Kant had shown metaphysics to be impossible. It was Charles S. Peirce who earlier had argued that metaphysics is hypothetical and thus not subject to Kant's critique. These issues are discussed throughout my *The Highroad around Modernism* and *Normative Cultures*. See also Wolfhart Pannenberg's *Metaphysics and the Idea of God*, as well as the beginning of vol. 1 of his *Systematic Theology*.

souls of those who participate in them. Religious rituals in some sense or other epitomize what the religion takes to be the important work of the people, at least in that situation. In mature religious communities, congeries of basic religious symbols affect and shape much if not all personal and communal behavior. Christianity, for instance, conjoins the crucifixion and resurrection symbols to shape the way much of experience is anticipated and treated with both resignation and hope; the symbols of love in Jesus' teachings and community of disciples shape fundamental attitudes of kindness toward others, at least a little bit (and perhaps only to selected others).

The question of the theological truth of symbols as shaping practice is whether the practices embody the value or important elements that the shaping symbols could carry. This has two parts. The first is the question of whether the practices of individuals and communities are in fact shaped by the symbols that would be relevant. Christians long have believed that their practices of treating other people, even enemies, should be shaped by the various relevant forms of love and kindness, and yet for most of Christian history have exempted practices toward Jews from having the values of love. Christians have not applied the symbols to the relevant practices in these and many other cases. Similar deficiencies are found in other religions. The second part of the truth of symbols guiding practice is whether the value the symbols would carry over actually does come to inform the practice. Hypocrisy is when the symbols are imputed to inform the practice but pragmatically do not.

Much of theology has to do with both of these senses of the truth of symbols in practice. The practical mode of theology is to articulate basic symbols as the deep structures to which communities are committed in principle, and then to determine how those symbols ought to apply to practice so that the communities are faithful to their deep structure. To belong to a religious community is to be invested with its symbols, clothed in them, so that one's practices play out the roles and initiatives within the community defined by them. Christianity is a religion that symbolizes such investment with models of conversion—putting off old clothes and putting on new ones.[24] Judaism rather emphasizes growing into the clothes of the family, the people of Israel. Islam insists on conscious affirmation of the basic symbols of the faith as well as the way of life following from them. Buddhism emphasizes the coming to existential realization of the real

---

24. See Carl G. Vaught's wonderful essay on Augustine's "putting on Christ" in his "Theft and Conversion." For a more complete view, see Vaught's two-volume study of Augustine's *Confessions, The Journey toward God in Augustine's Confessions* and *Encounters with God in Augustine's Confessions*, esp. the latter volume, pp. 90–99.

meaning of the basic symbols. Confucianism sets the goal of the sage to be commitment to a self-transformative process to be able to engage reality with the basic symbols and to form the community on the inspiration of that. Daoism stresses the use of the basic symbols to attain greater attunement with reality. Various forms of Hinduism exhibit all the above approaches and more.

The role of symbols guiding practices needs to be understood in terms of the density of interpretation in human life. Not only do we interpret the world consciously, relevant to our purposes and explicit attention, but at all times we comport ourselves in indefinitely dense ways with respect to our physical and social environments. Like driving a car, when we read the signs of the road, of other drivers, of the kinetic movement of the car, and a thousand other details while musing about something else, most of these interpretations are below the level of consciousness. Like learning to drive a car, the interpretations at one time might have been conscious, but they sink into a background of constantly shifting interpretations. So with interpretations employing religious symbols. Whereas we might not be thinking about anything at all explicitly religious, the way we take our world can be shot through with religious symbols that yield up the value they can carry over from their objects. Our practices are not so much explicitly directed by intentions to conform to the values conveyed by religious symbols as they are ways of harmonizing the myriad interpretations that bear religious significance into coordinated movements.

The importance of the truth of religious symbols in practice goes far beyond what the Yale School anticipated. As the pragmatists saw, the long-run testing of any hypothesis lies in whether it most richly discriminates what is most important to discriminate in life to guide living. Of course it takes an elaborate system of cross-checking to see whether a theological system in fact discriminates that well, part by part. Hence the testing of theology in practice requires the dialectical system. Tests are always made with regard to specifics in interpretation, so the specific doctrines and claims are required, both as networked within a system and as loosened up from the network, to have critical purchase on the system as a whole. And, to be sure, the vital symbols that guide life must include the primal witnesses of the religious imagination of the traditions at hand. So all the modes of theology are involved in the testing.

Given the scope of theology as symbolic engagement, the arena for practical testing cannot be limited to particular religious communities in which theologians participate firsthand. Because they are vulnerable to criticism from theologians in other religious communities and from practitioners of all the disciplines that might bear upon ultimate matters, the community in which practice is the test of the theology must be inclusive of all. In the end, the testing community includes the whole of human civilizations insofar as they interact in ways bearing upon ultimate matters. For this reason, the theological question of the *public* for theology is very complex, because participants live practically in that public in different roles and ways. This is far more complex than simply building a conversation across cultures and disciplines to make one's theology properly vulnerable, although that requirement is the engine that determines the field of relevant practice for the testing of theology, the topic of chapters 7 and 8 below.

Theological Truth and Context

I can now express the problematic of truth in theology as symbolic engagement schematically in terms of three sets of variables: semiotic, modal, and contextual. The semiotic variables have to do with the way interpretation itself structures the carryover of ultimate importance into interpretive life. The modal variables are imagination, assertion, dialectical systematic theorizing, and the symbolically guided practice of living before the ultimate. The contextual variables have to do with the loci of theological thinking.

The *semiotic variables* concern the formal structure of an interpretation in which the actual interpretation carries over into the interpreter the value or importance of the object in the respects in which the interpretation takes signs or symbols to stand for the object. At least five connected semiotic variables are important to notice and track: interpretive *context*, the network *meanings* of the signs, the modes of *reference* of the signs in the interpretation, *respects* of interpretation, and *readiness* of the interpreters. To ascertain whether carryover of the relevant value in the object has occurred, all these variables need to be identified. The identification is usually not explicit, insofar as most of these things can be taken for granted when they are understood; vast confusions arise in theology, however, when they are misunderstood.

The context of an interpretation is always concrete and particular, although of course it contains universals in its symbols, habits and regularities, and ritualized elements. Two elements enter into any context, the setting and the purpose. The settings, of course, include all the settings of religious life that might have theological reflection. But they also include all the settings occupied by any person or institution that constitutes part of the public of theology. The settings for theology collectively are its proper public. The purposes that shape interpretations within the settings are extremely diverse, from highly theoretical to extremely practical, from communicating with children to raising money for a religious charity.

Although the contexts shaped by setting and purpose are indefinitely varied, for understanding a schematic structure for testing theology, the four loci of theology are the most important and will be discussed separately shortly.

The meanings of the signs in an interpretation, especially of religious symbols, are defined by semiotic systems or codes. In religions, the basic symbols are defined within networks of other symbols that have residence, consistent or not, within a larger semiotic code that supplies the grammar of the networks' interactions. The symbols of sacrifice in the theology of the Christian writer St. Paul, to use an example already mentioned, come from at least three different networks of symbols. One is the network arising from the Exodus crisis in which Israelites in Egypt sacrificed lambs or goats and smeared the blood on their doors to prevent the Angel of Death from destroying their firstborn. Another is the network arising from the Levitical atonement sacrifice in which the sins of the people were put on a goat (or lamb?) that carried the sins away into the wilderness. Yet another is the apocalyptic imagery of Jesus as a sacrifice to redeem sinners from the Devil who has juridical right to them in the battle between God and Satan. Each of these networks has its own logic that must be understood in assessing particular interpretations, even though the symbols of sacrifice are common to all. To test the truth of an interpretation, the exact meanings (or inexact range of meanings) of the symbols involved need to be identified to avoid confusion. Much theological debate has to do with how the terms ought to be defined, a necessary task for assessing whether the terms are used correctly in an interpretation to carry over the truth. Debate about how the symbols ought to be defined in their various networks takes place within encompassing semiotic systems.

The modes of reference in an interpretation are those of icon, index, and convention. The iconic mode refers by saying that the object is like the sign or symbol in the respect in which the sign stands for it, as a street map refers to the layout of a city. Any description, however, is iconic if taken in the iconic mode of reference. A physicist's theory says its mathematical formulations mirror the relations of the physical world. A journalist says the newspaper account tells the story as it happened. But not all signs that have the form of description in fact refer iconically. A novel, for instance, is an elaborate sign that, in its fictitiousness, does not refer iconically to events but rather refers indexically by transforming the readers so that they pick up on something important in reality they would not have gotten otherwise. The sense in which fiction or art is "true" is much more indexical than iconic. Religious symbols are often referred more indexically than iconically. Disputes within many religious traditions between supernaturalists and others have to do with whether supernatural symbols must be referred iconically rather than indexically. All religious symbols refer conventionally, and this is defined by their networks of meanings.

The respect in which signs stand for their objects within given interpretations also needs to be identified. Most often, the respect is embodied in the intention in the act of interpretation itself. But sometimes there is confusion. For instance, Krishna in the Bhagavad Gita and Christ in the New Testament are both referred to as "Lord." In both cases, the terms derived from hierarchical political and social structures in which people owed allegiance to certain people above them, a structure that the Christian Middle Ages made very explicit. Yet would early Hindus or Christians think that the Lordship of their objects of devotion stood for those objects in a political respect? Possibly, if the political matters involved ultimate allegiance. But not necessarily, since they clearly had other lords in the political arena; Jesus explicitly said to render to Caesar the things that are Caesar's. Rather, in both cases it would seem that the respect in which Lordship stands for Krishna and Christ respectively has to do with a cosmic power that strangely is worthy of devotion. That the devotion can sometimes conflict with political authorities only shows how complicated the respects are in which allegiance is parsed. As chapters 4 and 5 will argue, the respects in which signs stand for objects are the categories in which alternative signs can be compared. These respects need to be identified if the claims of an interpretation to carry over what is valuable in the respect in which the sign stands for the object is to be tracked and assessed.

The readiness of interpreters is a semiotic variable having to do with effects of the stage of life and the existential state of the interpreter on whether a putative interpretation can be engaging. A child might know all the symbols and participate in correctly formed acts of interpretation in a liturgy and still not find the interpretation engaging in the way an adult would. Furthermore, because the effects of indexical reference often take a long time to work, as in the development of devotional life, even adults find great variation in the meaningfulness of interpretations. Elderly people, too, find that interpretations that once were meaningful change in their powers to engage. As to existential state, the signs in a religious culture develop to suit the leading people at the appropriate stage. But some people might have existential characteristics that prevent them from engaging with the signs that work for others and whose meanings, modes of reference, respects of interpretation, and contexts they know. For instance, persons who were sexually abused as children by their fathers are not likely to be able to engage God as father even though they know theoretically the differences between God and their father. In spiritual discernment, the determination of the stage and state of the interpreter is extremely important, often more important than sorting out the exact meanings and modes of reference of the symbols in the interpretations.

In order properly to assess the truth of an interpretation, confusions about all the semiotic variables need to be avoided. Although often the variables can be taken for granted in commonsense ways, in theological disputes they often are the hidden causes of misunderstanding and false disagreement or false agreement.

The *modal variables* are the different senses of truth in imagination, assertion, systematic dialectical theorizing, and practical living guided by symbols. With regard to testing the truth of symbolic engagements, the four modes have a nested or hierarchical arrangement. Images are true if they pick up on what is important religiously and bring that into interpretations. Knowing whether they are true, however, depends on whether a case can be made for them as assertions about what is important to recognize. Assertions are true if they carry across into the interpreters what is valuable in their objects in the respects in which their symbols stand for the objects. Knowing whether they are true depends on making them vulnerable to as many potential critical tests as possible, which requires evaluating them within a dialectical system of analysis. A dialectical system is true if its structure guides interpreters to evaluate the contexts of its contents properly so that the truth of the various assertions it systematizes is recognized in context, and so that assertions true in one context can be recognized as false in another. Knowing whether a dialectical system is true depends on two factors: the cogency of its internal dialectic and its fruitfulness in guiding the practice of life in ultimate matters. Whether a systematically guided practice is true, and in what respects, consists in its carrying over into life what is ultimately important and shaping life so as to bear that importance. Knowing whether a systematically guided practice is true depends on long-term assessment, dialectically guided, of the richness of the religiously patterned life in ultimate matters.

In each of these modes the semiotic variables might need to be handled differently from the way they are understood in the other modes. Contexts are various and will be discussed shortly. As to meaning, consider the symbol of sacrifice, for instance. In the imaginative mode, ascertaining its truth would involve determining whether it articulates something important in religious or social life, and inquiries associated with Rene Girard, for example, would be relevant areas for testing. Girard holds that sacrifice is a nearly universal phenomenon because all societies are under great internal pressure for the sake of social control, and sacrifice releases the pressure.[25] In the

---

25. See Girard's *Violence and the Sacred*.

assertive mode, sacrifice would be treated like a doctrine, as in the Chinese doctrine of the emperor as Son of Heaven with sacrificial ritual roles, or the Jewish and Christian doctrines of atonement. In the dialectical systematic mode, sacrifice would have a polyvalent meaning derived from its various uses as an image, from doctrinal formulations, from ritual practices as understood comparatively from all cultures, from its thematic roles in literatures of various cultures, and so forth. In the practical mode, sacrifice would find its meanings in the various patterns of life involving sacrifice, both good and bad, all as shaped by relevant images, assertions, and systematic understandings of sacrifice. The other semiotic variables—reference, respect, and interpretive readiness—also are shaped differently in the four modes of engagement. These will be discussed as they arise in subsequent chapters. To assess whether a theological interpretation is true requires understanding its modal character as imaginative, assertive, dialectically systematic, or practical.

The contextual variables especially important for theology as symbolic engagement are the four theological loci: (1) the expression of primary revelations and witnesses; (2) developing articulated teachings, doctrines, and claims usually associated with theology, including the cases made for them; (3) constructing and criticizing systematic theologies, worldviews, and theories of religion adumbrated by scientists and secular scholars as well as by religious thinkers; and (4) the practice of symbolically directed spiritual exercises, liturgies, communal practices, and the personal lives as these are shaped by and in turn test all the others. The fourth includes practices relating to ultimacy in all domains of life and inquiry and in all cultures, not only in those associated with institutional religion. These four provide the main contexts in which theology is done. Each has a family of settings peculiar to it, and purposes that are distinct from though related to the purposes in the others.

Recognition of the semiotic, modal, and contextual structures of theological interpretations is necessary for understanding them and for being able to ask whether they carry across into the interpreters, so contextualized, the appropriate value or importance of the ultimate matters that are their objects. Assessment of the truth of a theological interpretation needs to be sensitive to all these dimensions. The complexity of this enterprise, surely matching that of any mathematically articulated science, might be one reason why so many theologians back away from claiming that their theology is true, or merely assert it to be true because they will to identify with it.

The multitude of distinctions made in this chapter, often without much illustration, will be further explained and illustrated in what follows.

CHAPTER 3

Theological Imagination

Imagination as Synthesis

Imagination in Western thought has an ancient pedigree and came into its own as a fundamental philosophical concept with the late eighteenth- and nineteenth-century Romantics. Plato was its first great theorizer and he contributed two extraordinary ideas about it. In the *Republic*, he illustrated a parallel between modes of cognition and modes of reality in his diagram of the Divided Line.[1] He said to divide a line (think of it as vertical) into two unequal parts (think of the larger section on the bottom); then divide each of those parts into two parts in the same ratio. You would then have a line of ascending smaller segments (Plato said). On the right hand side of the line, starting from the bottom, list four cognitive modes or faculties: imagination, common sense (*pistis*), theory, and dialectic. Corresponding on the left-hand side are their respective objects: images, the concrete world of change, forms structurally considered, and forms dialectically considered. The faculty of imagination was especially well developed in poets, and they

---

1. This analysis and use of Plato's Divided Line will be developed and made more complicated several times in the following chapters. See the brilliant analysis of the Divided Line in Robert S. Brumbaugh's *Platonic Studies of Greek Philosophy: Form, Arts, Gadgets, and Hemlock*, part 1, esp. chap. 3. Plato used many models to make his points but was insistent on "breaking" the models so that people would not confuse the model with the reality. In the instance of the Divided Line, for example, notice that if the ratio of the two parts of the greater division is replicated in the divisions of each of those parts, the two middle segments of the four would always be equal in length, contradicting the direction to make them progressively smaller.

provided images for thinking about things. The Divided Line, which occurs in the middle of the *Republic*, is a key to understanding its structure. In book 1, Socrates' first interlocutors, Cephalus and his son Polemarchus, argue by quoting the poets. In the latter part of book 1, Thrasymachus, the next interlocutor and a professional Sophist, gives arguments from common sense. In books 3–5, Glaucon and Adeimantus, Plato's half brothers and proud theoreticians, present hypothetico-deductive theories of society and self to explain justice; in the rest of the dialogue, Socrates toys with them dialectically. In the *Republic*, Plato discusses not only poetic imagination and images, but also images as items of perception taken out of a commonsense-integrating context, such as reflections of trees in water, shadows cast by objects moving in front of a fire, and so forth. Commentators have pointed out that Plato distrusts imagination, or at least poets. They usually fail to point out that he believes imagination is the beginning and foundation of knowledge.

Plato's second insight into imagination comes in the dialogue *Phaedrus*, which generally is about truth in art. Plato's point to the youth Phaedrus, whom he seduces with a poetry superior to Phaedrus's previous model (presented by a would-be seducer), is that imaginative claims in art (especially rhetoric, the art in question) need to be subjected to dialectical criticism. In passing, however, Plato has Socrates give an argument that life in the soul consists in its ability to engender action spontaneously. In context, this is a philosophically spurious but rhetorically successful argument to prove the non-mortality of the soul, which Socrates wants Phaedrus to believe in order to accept certain consequent points. The larger point is that the soul has spontaneous powers to produce images, beautiful images, that themselves shape action. Commentators have hit upon the idea that this argument is supposed to be a proof of the immortality of the soul and, as a proof, it is a bad one. The real contribution is the notion of spontaneity in imagination relative to the (image) idea that thought proceeds logically.

Immanuel Kant inherited these Platonic ideas, whether or not he recognized their origin; or perhaps he simply imagined them anew. In the "Transcendental Deduction" of the first edition of his magnificent *Critique of Pure Reason*, he gave a brilliant account of imagination as the synthesis of otherwise merely causal elements into the fundamental structure of experience. For him, imagination is the secret source of both the forms of intuition in perception and the concepts by which perceptions are organized. In his thought, this means that the forms of intuition, space and time, are the result of imagination deep within the human soul, as well as all the concepts that we can recognize as logically related. For Kant, the human sense of thinking as an act is the spontaneous production of images (forms of intuition and concepts of various sorts) that integrate things according to a rule. The rule is the unity of the imaginative product. Kant combined Plato's separate notions of image production in poetry and the arts with spontaneity.

Following Kant, Romantic thinkers such as Hegel, Kierkegaard, Schleiermacher, Goethe, Coleridge, Wordsworth, Ruskin, Emerson, Peirce, James, and others, just to list some in the German- and English-speaking worlds, developed various views of imagination as the Holy Spirit creating within what they imagined as the mechanical world of nature. Many of these Romantics thought to use imagination to transcend traditional institutional religion.[2]

In our own time, Ray L. Hart has systematically formulated the theological use of imagination in his *Unfinished Man and the Imagination*. Beginning with the hermeneutical theory of Hans Georg Gadamer, Hart has pressed this "interpretation" or "common sense" orientation back to its ontological constitution in imagination. Although articulated in the discussion of "being" as framed by Heidegger, whom Gadamer follows so much, Hart's argument gets back to the basics of imagination. He argues that revelation and human self-constitution are correlated in imagination. As Fritz Buri has said so well, the entire cottage enterprise of "imagination in theology" has arisen from Hart's work.[3] Other major theologians of our time have written extensively on imagination, for instance, Gordon Kaufman in *The Theological Imagination: Constructing the Concept of God* and David Tracy in *The Analogical Imagination: Christian Theology and the Culture of Pluralism*.[4]

In the meantime, naturalistic thinkers (whom the Romantics are slow to recognize, pace Wordsworth) have developed models for cognitive processes, including imagination. Charles Peirce, who might be regarded as both a Romantic and a naturalist, argued for the spontaneous emergence of elements, which he called "Firstness," in contrast to opposition ("Secondness") and mediation in signs ("Thirdness").[5] William James was wondrously open to novelty in imagination, and John Dewey, though more indebted to scientific models, pioneered in the development of ideas of

---

2. See James Engell's *The Creative Imagination: Enlightenment to Romanticism* for a study of the Romantic elaboration of imagination.

3. For a discussion of "theology of imagination," see Fritz Buri's "American Philosophy of Religion from a European Perspective: The Problem of Meaning and Being in the Theologies of Imagination and Process." Buri credits Ray Hart's *Unfinished Man and the Imagination* with initiating this movement in theology.

4. See Garrett Green's wonderful study of imagination in theology, both historically deep and dialectically acute, *Imagining God: Theology and the Religious Imagination*.

5. Peirce's most famous discussion of imagination is in his essay "A Neglected Argument for the Reality of God." There he argues that, in "musing" on a problem such as the one and the many, free thought would instinctively come up with good guesses in about forty minutes. See CP 5.452–91.

human creativity giving rise to aesthetically controlled novelty.[6] By the end of the twentieth century, cognitive scientists and neuroscientists were speculating models of brain activity that could be correlated with religious experience and imagination.[7]

The following is a philosophical hypothesis about imagination that is sufficient to address its theological usage.[8] Readers who care more about what imagination does in theology than what it is more generally can skip to the next section.

The function of imagination is to cause the elements of reality, with all their various causal properties, to be synthesized into the processes of experience so that experiencers or interpreters engage the world. Reality impinges on experiencers in a great many ways, from bombardment by cosmic particles to the force of gravity, the mechanical interactions of commonsense objects, metabolic processes, neurological processes, and the various bearings of ultimacy. Imagination is the specific set of causal processes that responds to all these by synthesizing them into experiential elements. Cognitive scientists and neuroscientists offer hypotheses about what these imaginative causal processes are, and they probably are an advance upon Kant, who treated the synthesizing spontaneity of imagination as a secret and mysterious source underlying objects on the one hand and mind on the other.[9] The present hypothesis does not separate objects and mind as different modes of being and hence needs no hidden ground for their connection. Rather, there is a continuity of causal processes in which interpreters take in reality with experiential form and respond to it with the intentionality and semiotic patterns of interpretive, purposive experience.[10] This is the root notion of engagement.

Imagination has at least four dimensions that should be mentioned. The first is synthesis as such, and Kant's analysis in "A Deduction" in *Critique*

---

6. See Dewey's *Art as Experience*. For a subtle discussion of Dewey's views of imagination in religion as well as his whole philosophy of the transcendent, see Victor Kestenbaum's *The Grace and the Severity of the Ideal*.

7. For interesting speculative approaches in cognitive science, see Terrence W. Deacon's *The Symbolic Species: The Co-evolution of Language and the Brain* and Gilles Fauconnier and Mark Turner's *The Way We Think: Conceptual Blending and the Mind's Hidden Complexities*. In many respects, the latter volume expresses in the contemporary witty language of cognitive science the logic of transmutation that Whitehead laid out in *Process and Reality* (1929), esp. part 3.

8. This theory of imagination is worked out in great technical detail in my *Reconstruction of Thinking*, chaps. 5–8.

9. This point was central to Heidegger's interpretation of Kant in *Kant and the Problem of Metaphysics*. Kant wrote, "This schematism of our understanding, in its application to appearances and their mere form, is an art concealed in the depths of the human soul, whose real modes of activity nature is hardly likely ever to allow us to discover, and to have open to our gaze." *Critique of Pure Reason*, B180–81.

10. This is the point of the title of Warren Frisina's *The Unity of Knowledge and Action: Toward a Nonrepresentational Theory of Knowledge*. I argued the case at length in the philosophy of nature in *Recovery of the Measure*.

of Pure Reason provides the clue.[11] He distinguished three syntheses. The first, the synthesis of "apprehension in intuition," is the combining of stimuli to constitute a field in which all are together without losing their characters. He was particularly interested in space and time as fields, but using his theory, we can recognize countless other fields as well, including conceptual fields. The second, "reproduction in imagination," is the synthesis by which one can run through elements in a field so that the earlier are not lost when the later are reached. Instead of "now, now, now," or "here, here, here," reproduction in imagination gives us "now, again, and yet again," and "here, there, and still further." The dynamism of experience is based on imaginative reproduction. The third Kantian synthesis is "recognition in a concept," by which is meant synthesis according to a rule that relates the items synthesized in a field and reproduced. In counting, reproduction alone would give us "one, one, one"; with the plurality recognized according to a concept, we have "one, two, three." In this way, the dynamism of experience has continuity. The three elementary Kantian syntheses involve much transmutation of the original items synthesized in order to fit them into the continuous dynamic fields of experience.[12]

The realities synthesized in imagination can have many kinds of value, or disvalue, for each other, in themselves, and in relation to the experiencing interpreter. The synthesis of imagination adds to whatever values are included the extra value of gathering them together in the continuous dynamic fields. In the carryover of value involved in true interpretation, there are thus two "moments" of value, one in the things synthesized and the other in the synthesis itself. The second provides a place for error: the value achieved in the synthesis might distort the values in the things synthesized, as would be the case with imagination that involves denial; the denial might be of very great value for the interpreter, life saving perhaps, and yet it would lead to error about the value carried over from the objects.

In general, imagination as the bare gathering of things into continuous, dynamic fields is the province of religious imagination, as will be explicated in more specific detail in the next section.

Imagination as mere synthesis is an abstraction from concrete experience. In concrete experience, the synthesized fields have qualities. Now to assert that something has such and such a quality is an assertoric judgment, which will be discussed in the next chapter. But the judgment is based on

---

11. See Kant's *Critique of Pure Reason*, pp. 98–110, for that portion of the "A Deduction" dealing with the three syntheses.

12. See Whitehead's *Process and Reality*, part 3, for an analysis of transmutation by which a multiplicity of things is represented by some one thing, which is synthesizable with other things into a dynamic, continuous field. Fauconnier and Turner's notion of "blending" is a variant on this.

what might be called an imaginative perceptual interpretation. By means of imagination, the items in the field are synthesized as having qualities of various sorts. The imaginative interpretation just takes them to be as the qualities present them. Imagination synthesizes the items in the field with qualities, which at this point can be called "images." The qualities emerge from the synthetic work of imagination on the items in the field, and illustrate what Whitehead called transmutation, the use of one thing to integrate or stand for a multiplicity of things.[13] The images for basic experience come in large measure from imaginative syntheses of the optical, auditory, olfactory, touch, and kinetic systems of the body. But we can also "perceive" the relaxed atmosphere of a family at the table, or the tension in a crowd; Peirce argued that we perceive God if we but reflect on the ultimate multifariousness of things.[14] These are imaginative perceptions, and might in fact be false; to assert them as true perceptions is a matter of assertoric judgment.

At the level of imagination, perceptive synthesis has an implicit norm of assigning qualities that jointly are valuable. Not only is there the value of having the items in the field together, there is the value of putting them together in such a harmony as to achieve interestingness.[15] The general term for this norm is beauty. Perceptual imaginative synthesis is not cut off from the things synthesized, and so some element of the beautiful is the degree to which the beautiful perceptual synthesis is true to (that is, carries over) the values in the items. Imaginative qualities, images, then are normed by how beautiful they are, by how they make what they synthesize interesting. Art is the civilization of the work of imagination in perception, providing more interesting images for perception.

The imaginative field of experience is more than merely qualitatively diverse, dynamic, and continuous. The field is punctuated by objects that stand out from backgrounds, that "appear." These appearances might be physical objects in visual and auditory fields. Or they might be objects in any field that can become the focus of attention. Attention is focused by form. We attend to those things whose forms we recognize. The notion of form has been a central philosophical problematic since Plato and Aristotle, and theology as symbolic engagement involves a very particular and rich hypothesis about the nature of form. Although this is not the place to develop the full hypothesis about form, it proposes that form itself is to be understood as the synthesis by which things with the values that ought to

---

13. See Whitehead's *Process and Reality* p. 27, and part 3, chap. 1.
14. See Peirce's "Neglected Argument for the Reality of God," CP 6:452–93.
15. See Whitehead's brilliant discussion of beauty in *Adventures of Ideas*, chaps. 17 and 18, and of importance in *Modes of Thought*, chap. 1.

stand out or appear against a background do stand out. Form is the together-ness that carries over the values of things such that they can stand out in our attention from the imaginative field. In this sense, form is a function of car-rying over value rather than value being a function of form.[16] Imagination synthesizes forms to organize the stimuli and impingements of things into "things" that can be engaged. Without form defining the boundaries of things, their relations to one another and to their backgrounds, the differen-tial engagement of things would be impossible. Form has the intrinsic value of making differential engagement possible. Because of form, we can pay attention. For many thinkers, form is of the essence of images—images are forms. That was not the way Plato used the terms, though the point is not far from his hope that all form could be understood mathematically.

In concrete experience, imagination involves all these levels of synthesis at once. Together, this complex of imaginative activity constitutes elemen-tary engagement. Imagination involves not only the perception of appear-ances against a dynamic and continuous experiential field. It also involves the synthesis of this with purposes and intentions. We imaginatively engage the world noting the food in it because we are hungry. We imaginatively engage reality noting the ultimate because we long for ultimacy. At least that is what Augustine argued in the fourth sentence of the *Confessions* with this famous line: ". . . restless is our heart until it comes to rest in thee."

World Definition: Finite/Infinite Contrasts: Ultimacy

Peter Berger, the eminent sociologist of knowledge, uses the felicitous phrase "a sacred canopy" to describe the fundamental images by which reli-gions define the world, including its sacred and ultimate dimensions.[17] The web of images is like a large tent under which the adherents of a religion can gather and have the cosmos make sense to them. The web for any reli-gion is extremely intricate and might include images of the geography of the cosmos, of sacred times such as a golden age in the past or the future, narratives such as the Jewish Exodus story or the Christian redemption story, models for saintliness and virtue, and, of course, direct images of ultimate

---

16. The complex hypothesis about form, including the point that value defines form rather than the other way around, is defended at length in my *Reconstruction of Thinking*, chap. 7. The detail of that analysis is important for assessing the general claim that form is the synthesis of value that allows things to appear against a background as a focus of attention. That general claim in turn is important for the causal theory of imaginative perception developed here as applicable to primary witness. That imagi-nation is perceptual, of course, does not mean that it is infallible, as some modern European philoso-phers had hoped. Imagination is fallible even when causal.

17. See his *The Sacred Canopy* and also his *The Social Construction of Reality* with Thomas Luckmann. My exposition of the notion of sacred canopy draws on sources other than his, although the basic idea comes from Berger.

realities such as gods and cosmic principles such as Dao. The sacred canopy for pre-Axial Age religions imagines human life as intricately part of a relatively seamless whole of nature and spirits, what Berger calls a "mythic matrix."[18] Axial Age religions have sacred canopies exhibiting more transcendence for the ultimate and more solidarity of the human over against nature.

Berger points out that a sacred canopy is encountered as something objective handed down through tradition, usually family tradition, and internalized as people come to have a repertoire of images to engage their situation in reality. As internalized, people take the sacred canopy to be the way things are. They experience the world through the canopy's images in its broad general outlines. People act upon the basis of the internalized sacred canopy, thereby objectifying it again externally in the deeds and symbols of their religious culture.

The analogy of a sacred canopy might suggest that the network of world-defining religious images is static, when in fact it is constantly changing. The dialectic of external tradition being internalized and personalized and then directed outward in behavior would guarantee constant modification by itself. Sometimes the modifications are not much noticed and a claim can be made, or assumed to be true, that the current canopy is what has "everywhere and always" been believed. At other times, great events or discoveries "rend" the sacred canopy, requiring that it be mended or abandoned. The Copernican revolution in astronomy was devastating to the sacred canopy that made the Earth and its history the significance center of the cosmos. The divisive and losing fortunes of Israel after the death of Solomon tore great holes in the sacred canopy of the Chosen People. The empires of India and especially China, convinced that they were the repositories of the ultimate cosmic powers, were radically shaken in their sacred canopies by their defeat at the hands of the Western imperial nations. The decisive defeat of the Ottoman Empire and other Muslim nations by the imperial European powers has put extraordinary strains on Islam's sacred canopy, according to which everything that happens is God's will, an image that was not difficult to sustain during the days of Muslim expansion and highly civilized rule. Of course, these events and cultural changes are far more subtle and nuanced than mentioned here; nevertheless, the point holds about the dynamic quality of a religion's sacred canopy and about some of the traumas reality gives to those images.[19]

---

18. Berger discusses the mythic matrix in *Questions of Faith*, a more recent book than *The Sacred Canopy*.

19. Wesley J. Wildman has argued that theology has two modes—the articulation, rationalization, and expression of a sacred canopy in practical ways, and the creative work of dealing with reality when the sacred canopy is rent beyond quick repair. The latter is more interesting. See his "Theological Literacy: Problem and Promise."

What does it mean to say that a sacred canopy defines a world? Theology as symbolic engagement develops Berger's point the following way. The network of images in a sacred canopy articulates ways of answering basic questions about what reality is. For instance, there is a fundamental question about existence itself: Why is there a world? Creation imagery, divine or otherwise, often defines a religion's approach to this fundamental question. Is there wholeness or fragmentariness in the cosmos? Religious geographies address this issue. What is the ultimate nature and source of value, and how do we understand the tension between good and evil? Sacred canopies address this. Is there purpose for human life in the larger cosmos? What are normative kinds of affiliation? To family, clan, humanity? How does humanity relate to nature? What is the human spirit, and what is death?

All these and other basic questions require some settling in order for the affairs of daily life to proceed. How those questions are answered provides a kind of ultimate set of orientations within which more proximate affairs have significance. Most people do not think about these ultimate questions in their daily lives, but they do presuppose some ways of answering them in order for their daily lives to find orientation in the larger reality of the cosmos. A religious tradition provides answers in the form of the network of images in its sacred canopy. Theologians do think about these questions, both in the terms provided by some sacred canopy and in the search for new images that acknowledge new, sometimes canopy-rending realities. Most religions have festivals to reenact, teach, and celebrate the salient points in their canopy's imaging of answers to the basic questions: rites of birth and death, coming of age, family and civic identity, fertility and changes of the seasons, and the proclamation of the founding myths, texts, and motifs of thought characterizing their network of world-defining images.

The temptation to think of a sacred canopy as a mere human construction in contrast to worldly reality should be resisted, although the modern epistemological tradition of the West would suggest that subjective mind versus objective world mentality. Rather, the sacred canopy needs to be regarded as in causal continuity with the reality whose fundamental features it images. The images are imaginative constructs within human semiotic causality that allow for reality to be grasped as a dynamic and continuous experiential field, for it to be perceived at all, and for important things to appear within it. More particularly, the shaping of the fundamental structures of experience by a sacred canopy is a necessary kind of imaging for the world to appear experientially within which ordinary affairs take place. Without being able to assume some stance toward existence, continuity, value, relations with nature and other people, and the background meaning of life and death, people would have no orientation within which to make a living, enjoy friends and family, or exercise artistic creativity. This point holds for modern secular elites as much as for traditional religious people. The modern secular elites derive much of their sacred canopy from science and the imaginative inventions of culture, and they might object to calling it "sacred" because they regard their canopy as hypothetical and not derived from "revelation." Some elites also give very negative answers to some of the basic questions, for instance, that there is no real value in the world, no meaning to life, and so forth; these negations still are real images for answering the basic questions. In a fundamental sense, even the secular canopies are sacred.

That sense can be exhibited in the following analysis, which is an hypothesis explaining more theoretically what the world-defining issues are about. Let us suppose that the "object" engaged in an interpretation employing a fundamental religious image is a world-defining character. That "object" is *finite* in the sense that the character is determinate. For instance, the world, though contingent, is existent; the world has value of such and such a sort; life has this kind of meaning and not that; human affiliation is normatively to be this but not that, and so forth. On the other hand, if there were no world-defining character in that respect, that respect of the world would be nonfinite or *infinite*. This is different from saying that the world-defining character would simply be different. For instance, with respect to normative human affiliation, one religion (for example, Confucianism) might say that it is family love, whereas another (Mohism) might say it is universal love; in this respect, the fundamental images of the religions can be compared. But if there were no image in this respect at all, there would be no normative human affiliation; normative human affiliation would be nothing, nonfinite, infinite. If there were no image for fundamental value in the universe, with respect to value the universe would be empty, nonfinite, infinite. If there were no image of the grounding of contingent existence, in respect of the category of existence the world would be conceived to be empty, nothing, just the unformed realm of infinity. The "objects" articulated in fundamental world-defining religious symbols are finite/infinite contrasts.

A "contrast" is a reality that has two or more characters that simply fit together without further mediation.[20] A finite/infinite contrast is where one side is a positive character, for example, the creation of the world, intrinsic value in creation, life with the purpose of harmonizing with nature, and the

---

20. "Contrast" is defined technically in this way by Whitehead in *Process and Reality*. I have employed the notion extensively in defining religious symbols; see *The Truth of Broken Symbols*, chap. 2.

other side is the absence of character in that respect, or infinity. A world-defining contrast has to be a finite/infinite one. It cannot be only finite, because the very meaning of the contrast as world defining is that without it, the world would not be defined in that respect. It cannot be only infinite, because there would then be no respect of world definition defined. The two must go together in a contrast.

A finite/infinite contrast can be a logical object in an interpretive engagement, although it cannot be an object in the way of a commonsense thing in the world. A commonsense object is determinate by virtue of being this rather than that, with features distinguishing it from other determinate things. It can also be determinately existent in the sense of being here-now rather than absent, a real thing of the sort it seems to be rather than a fiction of that sort, and so forth. The finite side of finite/infinite contrasts is also determinate with respect to other determinate things—that is necessary for it to be determinate at all. But its contrast as a world-determining character is with what would be the case if there were nothing determinate in that respect at all. Therefore, images of world-defining elements are explicitly kataphatic, ascribing a positive character to the objects, and at least implicitly apophatic, referring to what would be the case were reality not to be defined in that respect. Theology often explores the apophatic side, especially in mystical traditions. Religion in the sense of having images of world-defining characters can only come on the scene when human experience has evolved to the point of having something like the subjunctive mood in grammar, of imagining facts and counterfactuals together. Ontological wonder is the deep mood of theology that grasps the objects of foundational images for what they are, finite/infinite contrasts that define basic respects in which the world is defined.

In this technically defined hypothesis, the "infinite" side of a finite/infinite contrast simply means lack of determination in that respect, lack of finiteness. As such, it is pure, uninteresting nothingness. Nevertheless, in many religions, both axial and pre-axial, the fundamental images in fact assert that the finite character arises as a creature and the infinite side is the creator. The existence of the world, for instance, is caused by an infinite creator or very fecund nothingness, as in Zhou Dunyi's account of the arising of finite things or in many Mahayana Buddhist representations of nothingness, in the Brahman without qualities grounding the Brahman with qualities, and in creation ex nihilo theories in West Asian religions. These images give a somewhat positive though still indeterminate aura to the infinite in a finite/infinite contrast. The infinite is viewed as source. This is often true of images of value, deriving from an infinite creator, and of images of the meaning of human life and so forth. Nevertheless, not all religious images need give this positive assessment of the infinite side of a finite/infinite contrast, as many secular ones do not.

The reason all images of finite/infinite contrasts can be called "sacred," although this is not a necessary usage, is that they all at least implicitly refer to the counterfactual condition—what if there were no character in this respect? This is uncanny, world questioning. That is a fundamental meaning for sacrality, as Eliade, Otto, and others have shown.[21] This uncanny or sacred element is present, for instance, in Stephen Hawking's wonderment at the end of A Brief History of Time, surely a secular mathematical physicist's work:

> Even if there is only one possible unified theory, it is just a set of rules and equations. What is it that breathes fire into the equations and makes a universe for them to describe? The usual approach of science of constructing a mathematical model cannot answer the questions of why there should be a universe for the model to describe. Why does the universe go to all the bother of existing? Is the unified theory so compelling that it brings about its own existence? Or does it need a Creator, and, if so, does he have any other effect on the universe? And who created him?[22]

Hawking's imagined unified theory is, for him, among other things, an image for the finite/infinite contrast in respect of the world's existence.

The hypothesis about finite/infinite contrasts as world-defining characters imaged in religious sacred canopies makes possible a more functional definition of "ultimacy" as the subject matter of theology. Ultimacy is the trait of being a finite/infinite contrast. The world's imagination has produced countless images of finite/infinite contrasts, and many competing sacred canopies exist that detail fundamental respects in which the world is determined as such. The list of foundational respects of world determination recited above is only partial: existence, wholeness, value, purpose, relations of humanity to nature, normative human affiliations, the nature of the human spirit, the meaning of death. To make the list more nearly complete would require enormous empirical study. Each respect in which the world might be determined in this sense is a finite/infinite contrast whose images reflect that character. Each is ultimate in that, without some determination in that respect, there would be no definition of the world in that respect. The respect of contingent existence itself has a kind of priority among these respects in that they all presuppose it; perhaps contingency is

---

21. See, for instance, Eliade's The Sacred and the Profane and Rudolf Otto's The Idea of the Holy.
22. Stephen Hawking, A Brief History of Time, p. 174.

unique among finite/infinite contrasts in this way. The images articulating this contingency are not all alike: surely those of the pre-Axial Age religions of the mythic matrix differ from the Axial Age religions that first come to conceive of "cosmos."

Everything in ordinary experience that is oriented by an underlying image of a finite/infinite contrast has a religious dimension and can be an "ultimate matter." For instance, it is a good thing to feed one's small children, and the forces that prevent that, as well as parents who forswear the task, are evil in various senses. However existentially important—and it's a matter of life and death for the children—the obligation to feed one's children by itself is not a religious or ultimate matter. But that prosaic task is oriented by images of the finite/infinite contrast defining value in the world from which obligation comes and by the images of the finite/infinite contrast of normative affiliation that link parents to children. Thus, there is a religious dimension to neglecting obligation or responsibility to children. Because the religious dimension can be taken for granted under ordinary circumstances, most ordinary activities are not ultimate matters. Yet they presuppose the relevant ultimate matters and, in times of crisis, ordinary experience suddenly opens out into its ultimate dimensions. This is so especially when the taken-for-granted sacred canopy is blown away and no longer functions: the religious imagination abruptly faces the chaotic abyss of the night sky. Because every ordinary thing is oriented by images of finite/infinite contrasts, religious virtuosi can learn to see the ultimate in the most mundane of activities. That each thing is to be appreciated such as it is, for Buddhism, for instance, comes from the fact that each thing is imaged in a field, given characters, and presented as an appearance against a background in orientational reference to the ultimate characters that define the world experienced.

Theology's dealings with ultimacy can be sorted roughly into three types. First are the various articulations of ultimacy itself, namely, the imaginative invention of appropriate foundational images, the critical conceptualization of these and inquiry into their validity, the systematization of all this in light of whatever is found to be relevant, and the conception of the practical bearings they have on how to live life. Second are the various articulations of how ultimacy bears on human life to give it a predicament. Human life has special problems because of the nature of ultimacy, and resolving those problems is of ultimate concern in the anthropological sense of ultimacy. Crudely put, the West Asian religions see an ultimate demand for righteousness that people have difficulty, if not an impossibility, meeting; the South Asian religions see suffering as a kind of ontological contradiction to ultimacy, with the ultimate human task being the overcoming of suffering;

the East Asian religions see disharmony as the human predicament, with a return to harmony as life's goal. The third sort of theological dealing with ultimacy is in articulating patterns of life—how to be religious, if you will—that properly relate human individuals and communities to ultimate matters. These three are obviously related to one another, but in different ways in different traditions. All of them can be pursued through the images of the theological loci of primary witnesses, defense of doctrine, system building, and practical embodiment.

Invention, Convention, and Truth

The argument of this chapter has focused on images of world definition of primal, elementary sorts, those articulated in the myths and sometimes-fanciful symbols of scriptures and rituals. These images are networked into sacred canopies that serve more or less well to orient ordinary activity and that define the ultimate dimensions of things. But imagination is not limited to these kinds of images. In assertoric interpretation, ideas are needed for clarifying and testing the primal images of witness, and these ideas need to be produced by imaginative activity, that is, by synthetic energies that come up with new forms of thought. Imagination is also required for systematic thinking and for the exercise of practical reason. Every new concept or theoretical construct, or practical implication, is an "image" in the sense that it must be invented in order to be put to work, examined, and criticized. We do not hesitate to call the geniuses of religious thought, in theory as well as in primary witness, masters of creative imagination. If the inertia of previously given thought patterns were automatically successful in guiding ordinary life and its crises, people would barely be conscious of theological matters: imagination is required where inertia breaks down.

Imagination is inventive wherever it works. It invents primary images of the sacred canopy, the concepts for articulating them doctrinally and critically examining them, the theories for relating them to all to which they should be vulnerable for correction, and the patterns of practice following from them. Nevertheless, we should not think of imaginative invention as constructing an inner world that may or may not mirror an outer world. Imaginative invention is part of the process of engaging realities. It arises as a human (or at least intelligent) semiotic causal response to the impingements of reality around us. Human beings evolve to imagine just as they evolve to digest. This is as true of imaging the ultimate conditions of reality as it is of imaging prey and predators.

Precisely because the invention of images for symbolic engagement is an interpretive organism's response to the environing reality, at the primary level it can be called the perception of things that appear. The word "witness," though it arises in only a few religious traditions, is a good one for all. A "primary witness" is an interpretation based on an imaginative invention that allows something ultimately important to be perceived. Some traditions call this "revelation" in the sense that it comes from the divine or ultimate with the authority of a perception. Revelation also has fancier senses having to do with parsing the notion of authority through texts and institutions, but the basic sense of revelation has a validity: suddenly our eyes are opened and we see something otherwise obscured. The notion of revelation might hide the human activity of imaginative invention, as if the images were delivered wholly formed by an external source, like God writing the Ten Commandments for Moses or the angel dictating the Qur'an to Muhammad. Nevertheless, the power in the novelty of imagination suggests forces deeper than ordinary human thought processes. The Romantics identified the deep springs of human imagination with the divine.

We deploy primary witnesses in religious life as assumptions, forming patterns of worship, community life, spiritual exercises, and the like. Yet we also subject the witnesses to refinement and critical analysis. We sometimes make them explicit as assertions about what things are, and sometimes question their truth. Moreover, we take them up into the rest of life and subject them to that larger sense of criticism that comes from seeking out vulnerability; we test them in practical living. The critical formation and testing of doctrine is every bit as much a form of engagement with the doctrines' religious object as primary witnessing. Dialectical systematic theorizing is also a form of engaging, one that engages a huge scope of objects as made accessible through its large public. And of course practical living is a kind of engagement with ultimacy. Modern modes of criticism have not been easy on traditional sacred canopies. Nevertheless, the question of truth can be pressed while still acknowledging the causal, perceptual character of the primary witnesses.

It is important to stress the causal, perceptual character because the inventive element in imagination is easily misconstrued. Thinkers such as Gordon Kaufman, Sheila Davaney, and William Dean have carefully pointed out this invention and have analyzed it as historicist construction.[23] They are entirely right about the historical contingency and human imaginative origin of theological images and ideas at all levels. Yet often they fall into the Cartesian assumption that, because it is a subjective human construction, it

23. Kaufman has had a long career making this point. See his *God the Problem, An Essay on Theological Method, In Face of Mystery,* and *In the beginning . . . Creativity.* See Sheila Greeve Davaney's *Pragmatic Historicism: A Theology for the Twenty-First Century* and William Dean's *American Religious Empiricism, History Making History,* and *American Spiritual Culture.*

is out of causal connection with reality. Although they would never say that because our conception of "father" is a construction, there are no real fathers, they often suggest that because our conception of God is a construction, we cannot assume that it refers to anything real. They say that crucial theological conceptions are mere constructions that we invent to make sense of a world that really is not to be referred to as the conceptions say. The error here is to assume that theological images and concepts have no real reference because real reference would have to be iconic. That is, the only real reference would be to say that the real objects are like the concepts or images of them. As late modern thinkers, these theologians quickly reject the supernaturalism involved in most religious images within the sacred canopy of Christianity, and so reject iconic reference. Such images might not refer iconically, however, but rather indexically.[24] Their indexical reference is the establishment of a causal relation that changes or reorients the interpreter so that what is important in the object can be carried across into the interpreter.

Our argument about the causal properties of imagination has now fleshed out some elements of the causal relation in indexical reference. An image does not have to be taken to say that the object has some kind of isomorphic likeness to the image. It can rather say that treating the object as the image depicts can cause the interpreter to pick up on what is valuable or important in the object; if the interpreter does pick up on what is valuable, in the respect in which the image stands for the object, then the interpretation is true. Whether or not an image's reference in the interpretations assumed in a sacred canopy is indexical is an issue to be determined by triangulating in on the interpretation from a variety of other perspectives. Chief among these perspectives is metaphysics, as will be argued in chapter 5. Theologians who emphasize the constructive character of theological ideas and deny them real reference do so perhaps because they believe metaphysics is futile. I will argue in what follows that metaphysics is not futile at all.

Images at the primary level and all other critical levels are not standalone expressions of imaginative genius. They create and are surrounded by the conventional semiotic systems within which they have some kinds of public meaning. Imaginative creativity adds to, sometimes radically altering, the conventional semiotic systems of the community within which it

---

24. Dean could accept this point. In *The American Spiritual Culture*, he defines God as a "sacred social convention," the human responses to which he likens to more traditional responses to the biblical God. In the language of theology as symbolic engagement, Dean's claim is that "God" does not refer iconically to anything like a divine person, although it refers indexically with all sorts of divine-person traits to a social convention.

arises. At the same time, the newly created images and concepts relate to the conventions already on hand. Otherwise, they would not be recognized as responding to issues in the religious world that are meaningful. Moreover, the images even in primary witnesses are as much reconstructions as wholly new constructions out of previous traditional images. The Upanisads, for instance, built with novelty upon the older Vedas; Christians initially grasped Jesus in the terms of the Septuagint and Hellenistic religion, as in St. Paul's sacrificial atonement theory.

The conventions for primary witnesses are those that shape the particular religious community that receives those witnesses, and may not extend beyond them. Insofar as the elements of the primary witnesses are derived from other communities, the conventions extend that far too. But, as in the case with Christianity inventing symbols for Jesus that were derived from Judaism but which other Jewish sects rejected in the ways they were imaginatively combined for Jesus, the older communities might refuse precisely what is the new witness for its own community. In a strict sense, the conventions within which a witness is received as a perception-defining element of a partially new sacred canopy for communal life are limited to that community. This is much of what the Yale School means with its claim that each community has its own cultural-linguistic deep theological structure: the community accepts these primary witnesses as its founding imaginative perceptions.

As the imaginative perceptions of the primary witnesses of a given community are subjected to clear articulation and criticism, however, the conventions for imaginative expression are expanded to include all the publics that help define plausibility structures. This is true for the treatment of doctrines within large religious traditions and for the systematization of theological ideas that learns from other religions, the sciences, arts, and normative practices. The argument in this chapter, for instance, has treated images of primary witnesses with the conventions of semiotic theory and history of religions.

In the long run, the conventions to which the articulation of the products of imagination must conform amount to the publics within which those products might function in true interpretations. Imagination conforms to and reshapes the conventions giving bones to the elaborate scope of theology.

In what sense are products of imagination true? According to the hypothesis about truth being the carryover of what is valuable from the object to the interpreter in the respect in which the signs stand for the object, images need to carry over the relevant value in order to be true. Assertoric judgments are true or false when the interpreter intentionally asserts that reality is as the interpretation says. Imagination per se is not true in that sense. Images can function as signs in an assertoric judgment, and in theories, and so on, and would be true or false there in this intentional sense. But images also function in the background interpretations that are not asserted, just assumed as comprising elements of the context of more assertive intentionality. Images function in assumptive interpretations simply as enabling engagement. They might be true or false about what they engage. Yet that truth is not known or asserted. It is assumed, and perhaps wrongly so. The assumptions about the world might be mistaken, even though they engage. But if they are true, which would need to be determined by making a case for an assertive interpretation using them, the images function as bearing truth in the assumptions, carrying across the relevant value.

Founding Religious Witness: Core Texts and Motifs

The argument of this chapter has focused on imagination as a mode of symbolic engagement. Although it has just been noted that imagination is present in all kinds of theology, from primary witnesses to the grandest systematic thinking and schemes of practice, imagination is most prominent in primal witnesses, the first of the four major loci for theology.

In some religions, the primary witnesses are the activities of charismatic leaders and teachers, the great founders of religious traditions such as Confucius, Laozi, Gautama Buddha, Mahavira, Patanjali, Moses, Jesus, Paul, John, Mohammed.[25] In other religions, great events supply the founding witness as they are interpreted, such as the Exodus. In yet other religions, primary traditions exist that simply appear as handed down, as in shamanism, or that have canonical form in texts such as the Vedas, whose authors are unknown or not lauded as personalities. Most traditions have primary witnesses of all sorts interacting. Moreover, no clean line exists between primary witnesses and layers of interpretation of those witnesses. Often the witnesses themselves take the form of interpretation.

Theology is involved in the primary witnesses at the point where the witnesses are expressed in the conventions of language that they themselves are set within a culture. These expressions are recorded in texts that are regarded as "scripture" in some sort of authoritative sense (religions have various senses of authority). Or they are embodied in rituals that are carried

---

25. The Christian writers Paul and John would be the first to say that they are not founders in the sense that Jesus is. Yet their imaginative work in creating original images and conceptualizations of Jesus has been decisive for inaugurating the Christian tradition in distinction from other forms of Second Temple Judaism. The writers of the Synoptic Gospels, perhaps, were more interpreters and editors of other sources than creators of original images, at least when compared with Paul and John.

down. Or they are expressed in motifs of thought, such as the Chinese conception of process as interactions of forces of yin and yang, which have no *locus classicus* but are used repeatedly throughout literature and practice. For convenience these all can be referred to as "core texts and motifs," counting rituals and other symbol-shaped religious practices as texts.

Core texts and motifs have conventional expressions that allow them to be recognized in a wide community and handed down to others. Sometimes there might be a significant distinction between the original, founding primary witnesses and the core texts and motifs in which they are recorded. Christian neo-orthodox theologians such as Karl Barth claim that the Bible is a human record of the primal witness of God's activity in history, particularly in Jesus; Evangelical orthodox (not neo-) theologians usually say that the Bible itself is the inspired primary witness. Islamic scholars have considered whether the "real" Qur'an is what is in the mind of Allah, what the angel spoke to Muhammad, what Muhammad told his followers of the angel's message, or the text in which his citations of the message are written down. Some Buddhists have lamented the decline from the living Buddha who embodied the dharma in life and teaching, to followers after his death, who remembered him and his charisma and had the texts of his teachings, to disciples generations later who had no living memory but only the texts, to an extended tradition in which the texts themselves had been corrupted in transmission. These subtle distinctions illustrate the complicated interaction between original imagination, its conventional expression, and its recording and subsequent interpretation in core texts and motifs.

Regardless of these subtleties, the core texts and motifs themselves function in religions as the primary witnesses. The Jewish and Christian Bibles, the Qur'an, Hesiod's *Theogeny*, the *Mahabharata* (including the Bhagavad Gita), the Vedas (including the Upanisads), Buddha's sermons, Buddhist sutras and the Tripatika, the Analects of Confucius and the older texts he discussed, the Daodejing and Zhuangzi all are prominent core texts. They shaped people's imaginations deeply, were prominent in sacred canopies, provided the images for ritual and spiritual exercises, and were the sources for further theological reflection and the articulation of claims and assertions about ultimate matters. In addition to texts like these, which appeal to Protestant scholars as something like scriptures, there are ancient songs, poems, myths, and other images that are communicated without physical textual expression that also count as "core texts and motifs" in shaping a religious tradition.

The fortunes of core texts and motifs change continuously as they are handed around within traditions. They are interpreted in commentaries, expressed in other media such as the arts, and are made to be relevant to new situations in which ultimate matters need to be engaged. Tracing what happens to core texts and motifs in their historical fortunes is an excellent procedure for history of religions, because it allows scholars to back away from the fruitless task of defining the boundaries of traditions. Instead of generalizations such as "Hinduism" and "Buddhism," scholars can trace the fortunes of the Vedas, for instance. The Vedas themselves developed over centuries, with the later Upanisads telling tales of gods introduced in earlier literature. The Buddhists and Jains arose out of the culture shaped by the Vedas but rejected their authority, developing their own core texts and motifs connecting with the conventions of Vedic culture. In reaction to the denial of Vedic authority, the six orthodox schools of what we now know as Hinduism reasserted the authority of the Vedas, although interpreting them in quite different, often mutually contradictory ways. These orthodox schools, Nyaya, Vaisesika, Samkhya, Yoga, Purva Mimamsa, and Vedanta, each had its founding core text, usually associated with an author. Because these were remarkable new and divergent turns in the Vedic tradition, those core texts can be said to define their own traditions. Further, some of them underwent subsequent significant divergent development, as in the case of Vedanta, which developed an Advaita school with core texts by Samkara and the Vishistadvaita school with core texts by Ramanuja.

Meanwhile, Buddhism migrated into Tibet, where its encounter with the native Tibetan religion produced the great imaginative synthesis sometimes known as Tantric Buddhism. Buddhism also spread along the Silk Road.[26] At the Silk Road's western end, the great classic, *The Questions of King Milinda*, was a dialogue between a monk, Nagasena, and the king, who was a Greek ruler (Menander in Greek) over part of Alexander's Indian conquest; the dialogue is close to Socratic in form and in fact parallels some of the argument of Plato's *Phaedo*. At the eastern end of the Silk Road, Buddhism encountered Daoism, Confucianism, and Chinese shamanism, resulting in schools such as Hwa-yen and Chan (Zen) Buddhism. These schools of Chinese Buddhism of course carried on Indian core texts and motifs, including Vedic ones (though without authority), but they were extraordinary imaginative syntheses, expressed in new core texts and motifs of thought, with Chinese cultural conditions.

The ancient core texts and motifs of Daoism and Confucianism themselves had been founded against the background of earlier Zhou Dynasty literature, and they flourished into the Han Dynasty with many other schools. With the coming of Buddhism, Confucianism lost its dominance

---

26. See Jeffrey Hopkins's *Tantra in Tibet*.

at court and began to absorb Buddhist interests in personal spiritual cultivation through meditation and also metaphysical interests in being and
nothingness. Daoism absorbed those Buddhist influences plus the social
forms of monasticism and created the new core texts of what we know as
medieval or religious Daoism. The great founders of Neo-Confucianism at
the beginning of the Song Dynasty imaginatively integrated both Buddhist
and Daoist themes while citing always the authority of the ancient
Confucian core texts.

An analogous story is to be told of the fortunes of the core texts of the
Hebrew Bible, its development in commentarial rabbinic Judaism, including Cabbala, its Christian and Muslim variants. The nodes of new core texts
and motifs that marked its divergences also were imaginative integrations
with the core texts and motifs of other religions; for example, the dualistic
apocalypticism of Zoroastrianism, the pagan motifs of Hellenism, and the
Germanic and Celtic religions of pre-Christian Europe. When Christianity
flourished in China during the Dang Dynasty, it translated the beginning of
the Gospel of John: "In the beginning was the Dao"; perhaps that does not
count as a new core text, but it was part of an imaginative node that established a new branch of Sino-Christian religion.

The importance of the history of core texts is not only to show the deep
involvement of religions with one another. It is also to observe that at every
node in which a new core text or motif arises that marks a new direction or
branching of a tradition, a new imaginative symbolic engagement occurs
with the ultimate matters of the religious object. Sometimes this new
engagement has the imaginative force of a new primal witness; this surely
was the case with Buddha's development of the Vedas, and possibly also the
responses of the six orthodox schools of Hinduism. It also was the case with
the Christian and Muslim core texts and motifs building on the Hebrew
Bible. But sometimes the new core texts were in the form of the development of doctrine, especially in the commentarial traditions, for instance, in
the proliferating schools of Buddhism in its first millennium and in the
patristic period of Christianity. Sometimes the doctrines were integrated
into brilliant new systems, as in the masterpieces of Nagarjuna, Vasubandu,
Augustine, and Thomas Aquinas. The imaginative core texts of doctrine
and system might have affected common practitioners differently from the
ways primal witness core texts affected them. But they were genuine
moments of creative imaginative symbolic engagement for the elites who
followed them.

To talk about the imaginative new engagements in practice as opposed
to the development of textual traditions is difficult, because new engagements

often are in response to changed conditions rather than merely being new ways of embodying the primal, doctrinal, and systematic literary traditions. Nevertheless, the authenticity of important innovations in the practice of religion is often tied to the connection between the literary traditions and the new conditions. One thinks of the innovations of monasticism in Buddhism, Daoism, and then Christianity; or the formation of temple worship in ancient Israel, and then synagogue worship after the Second Temple was destroyed; or the Constantinian modeling of the Christian Church on the hierarchy of the empire's military/political system, and then the radical leveling of that hierarchy in the Protestant Reformation; or the development of extraordinary exclusivism in Islam, compared with the syncretism of Chinese religion. In all these cases, the nodal changes involved a new symbolic engagement with religious realities in new circumstances.

Nevertheless, there is a primacy to the primary witnesses, which are aptly named. Religious practice, both individual and communal, requires engaging the world-defining realities, the finite/infinite contrasts, through the symbols of the primary witnesses. In early stages of the development of a tradition, this might be mainly through imitation of the primary witnesses themselves. In later stages, it is more likely to be through interpretive reassessments of the primary witnesses through doctrines, systems, and religious patterns of life. For religion to be vital, to be meaningful in the sense of genuinely engaging, it needs to grasp the religious realities like something appearing in perception, with the causal force of that.

In times such as our own, when our own background imaginative assumptions about the world are vastly different from those in which the defining core texts and motifs of our traditional religions were formed, the white heat of imaginative engagement tends to be in the elite creativity of doctrine and system. In reaction, there are often "conservative" countermoves to return to the sources in the primary witnesses. Fundamentalisms are among these countermoves, distinguishing themselves from others by their militancy and sense of defensiveness.[27] Whether the conservative countermoves are justified depends on whether the primary witnesses can carry across that truth proper to imagination to their contemporary interpreters.

Abstracted from their interpretation, the perceptive power of primary witnesses lies in providing imaginative ways of engaging religious realities.

---

27. See the introduction and first chapter (by Nancy T. Ammerman) of *Fundamentalisms Observed*, ed. Martin Marty and Scott Appleby.

Those ways subsequently can be interpreted to be true or false. The truth of the primary witnesses is whether their mode of engagement in fact carries over the value relevant to the respect in which the witnesses interpret their object. The primary witnesses are true if they make accessible for engagement that which otherwise would be missed or obscured, and do so in such a way as to carry across the relevant value into the interpreters, regardless of whether the witnesses are assumed or asserted.

CHAPTER 4

Theological Assertion

—⟨⟨⟨⟩⟩⟩—

Interpretation as Engagement

A major thesis of this book and the pragmatic tradition from which it springs is that all knowing is interpreting.[1] Many modes of interpreting exist, of which theology as symbolic engagement highlights four: imagination, critical assertion, dialectical systematic theory, and practical reason. All the many modes of interpretation, nevertheless, take a general triadic form: every interpretation involves an object, a sign, and an interpretant or

---

1. Although not to be pursued in this text, the claim that all knowing is interpreting stands as a sharp alternative to the main line of the Western philosophic tradition since Descartes, for which all knowing is representation by mental ideas of objects, some of which are extra-mental. The problem of representative knowledge is that of finding some neutral ground on which to stand to judge whether mental representations accurately represent extra-mental realities. Hermeneutical phenomenology of Gadamer's sort makes a valiant effort to connect the mental and extra-mental with an interpretive process; yet it fails to articulate anything in that process that makes causal connection between non-mental things and consciousness of them. To say by contrast that all knowing is interpretation is to treat knowing as an action, continuous with interactions of perception and internal and external behavior. Thus, knowing as interpretation is subject to moral-like norms appropriate for actions, and is to be judged in terms of what makes actions appropriate and successful. Charles Peirce said that logic is a species of ethics, which in turn is a species of aesthetics (CP 5.129–43). John Dewey characterized knowing as interaction (in *Experience and Nature*, for instance). Alfred North Whitehead provided a microanalysis of knowing as interpretive action (in *Process and Reality*) according to which action arises through prehension of the past and aims to determine the future. All these thinkers were running against the grain of Western thought. In the Chinese tradition, however, knowing was always understood as a kind of interpretive action, the function of which is to comport the knower deferentially and appropriately to the environment. This story is wonderfully told in Warren Frisina's *The Unity of Knowledge and Action*.

interpretive act that takes the sign to stand for the object in a certain respect.[2] Signs considered in themselves have meanings, which are to be understood in terms of semiotic codes.[3] The relation between signs and their objects is reference, of which three modes have been discussed: iconic, indexical, and conventional. The interpretive act that connects them, so that the sign stands for the object in a certain respect, has a mediating intentionality that arises from the interpreter's context, including the interpretive purposes. Meaning, reference, and context are the topics for this chapter, following this section on the interpretive act.

Interpretive acts, being acts, are always particular, and thus in some context or other. This is so even when the acts are long drawn-out processes with many phases, as is always the case for dialectical system building. Moreover, the contexts for interpretive acts always call for engagement of the objects interpreted. If the imaginative construction of the signs involved is effective, regardless of whether they are true, then the engagement takes place. Yet the interpretive act might still be mistaken in taking the signs, however engaging, to stand for the object in the respect in question. The truth of the interpretation lies in whether the interpretation carries over the value in the object into the interpreter in the respect in which the signs are taken to stand for the object. The value of the imaginative signs per se, regardless of their truth, as argued in chapter 3, lies in whether they engage the object in such a way as to let it appear in some kind of dynamic and continuous perceptual field. Perception is not limited to visual images but to any experience in which the force of the reality presenting the object is felt in a causal way under the forms of experience. The causal character of imagination in engagement is another testimony to the particularity of engaging interpretations in context.

If interpretations are always particular, how can they be couched in general signs and expressed, sometimes, in propositions? To answer this question, a distinction needs to be drawn between the *extension* of interpretation and its *intention*. The extension of an interpretation is its form within a semiotic system, and that form is general. A semiotic system is a system of signs that exhibits their possible normative connections. So, a semiotic system includes codes by which signs are defined in terms of one another. Moreover, it includes rules of grammar, as it were, taking language as a paradigmatic semiotic system. All the structures of mood, tense, and even "metaphoric reach" are included within a semiotic system.

---

2. As noted in chap. 2, this language comes from Charles Peirce; see the discussion there for primary and secondary references.

3. For a theory of semiotic codes, cognizant of Peirce but not following the whole of his semiotic theory, see Umberto Eco's *A Theory of Semiotics*, chap. 2.

Although language is the easiest semiotic system paradigm to discuss, there are "languages" of gesture, of music, of movement, and so forth. Perhaps the most encompassing paradigm of semiotic structure is ritual in its large Confucian sense.[4]

The *extension* of an interpretation is its expression within the semiotic system of which its signs are parts.[5] All of its parts are elements of the semiotic system, and hence are signs and their rules for combination. The object of the interpretation is a sign, the signs in the interpretation that stand for the object are signs, and the interpretive act itself that intends the object by means of the signs is expressed as a complicated sign, which Peirce called an "interpretant." All parts of the extension of an interpretation are conventional because they are elements of some semiotic system, and all of them are "universal" in ways appropriate to their semiotic function.

The *intention* of an interpretation, by contrast, is the act of taking the signs embedded within their whole semiotic system to stand for the object. The real object is engaged, not the representation of the object in the extensive expression of the interpretation. The entire extension of the interpretation is the complicated sign that mediates the object to the interpreter so that the value in the object is carried across, if the interpretation is true. Moreover, the entire semiotic system is involved in that mediating position. No interpreting sign stands alone: its full reality is the whole semiotic system within which it has its extension. In this sense, we say that culture, meaning the entire semiotic system, is the medium through which we experience reality. The intention of an interpretive act, its full character, is the engagement of the object by means of the sign in its semiotic system. The *form* of that engagement can be expressed as the interpretation's extension within the semiotic system. Interpretation *itself*, however, is not the possible extensive combinations of signs or the possible interpretations expressed extensionally, but rather the concrete engagement of reality with the signs semiotically structured. The function of the universality of the interpretation's extension in the actual intentional interpretations bears the universality in actual interpretation.

Most of the time when we discuss interpretations, we identify them with their extensive expressions. In fact, we cannot talk about particular interpretations at all without expressing them in their extensions. But no

---

4. See the ritual theory, for instance, of Xunzi.

5. In symbolic logic, for instance Whitehead and Russell's *Principia Mathematica*, such an extensive expression would be called a "proposition." Although that term associates semiotics too much with language, Whitehead himself uses "proposition" in the properly general sense of an expression in a semiotic system in *Process and Reality*. Curiously, Whitehead never developed the potential in his philosophy for a full theory of semiotics. The best statement is in his *Symbolism*.

interpretation in its extensive expression is true or false, except in terms of the rules of definition, grammar, consistency, and so on that norm semiotic correctness. An extensively expressed interpretation is true or false of its object only when it is intentionally used to engage that object. For this reason, truth or falsity apply only to actual interpretations, and therefore are always and only contextual.

In theological (and other) discourse, we ask whether a certain interpretation, a judgment, is true. Strictly speaking, we should determine the specific context in which that interpretation is made intentionally. But for ease of communication we suppose a kind of subjunctive mood for the question of truth: Would the interpretation be true if intentionally asserted within a range of contexts? Sometimes that range is taken to be universal; in theology it often is a mistake to assume this is the case, as feminist critics have pointed out. Theologians from religions other than one's own also make that criticism.

The failure to distinguish and keep in mind the distinction between extension and intention has led some postmodern thinkers to assume that we engage no realities, only signs of realities.[6] They believe we are boxed in to activity within semiotic systems and fail to see that the systems themselves are the adaptive "signs" that humans have evolved to engage reality with discernment relevant to human purposes. This is a modern version of Descartes' hypothesis that we know only our own mind, and that whatever we know, by definition, is just part of the mind. Modern Cartesians, of course, would reject the distinction between extension and intention because they would see the latter as leaping illegitimately outside the mind or consciousness. David Weissman has carefully rebutted this Cartesian hypothesis.[7] The pragmatic tradition offers a better hypothesis.

An interpretation engages its object by means of its signs that it takes to stand for the object *in certain respects*. Peirce did not develop the importance of the notion of "standing for in certain respects," although it was at the heart of his sense that mediation requires more than the terms mediated (the object and the sign). As indicated earlier, the "respect" in which a sign stands for its object is a category: within this category, the object is a such and so. In theology, the meta-level discourses often attempt to tease out the categories within which primary witnesses interpret their objects. To attempt to "list" categories as Aristotle did would be to fly in the face of a generation of scholarship that has shown how multifarious the categories of interpretation are within religion, let alone within the wider culture.

6. Derrida is the most noted and controversial philosopher on this problem. See his *Of Grammatology*.
7. See his *Intuition and Ideality* and *Hypothesis and the Spiral of Reflection*.

With that caveat in mind, the formal claim can be made that interpretations are theological to the extent that their categories of interpretation are respects in which finite/infinite contrasts are interpreted. These are the respects in which the interpretations of ordinary and extraordinary things bear upon the ultimate.

How should we understand the respects in which theology legitimately makes its interpretations? Today this is a question of extreme importance, because of the claims by many that religion should stay out of politics, economics, the values of domestic life such as moral issues of birth and death, and so forth. The obvious frontline categories such as the nature of ultimacy, the human predicament defined by relations to ultimacy, and patterns of life for living in face of the ultimate are important but insufficient as a list of theological categories. Everything else in life also receives its larger orientation in terms of the ultimate issues defining its sacred canopy. One of the most important projects of theology, usually located within religious studies, is the empirical examination within each religious tradition of how its particular symbolic expressions approach ultimate matters in certain respects and not others. Any large theological system requires a provisional hypothesis on these matters.

The hypothesis that truth is the carryover of value can now be enriched by the discussion of semiotic systems. The carryover is not the simple displacement of value from the object into the interpreter, as a Cartesian reading of Aristotle might suggest. Rather, the carryover is qualified by the biology, the culture, the semiotic systems, and the purposes of the interpreter. What are these qualifiers?

Whatever value the real object might have, as food, for instance, or as a dangerous predator, a supportive habitat, or an indifferent creator, that value, which is chemical, agential, environmental, or ultimate, needs to be transformed into what can be registered with human biology. Human beings have meat brains, with neurons and supportive tissues that process interpretations of value. In this respect, human beings differ from computers that have silicone "brains." Cognitive scientists can describe certain parallel functions between meat and silicone brains. Yet these parallels are often extremely forced and underestimate the potentials of both meat and silicone brains. The forms of what is important and valuable in objects, including the ultimate ones, needs to be translated or qualified into the forms of what can register that in human biology.

As has been argued, our meat brains have evolved to be cultural and cultured. The human biological organism is underdetermined with regard to culture. Cultures evolve with the invention and social introduction of semiotic systems, and many alternative cultures exist with different conventional patterns of interpretation and life that are possible for biological human beings. Cultures are vast arrays of semiotically shaped activities and products, such as architecture, economic systems, land use, and arts. The values of objects need to be qualified by forms that fit into cultural forms. Of course, cultures are constantly changing by accepting things that require the moderation of cultural forms.

Semiotic systems are the means by which cultures extensionally shape their significant, sign-shaped activities and products. The values in objects need to be carried over into forms that register within the conventions of a culture's semiotic systems, bearing in mind that those systems themselves constantly change to accommodate new conditions.

Finally, the individuals and communities within a culture, sharing the semiotic systems of that culture, have purposes in reference to which interpreted objects are encountered, taken up, and responded to. Engagement is not possible, in distinction from non-semiotic causal reactions, without purposes. Purposes are crucial in selecting the respect in which the objects are interpreted. Purposes might be quite peculiar to a particular interpretation, such as getting food for one's children tonight or making peace in Jerusalem. Or they might be general, underlying a whole medley of interpretations, such as generally providing for sustenance and seeking world peace and justice. The value in the object interpreted needs to find a form that conforms to the strictures of the multiplicities of purposes environing a given interpretation in order to be registered.

Now it should be apparent why the carryover involved in truth is not of form per se but of value. The forms required to register what is important within the interpreter or interpreting community would obviously be vastly different from the forms in the objects that achieve their values. Eddington's old supposed paradox of how a table could be a dance of electrons is no paradox at all. The value of that dance of electrons is that persons with meat brains and bodies can have dinner around it. This respect in which the dance of electrons is interpreted is quite different from respects that interest particle physicists (when they are not social and hungry).

Meanings

The meanings of signs are made determinate in semiotic codes at many levels. Some of these levels are involved with the subtlety of syntactic and semantic "grammar." Among the levels of most interest to theology are those in which religiously important signs, "religious symbols," are defined within networks of other symbols. To take an example already mentioned, consider the symbol of "sacrifice" in the Hebrew Bible that New Testament writers used to interpret Jesus. One network that defines sacrifice is the story of the Passover in Exodus 11–12. To counter the Egyptian Pharaoh's stiff-necked obstinacy in refusing to let the Israelites go free, God "passes" through Egypt to kill the firstborn in every family of human beings and animals. To spare the Israelites this horror, God tells them to slaughter a lamb (or goat) and smear its blood on the doorposts and lintel of the house in which the lamb was roasted and eaten. God would then "pass over" the houses of the Israelites. The paschal lamb thus was sacrificed to spare the Israelites from the murderous anger of God. St. Paul called Jesus the "paschal lamb" (1 Corinthians 5:7).

St. Paul also called Jesus a "sacrifice of atonement" (Romans 3:25), however, the meaning of which comes from a different symbolic network. Leviticus 16 prescribes the atonement ritual. Aaron the high priest is instructed to sacrifice a bull to God in order to atone for his own sins. Then he is to cast lots between two goats, one of which is to be designated for the Lord and the other for Azazel, a desert demon. The goat designated for God is sacrificed to purify the temple and people. Then Aaron places his hands on the other goat and transfers to it all the sins of the people; the goat is then led alive into the wilderness to carry away the sins of the people, presumably to be devoured by Azazel. Paul's references to Jesus as the sacrifice who "takes away the sins of the world" (see also John 1:29) find their meaning in the atonement network of sacrifice symbols.

The Passover network has nothing to do with Israel's sins, only with exempting the Israelites from the punishment wreaked upon all the Egyptians and their cattle because of Pharaoh's sin (caused by God!). The atonement network has to do with removing the sins of the people so that they could be in a holy relation with God; it has little if anything to do directly with death. St. Paul combined the two networks in a new sacrificial theology that said Jesus, like the atonement scapegoat, takes away the sins of the world so that God would not punish sinners with death, like the firstborn Egyptians (who were not killed because of their sins). The symbolic network of the Passover came from a narrative; that of the atonement came from a ritual prescription. The Passover itself became a ritual in the life of Israel and of Judaism today, but it celebrated God's strong hand in freeing Israel from Egypt and was not any kind of sin offering.

Symbolic networks have a kind of integrity of their own, as in the narrative or ritual instructions. They also can include other networks within them: both the Passover and atonement networks include the much older network associating sacrifice with propitiating the gods; human sacrifice was included, and that might lie behind the Passover sacrifice of Egyptian children. Networks of symbols can operate together without being made consistent. New Testament writers did not reconcile the Passover and atonement images of Jesus as a sacrifice but let them resonate together, as they still do in much Christian worship and thinking.

The symbolic network of the new and old covenants expressed in the Christian eucharistic liturgy further complicates the sacrifice imagery of Jesus in the New Testament (1 Corinthians 11, Matthew 26, Mark 14, and Luke 22). In Exodus 24, Moses ratified the first covenant between God and Israel by sacrificing oxen for the twelve tribes of Israel; he splashed half the blood on the altar and the other half on the people. As the sacrifice of oxen ratified the first covenant, the sacrifice of Jesus ratified the new covenant for the early Christian community, who celebrated the Eucharist. The blood sacrifice of ratification of a new relation between God and the people resonates with the Passover and atonement networks in Christian thinking about Jesus as sacrifice. That these networks are not consistent with one another does not mean that they cannot function liturgically and spiritually together.

The network of sacrifice imagery that has been most influential in Christian theology is that having to do with redemption. Jesus' death as Son of God is the very high price paid to redeem or ransom humankind from Satan to whom people have sold themselves by their sin (Matthew 20:28; Mark 10:45; Luke 1:68, 21:28; Galatians 3:13, and elsewhere). This redemption network, heavily influenced by Persian dualistic thinking pitting God against cosmic evil forces or personages, has little or nothing to do with taking away sins, only with taking away their punishment. Paul sometimes speaks of redemption from the bondage of sin itself rather than from Satan. Though not consistent with the other networks defining sacrifice, the redemption network resonates with them.

The discussion here has focused on symbols and their networks taken mainly from the level of primary witnesses. Similar points can be made about the revision of these symbols to form coherent doctrines and the further attempts to make them consistent with one another and with what else is known. For many theologians, the bulk of theology is the analysis of meanings of theological symbols as expressed celebratively (in Rowan Williams's sense), doctrinally, and systematically.

Theology as symbolic engagement calls attention to a different though clearly related sense of meaning: "content meaning" as different from "network meaning."[8] In the distinction between extensional and intentional

---

8. The language of content meaning versus network meaning was first developed in my *The Tao and the Daimon*, chap. 11, in reference to Buddhist notions of truth. See also *The Truth of Broken Symbols*, pp. 95–104.

interpretation made in the previous section, network meaning is a function of extension. Network meaning lays out the interconnection and definitions of symbols in terms of other signs within the semiotic code. Content meaning is the meaning the symbols have in an actual intentional engagement of their object. In content meaning, the symbols in their network meaning are used to carry across what is important in the object to the extent that the interpretation is true.

The importance of the distinction between network and content meaning lies in the fact that one can employ interpretations with correct network meaning and yet fail to engage properly because the content meaning is missing. This is the case in a simple sense in the example mentioned earlier when a person who as a child has been abused by her father is unable to use the symbol "father" to engage God, even though she knows the network meaning of "Father" in Christian theology does not suggest that God is like *her* father.

In a more complicated sense, however, the importance of the difference between network and content meaning stems from the fact that network meanings pile up on one another like Chinese boxes, and they resonate with one another even when they do not quite fit together. A person can trace out some of these overlaid and resonating network meanings while ignoring or being ignorant of others. To employ symbols with these meanings in an actual interpretive act, however, requires having them all lined up, as it were, so that all are effective in mediating the object to the interpreter. The symbols with network meaning that cannot be effectively coordinated with the others need to be altered or eliminated. Consider an example from psychology. Suppose, for the sake of argument, that Freud's theory of infantile sexuality is right and that children need to have successful experiences and build a repertoire of responses through each stage. Suppose further that an individual has an especially difficult time at the oral stage (perhaps because of a prolonged infection of the lips), surviving with enough nourishment but not learning the comfort, acceptance, ability to enjoy merging, and emotional warmth associated with oral contact. As an adult, the individual is otherwise emotionally healthy, but is incapable of enjoying kissing with the emotional pleasure and arousal that requires a happy passage through the infantile oral stage. The individual knows what kissing is about and perhaps masters the techniques, which is to say the individual can operate with the network meaning of kissing, even to the point of knowing that it is tied to infantile pleasure at nursing. But the emotional pleasure and arousal simply are not possible. The most the individual can hope for, with regard to the personal satisfaction of kissing, is to find a psychoanalyst who can help reconstruct the infantile experience. Perhaps that broken layer in the network of meanings that underlie kissing can be repaired and its networks of unpleasant symbols eliminated so that all those layers of deep biopsychic experience can be lined up. If they are lined up properly, the experience of kissing can engage the "kissee" with a vastly rich and deep experience of the kisser.

Engaging the ultimate with religious symbols is even richer and deeper than kissing. Precisely because the symbols have meaning in networks within networks within networks, overlaid, overlapping, and sometimes merely resonant with one another, all of them have to be lined up within an individual's or community's intentional repertoire in order for the religious object to be engaged effectively. The networks that inhibit or distort the others need to be eliminated or cordoned off. Knowing the network meanings is necessary but not sufficient. They have to be brought together as content meanings with all the emotions resident in the values they bear in order for the value in the object to ring clearly through all their levels and overtones.

For this reason, the spiritual process of engaging God with the symbols of any religious tradition requires a long discipline in order to do justice to the values the symbols can carry. Children can learn the symbols in network fashion, and perhaps have one-dimensional interpretive engagement with ultimate matters through them. Yet to be able to employ the symbols in their full richness and depths as content meanings takes extraordinary spiritual discipline. Most religious practitioners only get glimpses of what profound interpretive engagement with ultimate realities might be, and take the lessons of their religious virtuosi on faith. Sometimes the problems in spiritual development might be pathological, as in the case of the frustrated kisser: something broken needs to be mended. But most often, spiritual development requires first coming to terms with all that is implied in the networks of networks of networks that give meaning to an important symbol and then integrating this in a unified act that engages the religious object with the symbols in their content richness and depth.

For a Christian to engage (alleged) salvation in Jesus Christ through the symbol of Jesus as sacrifice, for instance, all four of the networks mentioned need to be understood and emotionally coordinated—the Passover, atonement, covenant-ratifying, and redemption networks. Each is itself a network of networks of networks. In imaginatively constructing the image of Jesus as sacrifice, Paul knew that to his mainly Gentile audience the Passover, atonement, and probably covenant-ratifying networks would be culturally alien and would have to be adopted at second hand. So in living with these symbolic networks, Paul hoped his readers would learn to see through them to what transforms their own experience to pick up on what is important in the ultimate matters of salvation in Christ.

If it was hard for first-century Gentiles to get this point, people for whom sacrifice was a common domestic and national occurrence, how much harder would it be for twenty-first-century Christians to work through what they might say about ultimate matters in the human condition, people for whom sacrifice is not only alien but disgusting! Nevertheless, twenty-first-century Christians can learn from the Passover network about the dark side of God, who would slaughter thousands of innocent children and animals to liberate his people for whom the sacrifice of a lamb per family was cheap. The cost of human evolution and of the maintenance of the Earth as a habitat is enormous, and the ultimate powers behind that seem indifferent to that cost. Simply to have evolved to the state where we humans can relate to God is to have accumulated incalculable bloodguilt. From the atonement network, contemporary Christians can learn that, when their sins are removed from their own account, they are borne by others—sin does not simply evaporate as if it does not count. From the covenant-ratification network, contemporary Christians can know that their transformation from alienation relative to the ultimate to reconcilia-tion in such a way that leads to holiness is costly in blood; it is not a simple benign change of masters. From the redemption network, contemporary Christians learn to acknowledge that evil is not just a matter of their rather trivial wills but has cosmic power and organization behind it, and that they participate in nature's violence, society's oppressive selfishness, and Azazel's demonic displacement of other people's sins onto hapless scapegoats. Together these sacrifice networks tell contemporary Christians that evil is so cosmic, sin is so serious, such vast burdens are borne by inno-cent people, and God the ultimate source is so implicated in this dark side, that the bloodguilt can be paid only by God. Most Christian theology thus struggles to provide a metaphysics of Jesus as God in whom God pays the price of blood guilt so that sinners, now redeemed from their participation in this guilt, can love the creator who brought it to be. Collectively the net-works of sacrifice symbols carry the Christian imaginative articulation of the depths of evil in the cosmos, the implication of creation itself in this evil, and the participation of people, both innocent and culpable, in the dark side of creation.

Without these sacrifice networks in play, it has been easy for Christians to construe God as a domesticated, well-intentioned Good Big Spiritual Person and to limit evil to the tepid sins of individual personal responsibil-ity, which is to betray the primary Christian witness. Although the image of God as personal has biblical roots, the image of God as an all-benevolent personal spiritual being developed along with Deism in Enlightenment pietism, when the sacrifice imagery had fallen from significant spiritual practice and was regarded as superstitious; that view of God is seriously superficial compared with the more classical view within Christianity.

Within the Christian set of symbols, primarily the sacrifice imagery, with its extraordinarily complex richness and depth of network meanings, is able to carry over what might justify the Christian claims about the ultimate dimensions of evil. Those claims about evil, of course, might be false. But the issue cannot even be addressed without the symbolic meanings to engage it. If those classic Christian claims about evil are indeed true, it would be interesting to ask whether other religions have other symbol systems that allow alternative recognitions of it; obviously, Judaism has those symbol systems, although not put together in the Christian way.

The argument here about meaning in some respects has paralleled the argument in the previous chapter about images. The parallel comes from the hypothesis that truth is the carryover of what is valuable or important in the object interpreted into the interpreter in the respects in which signs stand for the object. This causal account was reflected in the theory of imagination, according to which the synthesizing activities of imagination allow reality to be carried into human experience in experiential forms. An image is true to the extent that it allows the reality in its object, when used to interpret that object, to be engaged. The causal account is reflected in the theory of meaning according to which interpreters need to find the meanings and arrange them so that the interpretive engagement of the object can bear the value or importance across into the interpretation. The examples dealt with here have been meanings that are images in the primal witness of Christianity; they illustrate the importance of always retaining the symbols of the primary witness. A similar point could be made, however, about carefully crafted abstract theological concepts and systems of concepts. They are richer and deeper than they seem in superficial network definitions, and serious theology needs to line up the subtleties of those riches and depths.

Reference

Reference is the relation that signs have to their objects in interpretation. According to Peirce, as already mentioned, reference has three modes: iconic, indexical, and conventional (which he called "symbolic"). He derived these three modes from his theory of categories: Firstness, Secondness, and Thirdness.[9]

---

9. See CP 1.284–353, 5.41–119, and elsewhere throughout Peirce's work for extensive discussions and uses of the distinction between Firstness, Secondness, and Thirdness. Perhaps the most concise discussion is in the letters to Lady Welby, CP 8.327–79. The discussion of icons, indices, and symbols in terms of the categories is in CP 2.274–308.

Firstness is what a thing is simply in itself. The Firstness of reference, iconic reference, is when the object is like the sign; Peirce's example was the cross in church being an icon of the cross of Jesus' crucifixion. "Likeness," of course, is a very complicated notion, with ranges of meaning from one-to-one isomorphism (the sign as map) to likeness of basic structure (the sign as mathematical-physical theory), to subtle metaphorical description (the sign as artistic rendering in words or other media).

Secondness is what a thing is in dyadic opposition to some other. The Secondness of reference, indexical reference, is when the sign establishes a causal relation between the object and the interpreter. A pointing finger gets the interpreter to turn to look in a new direction. In theological interpretation, the indexical mode of reference transforms the interpreter so that the religious object is accessible for engagement. The rest of this section shall focus mainly on indexical reference.

Thirdness is the reality of a thing that mediates one thing to another. The Thirdness of reference is the conventionality of signs in a semiotic system such that they have signs as objects and other signs as interpretants. All language refers conventionally. Hence, any interpretations that we can talk about are treated as having at least conventional reference.

Peirce did not make the sharp distinction drawn above between extensional and intentional interpretation, although by interpretation he clearly usually meant the latter. Nor did Peirce construe truth in terms of the carry-over of value theory. So the account here extends Peirce's semiotic theory in ways he might not have wanted to follow.

The reference involved in most theological discussion is not to ultimate matters directly but to other theologians, to theological ideas, and to the situations in which theological ideas are true or false. Much theological interpretation is argumentative, worrying about the meanings of symbols, testing theological claims, probing systematic links and lacunae. Insofar as this is the case, besides every interpretation referring conventionally, most also refer iconically. This is especially true when a theologian attempts to make sure that the dialogue partner is understood correctly, when the concern is properly to register a complex theological claim or system to be able to subject it to one's own reflections, and the like. Indexical reference is also involved in theological argumentation where the object to be engaged is some other theologian: the interpretive signs must refer in ways that give the interpreter concrete access to the others' ideas, through their books, words, and so forth. In our time, among theological elites, the academic conference is the primary locus of theological engagement among positions and it involves indexical reference in the face-to-face encounters among theologians.

Lying behind most theological discussion, however, is the supposition that the arguments themselves engage the ultimate matters that are their topics. Not only are the ultimate matters represented within the extensional references of the argument, they are engaged in their own reality by the interpreting theologians individually or in community. Theologians argue about which of the assertions about the real ultimate matters best carry across what ultimately matters in the various respects of interpretation under discussion.

If religious symbols and assertions referred only iconically and conventionally, then theology would be debate about how best to *describe* ultimate matters. Theologians from ancient times until now, in West and South Asian religions, have likened their discipline to science, which aims to refer mainly iconically. Of course, the notion of science has radically changed from ancient to modern times, and has always differed somewhat between the great civilized cultures. Nevertheless, theologians have often thought that their job is to describe the religious realities that are their topics. And in every tradition there have been recognitions that at least some ultimate realities are not objects that can be described. Without adopting anything like the hypothesis of finite/infinite contrasts, theologians have recognized an apophatic moment in theology. Perhaps the most poignant in Western religions was Thomas Aquinas's reluctant claim that God is not a genus or in a genus, and hence cannot be described directly at all, only by analogy with generic and specific things.[10]

The reason to adopt theology as symbolic engagement rather than theology as description is that many of theology's key references to ultimate matters are dominantly indexical. This is to say, thinking about the ultimate matters in the ways articulated by the meaning networks of the signs causes the interpreter to be open to the real value in the object to be carried across in the relevant respects, even though the object is not "like" what the signs say. Sometimes theology is appropriately descriptive. In its metaphysical moments, it does aim for description when engaging ultimacy, and of course it aims for description when representing other theological images, assertions, and theories. But much of the time theology engages ultimate matters with symbols in interpretation that are radically non-iconic and yet can be true in the sense of carrying across what is valuable in the ultimate objects into the interpreter. Theology at the systematic levels, and in making cases at the assertoric levels, interprets *how* the indexical reference works in those interpretations that engage ultimate matters. Theology as

---

10. See Aquinas's *On the Truth of the Catholic Faith (Summa contra Gentiles)*, book 1, chap. 25, "That God is not in some genus," and chaps. 29–36 on analogous knowledge of God.

iconically referring description fits within theology as symbolic engagement. But the attempt to treat indexically referring interpretations within
theology as if they were descriptions leads to contorted fights about literal-
ism and metaphor that obscure, if not deny, the real efficacy of religious
symbols to engage truly.

The significance of Rudolf Bultmann's project of demythologizing does
not lie, as is usually thought by demythologizers, in finding some kernel of
the primary Christian texts that can be believed by modern people without
the mythic terms. Rather, his genius was to propose hypotheses about what
real issues were involved in the ancient world. Whereas the biblical texts
talked about supernatural entities and events, he argued, their real significance was in providing for human constitution in basic existential ways.[11]
Whether or not his particular existentialist hypotheses are right is not as
important as his recognition that talking about the supernatural matters
was not theologically important as iconic description—that description
modern science knows to be false—but was rather important for its existential power. In the language of theology as symbolic engagement, he had
identified indexical reference as different from iconic reference. The religious function of ancient supernaturalism, he showed, was not to describe
supernatural things but to effect existential constitutions of the sort he was
able to describe in the language of modern existentialism. Existentialism is
probably far too narrow a modern language for understanding what he was
getting at. Theology as symbolic engagement calls upon a far broader
repertoire of thought to understand indexical reference and how ultimate
matters are carried over into interpreters in ways that are often not iconic,
yet are real. Bultmann, of course, did not employ the language of iconic and
indexical reference.

Bultmann saw only half the potential of his project, however. He saw
that modern people could escape the unacceptable biblical supernaturalism that was scientifically mistaken while adhering to ancient insights
restated in modern terms. He did not see how the original biblical witness
was powerfully engaging, except for the fact it spoke the language and culture of its time. He did not analyze, as theology of symbolic engagement
does, how imagination, meaning, and indexical reference set people in a
vital causal relation with religious realities so that their import can be carried over. He did not see the extent to which his own language of existentialism was itself something like a primary witness in his day. Heidegger
gave a whole generation of people a new possible way of engaging the
depths of existence (Heidegger would not have thought of himself as either

---

11. See, for instance, his *Jesus Christ and Mythology*, chaps. 3–4.

a prophet or a theologian, though he was both). From the standpoint of the early twenty-first century, early twentieth-century existentialism is rarely a primary witness, but rather is viewed as narrow, divorced from ethics, and incapable by itself of expressing a full religious sensibility. Bultmann could have given an account of how his existentialism had primary revelatory force because he obviously believed and asserted that it did.

Had Bultmann provided an account of contemporary primary witness, he might have shown that theology needs to remythologize as much as demythologize. When modern people understand how the ancient primal witnesses were indexical references to what now can be expressed differently, though without the primal power of engagement, perhaps they can themselves use those ancient symbols to engage their own realities now. With a sophisticated enough theological understanding of the indexical reference in the ancient symbols, those symbols might be taken up with a "second naiveté" by moderns seeking to engage ultimate matters. The previous section, in its analysis of symbols of sacrifice in early Christianity, suggested that, although those symbols cannot be used iconically among the elite in the modern world, modernity has developed few alternative symbols to capture the character of evil and its implications. With only a few exceptions, such as imagery from the Holocaust, modernity still employs the ancient symbols in its literature, films, and other expressions. A proper extension of Bultmann's project would be to remythologize those sacrifice symbols (and other ancient symbols of evil) to give the primary witness of Christianity the power to engage people in late modernity. Theology has an interesting task to discern whether the primary witness of contemporary mass-death phenomena such as the Holocaust can be joined with Christianity's primary witnesses of redemption.[12]

Recognition of non-iconic indexical reference is important not only for Bultmann's problem of bridging vastly different imaginative cultural worlds. Its implicit recognition has probably been in all the large theological traditions of the world religions. In most of those traditions, for instance, a spectrum of ideas of ultimate reality exists that runs from highly anthropomorphic images to highly transcendent and abstract ones.[13] Perhaps the former were dominant in the pre-Axial Age religions, but they coexist in the great literate religions. The East Asian religions such as Daoism and Confucianism fixed the center of gravity of their rhetoric in the transcendent abstract symbols, although daily life in those religions is

---

12. The brilliant theologian Edith Wyschogrod has explored mass-death phenomena in her *Spirit in Ashes: Hegel, Heidegger, and Man-Made Mass Death*.
13. The idea of this spectrum has been explored by Wesley J. Wildman and me in my *Ultimate Realities*, chap. 7, pp. 164–71.

filled with spirits. The West Asian religions of Judaism, Christianity, and Islam fixed the center of gravity of their rhetoric in anthropomorphic images, although their theologians conceived of very transcendent divinities. The South Asian religions of Hinduism and Buddhism employ symbols from across the whole spectrum.

In the Hellenistic world around the Mediterranean in the first century, the notion of the High God was prevalent in just about all the major religions, not only those of Greek, Roman, and Semitic origin but also imports from Persia and Egypt. The High God was extraordinarily transcendent, beyond all distinctions that could be grounds for the charge of idolatry. Philosophers gave metaphysical interpretations of this; for instance, Plato's notion of the Form of the Good and Aristotle's notion of Thought Thinking Itself. By the fourth century, Christian theologians would define God the Father as simple and pure, with the Son exactly like that except derived from the Father.[14] These High God conceptions precluded any sense that God could have intentionality like a human person, thinking *about* people and things as objects, even taking up a differential relation to something in the world. If God is the creator of time and space, God cannot be spatially and temporally related to things as would be required for personhood. Such high conceptions of God are religiously remote if not impossible, however. And in religions with a High God, the first century saw symbols of mediators—angels and other finite spirits, religious virtuosi who could spiritually merge with the transcendent, and figures like Jesus Christ as represented, for instance, in Philippians 2: once in the form of God, he descended to take on the human form of a slave and then ascended back to be with the High God, making it possible for human beings to follow in some sense. In one way or another, the High God was anthropomorphized.

Now the theologians of that time and subsequently held to both the high transcendent notion and also to the anthropomorphic notions that were the stuff of religious devotion. Within Christianity, this was so of the great theologians such as Origen, Augustine, and Thomas Aquinas, down to Tillich. Aquinas could be very clear that God is the Act of *Esse*, pure, simple, and unrelatable to the world, and at the same time he could describe God in biblical terms that were highly personalistic. If all theology is only iconic, descriptive, Aquinas would be in contradiction, as would all the other theologians who affirmed both sides. But if theology is sometimes

14. For a sample of these discussions, see William G. Rusch's edited volume *The Trinitarian Controversy*. For an interesting contemporary discussion of the fourth-century debates, see Catherine Mowry LaCugna's *God for Us*, chaps. 1–2.

indexical, there need be no contradiction between the mainly iconic meta-physics of the High God and the indexical anthropomorphic qualities of the biblical God. Of course the relation between these two kinds of symbols needs to be explained. One main strategy for explanation was popularized by what is now called the Perennial Philosophy, especially in Neoplatonism, which emphasized different levels of comprehension corresponding to dif-ferent levels of reality. Aquinas's strategy lay in his theory of analogy: as God is the pure and simple fullness of being, any positive finite traits of the world also characterize God, though in infinite form. Tillich was explicit about the anthropomorphic images being symbols and was a self-conscious theologian of symbolic engagement, although he did not call it that.[15] Theology as symbolic engagement helps explain what has been implicit in theology all along, namely, that some symbols can be interpreted with mainly iconic reference and others with mainly indexical reference.

The problem indexical reference poses for truth is that some other lan-guage than the indexically referred symbols is needed to assess whether those symbols carry across what is valuable into the interpreter in the appropriate respect. Some other means is necessary to identify what is valu-able in the object and to assess its status in the interpreter. The truth of indexical reference needs to be assessed indirectly, and pragmatic criteria come into play: "By their fruits you shall know them." In the past, some people would have thought that iconic reference does not pose such diffi-cult issues of truth: you just have to check to see whether the interpretive expression is like the reality. That view reflects the Cartesian conviction that truth is a matter of mirroring external reality in mind. Philosophers have come to see the grave limitations of the Cartesian dualistic theory, however.[16] Where do you stand to compare reality with its representation in mind? Pragmatic criteria seem an attractive way of adjudicating that problem, even for philosophers who continue to be wedded to mind-object dualism.

Context and Critical Assertion

Whereas imaginative interpretation simply takes the engaged object to be such and so by means of the imaginative signs involved, without any sug-gestion that it could be otherwise, critical assertion affirms that the object is to be engaged in the signs' way and is not to be engaged in ways that deny the signs. Assertion implies a kind of dyadic consciousness: this and not that. This interpreting sign is right, and not the others that would deny this.

---

15. See especially his discussions of symbols in vol. 3 of his *Systematic Theology*.
16. The classic, recent refutation is Richard Rorty's *Philosophy and the Mirror of Nature*.

Implicit if not explicit in critical assertion is that there is good reason for asserting this determinate interpretation rather than one that construes the object differently. To assert something in an interpretation is to suppose that a case can be made for it, even if a case has not in fact been made.

Descartes had an elaborate theory for "making a case" for assertions, a theory in which intellectual intuition is heavily involved. Yet he said that judgments, or assertions, are made by will, not by the intuitive faculties of mind. He accounted for error by saying that the will sometimes affirms predicates of subjects when the case-making mind has not approved the connection.[17] Could it be that assertions are merely matters of will and not matters that involve an implicit or explicit critical claim for a case? Of course, Descartes' "faculty psychology," sharply distinguishing will from intuition, has been roundly rejected. His point about assertion being a matter of will rather than knowledge nevertheless deserves reflection.

In the pragmatic hypothesis of theology as symbolic engagement, the contexts for actual interpretations always involve human purposes.[18] Any given event, such as driving a car to work, involves a huge number of interacting interpretations, each with a purposive guiding dimension. The interpretations that are mainly imaginative and not assertive still organize their form according to values resident in the culture. One hopes that the perceptual culture of a driver is shaped by the values of an automobile culture rather than only by those of a denizen of the Amazon. When driving, of course, there is the added purpose of picking out what is important to notice about the road, the traffic, and one's own vehicle in motion. Such a purpose might have one orientation if the driver is late for work and needs to hurry through traffic, another orientation if the trip is leisurely. All such purposes involve finding interpretations that are true about the driving conditions: a mistake might cause an accident. Yet no purpose of that sort might register in the driver's conscious attention, operating rather at a more or less unconscious biopsychic level in the habits connecting eyes, ears, and kinesthetic sense to hands and feet. The driver's attention might instead be on what is expected at work, thinking through complicated problems, and interrupted only if some unexpected crisis happens on the road. Whereas some interpretations are engaging the road and driving conditions, others are engaging the issues of the job, with the massive

---

17. The argument is in his *Meditations*. The discussion of knowledge and will is in Meditation 4.
18. Other animals might make interpretations analogous to human ones. If the animals lack semiotic systems, they would not refer at all in the conventional mode, only iconically and indexically. To the extent they do have rudimentary semiotic systems, the analogy with human interpretation is all the stronger. Terrence Deacon argues, in the Preface to *The Symbolic Species* and passim, that animals do not have language in anything like the human sense.

complications of sets of interpretations involved in understanding the issues, contemplating the future, and so forth. Insofar as the driver is thinking out the job issues, the purposes involve something like attaining a systematic view of them, thinking them through from a variety of angles, wondering whether any other factors are relevant to consider, and so forth. The elements of the driver's context that involve thinking about the job are shaped by all the diverse purposes that would play into understanding the complicated situation.[19]

Contrary to Descartes' separation of the intuitive faculty that should approve assertions before they are made from the will that makes them, the pragmatic hypothesis provides a complicated analysis of the involvement of purpose throughout many levels of interrelated interpretations. When some function of purpose is made the focus of attention, it becomes what is usually known as will.

Theological assertions are shaped by many kinds of purposes, depending on their contexts. Practical purposes for the ordering of communal life and purposes of spiritual formation, for instance, might shape critical assertions quite differently. A Buddhist theologian seeking to guide a community might emphasize calm centeredness in the midst of bustling business by evoking iconic analogies with life in a monastery. To urge the mastery of monastic centeredness or emptiness regarding bustle, however, the Buddhist might enjoin concentrated meditation on wild images of dancing goddesses with waving swords and girdles of skulls, images with strong indexical and minimal iconic reference. The contexts of the practice of religion guided by theology will be discussed in more detail in chapter 7.

The locus of theology where critical assertion is most important is in the development, analysis, and assessment of what in several religious traditions is known as doctrine. Doctrine, in many forms and variations, is the attempt to say what is true and not false about ultimate matters. Religions differ widely regarding what they count as ultimate matters. Roughly, however, they have some views about what is ultimately real in an ontological sense, except in cases such as Madhyamika Buddhism, whose view is clearly assertive that there is not anything ontologically real in an ultimate sense. Religions have views about what is ultimate in the human condition, what its ultimate predicaments are, what its ultimate projects are. And religions have views about how to pattern life to live in relation to ultimate matters in all the proximate affairs of life, and how to mature in individual and

---

19. David Rothenberg points out that technology introduces human purposive semiotics beyond the body into machines that are also parts of mechanical nature. Such machines can embody "purposes" of their own that vastly complicate understanding the purposes involved in human interpretive behavior. See his *Hand's End: Technology and the Limits of Nature.*

communal engagements with all these ultimate matters. Doctrines engage all these kinds of ultimate matters, attempting to say what is true in each instance, with a consciousness of what is denied as false and implicit if not explicit arguments for why what is asserted is true and what denied is false.

The purposes involved in the development of doctrine are as multifarious as the contexts in which doctrinal assertions are important. Nevertheless, a rough list of typical purposes helps orient thought about the complexities of doctrine. Most theological doctrines intend to engage the ultimate matters (relating directly or indirectly to finite/infinite contrasts) by means of the symbols in the primary witnesses of some one or several living religious traditions. This purpose is especially prominent in modes of doctrinal theology that take the form of scriptural commentary; it is also true of scripture-first traditions such as Reformation Protestant Christianity and Islam. A second purpose is closely connected with this, however, namely to lift up the connections of the primary witness symbols to the ambient culture so that, first, the alternative possible doctrines can be implicitly or explicitly denied and, second, that the significance of the doctrine for the culture can be expressed. So doctrine guided by these two purposes complicates the language of the primary witness with whatever is necessary to spell out the embeddedness of the witness in the conventions of the larger culture. A more technical language can be introduced to sharpen up the symbols of the primary witness. Where the theologians' culture is different from that of the primary witnesses, this involves a special hermeneutical comparative purpose. Yet another purpose involved in doctrine is to establish a communicative language that connects with the theological interests of others who are concerned about the truth of the doctrine and the cases that can be made for it. This can develop so far as to be a kind of scholastic language that can be sharpened in a large theological community. Metaphysics is the language that attempts to be true across a very wide range of contexts that is employed in the special theological context of wanting a universal language. These moves, from the symbols of primary witness to a highly evolved scholastic and philosophical language, remain part of the overarching theological purpose of engaging the ultimate matters with true as opposed to false assertions.

Yet another purpose shaping theological contexts is to establish critical communication, with its own relevant languages, with all the domains of discourse that might help make cases for the truth of the doctrines. The reason for this purpose is that the best case to be made for any doctrine comes from making it vulnerable to correction from all relevant angles. Because of this, the critical assertions of doctrine lead inevitably toward dialectical systematic theory. Part of this dialectical purpose means shaping the cases for doctrines in light of the richness of a theological tradition, with all its modes of discourse from primal witness through commentaries and the rest, including the radical reversals of thought. A related part of this purpose is to bring to bear religious and theological traditions that have arisen from other primary witnesses, which requires comparative theology with all its relevant purposes. Another part of the dialectical purpose is to learn what one can from things outside "religion" that might bear on the ultimate matters under discussion. Subsequent chapters shall focus on the sciences, the arts, and practical normative disciplines.

To think of a doctrinal assertion as guided by only one purpose in its intentionality regarding what sign to use to interpret its object in its selected respect is vastly to oversimplify the context. The real context is shaped variously by a whole array of purposes, each determining some aspect of the "logic" of the doctrine. The kinds of purposes mentioned here are all very general. The discussion has prescinded from whether the doctrine is asserted in a theological classroom, in medieval Indian debates between Hindus and Buddhists before the king, or in free-floating theology in chat rooms on the Internet. All of these factors would give further determination to the context in which the doctrines are asserted, and each would involve the purposes peculiar to carrying on theology in those locations.

For theology as symbolic engagement and many other theological programs, however complicated the context for critical doctrinal assertion, however multifarious the purposes are, however diverse the special locations of theological discourse, the overall purpose and context is to engage the ultimate matters truly. Given the abstractness of so much theological debate, given that the arguments seem to be engaging alternative positions rather than the ultimate matters, and given the range of the public defining the scope of theological assertions' critical cases, it is easy to forget that the overall purposive intentionality is to engage the ultimate matters themselves, and to do so truly. While the focus of attention in a particular argument might be to determine the ancient meaning of an obscure word in a scriptural text or to refute some other theologian, the real context that gives meaning to the particular argument is the one of theological engagement with ultimacy. All the other purposes correlate to make possible the prosecution of that larger purpose. The hypothesis in theology of symbolic engagement is that this is the presupposition of all doctrinal theology.

Of course, theological programs exist that subordinate the purpose of truth-seeking to other purposes, such as sheer praise of God (celebratory theology alone) or community identity formation and defense. In certain circumstances, the purpose of inquiry or truth-seeking undermines those other purposes for theology. Moreover, when theology is viewed through the lenses of sociology, psychology, and anthropology, it is often seen only or primarily in its roles of social, personal, and cultural formation. The purpose of getting to the truth about theological topics does not easily register in a functionalist analysis of theology. The social science reading of theology reinforces those other purposes of theology while marginalizing the purpose of truth-seeking. Nevertheless, all those other purposes are unstable in the long run unless they can assume that their personal and social functions are based on what is theologically true regarding those assumptions. No doxological theologian deliberately wants to praise a false god. No identity-seeking theologian deliberately wants an identity that betrays the relevant primary witnesses and their valid interpretations. In the long run, the most practical dimension of theology is that it be normative, and all its other purposes depend on that.

With these complicated factors in mind, it is possible to review and bring to summary the hypothesis about critical assertoric truth in theology of symbolic engagement. The question of truth is whether the intentional interpretation of ultimate matters by means of the doctrine, considered in its complicated wholeness, carries across into the complicated interpretation in its complicated theological context what is valuable in the ultimate matters in the respects in which the doctrine stands for those matters. To do this, there are at least three critical moments.

The first moment is to identify just what the doctrine is when, taken as a whole, it is a sign by which the ultimate matters are engaged. The identification of the doctrine is the analysis of it as an *extensional* interpretation. Included within understanding the extension is an analysis of the meanings involved as discussed above, with all the complications of sorting out the networks defining the primary symbols, the conventional cultural connections, and all the other dimensions of the context. Included also for understanding the extension is an analysis of the various modes of reference involved, paying particular attention to the distinction between iconic and indexical reference as these affect the carryover of value. Finally, assessment would require identifying within the extension of the interpretation all the complications of the theological context, including all the purposes involved that select the respects in which the various signs are taken to stand for their particular objects.

The second moment of assessment, having identified the extensional structure of the doctrine with its meanings, references, and context, is to examine whether, when that doctrine is *intentionally* asserted to engage its objects, the relevant value is carried across into the theological interpreters.

This, of course, is an attempt to stand outside the complicated intentional interpretation itself to identify independently what the value is in the object and interpreters and how the extensional doctrine carries or fails to carry the value across. Theology in this moment works to triangulate the actual interpretation, judging it by as many independent tests as possible. The dialectical irony here is that this independent testing itself can be viewed as part of the larger context of the interpretation. If so, then the testing can be expressed as part of the extensional doctrine itself, with a new level of testing built into what is employed in the intentional assertion of the doctrine. This dialectic of standing outside the intentional interpretation and then slipping into the intentional interpretation now enlarged is a defining characteristic of dialectical systematic theorizing, to be discussed in more detail in the following two chapters. Ultimately, there is no external interpretive context within which a doctrine, understood in the complexity sketched here, can be tested that cannot itself be internalized to the doctrine in an enlarged context. Because the context, however enlarged by proximately external tests, includes within it all the tests for vulnerability of its parts, it is not a vicious circle. It is a circle, nevertheless.

The third moment of assessment beyond the extensional identification of the doctrine and the external assessments of its intentional carryover is the practical assessment of living with the doctrine. "Living with the doctrine" has two parts. One is living with the doctrine as something that shapes religious life. Overall feedback from reality is what corrects our interpretations at the most rudimentary level, as the road corrects our driving interpretations. The same thing corrects our interpretations at the level of ultimacy, however slowly and indirectly the feedback comes. Chapter 7 discusses this more thoroughly. The other part of living with the doctrine is letting it serve to guide the larger community, including those who are not part of the religious practice. This is to say, the doctrine needs to prove itself across the whole scope of theology, in its widest public. The dialectical systematic theory involved in doctrine internalizes what can be learned across that scope. The doctrine with that theory also must prove itself to all who are relevantly involved in the public and care to inquire. Chapter 8 pursues the implications of this.

CHAPTER 5

Components for Theological System

To assert something to be true of a theological topic is to have in mind as well what would be false to say. The assertion of one thing as true assumes a case can be made for that assertion over its alternatives. In the concrete event of a theological assertion, the making of its case might be more whistling in the dark than a full-blown brass band of arguments. Nevertheless, the complexity of the context within which critical theological assertions are made includes the purposes that open the cases for theology to all the domains from which it might learn. In this lies the basis, indeed, the ineluctable necessity, for dialectical systematic theory in theology.

No one doubts that religion itself, especially in its intellectual theological strains, is a component of a dialectical systematic theology. After all, the theological assertions needing a good case are what seek to surround themselves by the system within which they are vulnerable to all possible corrections and pass the tests. Religion, of course, is not the only context within which theology arises; secular and even antireligious interests might deal theologically with ultimacy. Jean-Paul Sartre had an elaborate theology of a God who he was sure could not exist. Even an atheist like Sartre, however, would have to take religion as providing some of the evidence for or against theological positions. What might be surprising to some theologians is the importance of including in theology what else is known about religion in the social and natural sciences and other disciplines of religious studies, for something can be learned about ultimate matters from all these perspectives.

The strong claim of theology as symbolic engagement, given the array of domains within which ultimate matters are symbolized, is that the sciences, the arts, and normative practical disciplines such as ethics, law, and politics also have important contributions to make. Each constitutes part of the scope required to make critical cases for theological assertions.

The present chapter constitutes something of a break in the argument of this book, which has treated two of the four modes of symbolic engagement: imagination (chapter 3), critical assertion (chapter 4), and will move on to dialectical systematic theory in chapter 6 and practical reason in chapters 7 and 8. Here the specific roles of religion, science, art, and practical normative disciplines will be discussed as they might be components of dialectical systematic theorizing.

Religion

Most theologians reflect on ultimate matters from within a religious tradition that has symbols of primary witness, core texts and motifs, and a history of theological reflection, perhaps a complex history of diverse theological movements. Moreover, a religion has rites and spiritual practices. Both domestic life and public life reflect patterned religious activity. The tradition likely has favorite stories that, although not "canonical," shape its self-understanding and practice. Saints and heroes punctuate its history and culture. Music, song, dance, architecture, and often theater provide components of the tradition's culture. Moreover, all of these have histories with various elements of growth, change, novelty, disappearance, and forgetting. Ninian Smart, in a brilliant comprehensive, comparative review, sorts religion into several dimensions: the doctrinal (including philosophical), the ritual, the mythic narrative, the experiential and emotional, the ethical and legal, the social, the material, and the political.[1] All of these things contribute to what a religious tradition provides its theologians. All of them may be subjects for theological interpretation, and all are resources for theology.

How a theology relates to these elements is, of course, a primary theological question. The orthodox schools of Hinduism, for instance, differ among themselves regarding how to treat the authority of the Vedas, although all affirm it, whereas the Buddhists recognize the Vedas and their cultural world but deny them scriptural authority. Confucianism has its rituals, mainly centering around veneration of family and ancestors, although in older times the imperial court rites were Confucian; in daily life, however, Confucianism blends with Daoism, Buddhism, and shamanism,

---

1. See his *Dimensions of the Sacred: An Anatomy of the World's Beliefs.*

sharing their rituals. How this blending has been effected has changed in different periods.[2] Similarly, the commentarial tradition of Judaism has changed over the years in the ways it relates to the Torah and also to its own antecedents. The Roman Catholic approach to scripture during the High Middle Ages was very different from that taken by the Protestant Reformers, and then by the Roman Church in the Counter-Reformation. Protestant Christians of the Lutheran, Calvinist, and Anglican traditions differed radically among each other regarding the place of art and architecture in worship, although all agreed on the importance of music of one sort or another. Arguments about which theological ideas from the past to lift up and which to disregard are central to both theological assertion and system. A good way to distinguish one theological position from another within a tradition is to see how differently they read that "common" tradition. This is especially so in traditions where theology predominantly takes the genre of commentary.

Theological positions define themselves over against both other positions within their own tradition and also other traditions and nonreligious secular thinking. Thus theological traditions have histories of built-in engagements of their alternatives. Sometimes these engagements have been genuine dialogues, though often they are monologues about the "others" and might be filled with caricatures. These histories, to be sure, help determine the intellectual and religious situation of theologians. They also provide resources for subsequent theological thought. But perhaps most important, they provide perspectives for understanding a theologian's own tradition that can call into question the tradition's self-understanding. Properly to grasp the boundary issues with other religious traditions and secular cultures requires crossing the boundary to see what one's tradition looks like from the outside.

Some theologians rightly claim that one cannot understand one religious tradition without understanding at least two, in order to get both insider and outsider views.[3] Of course, understanding of the outside religion needs to be profound and sensitive, or it will simply distort and prove less than helpful. Therefore, careful comparative theology is a necessary resource for taking stock of one's own theological situation. Comparative theology does not necessarily define the theological position one ultimately takes. But it needs to lie in the background out of which one makes a case for a theological position.

---

2. See, for instance, Judith Berling's *The Syncretic Religion of Lin Chao-en*.
3. This point is attributed to Wilfrid Cantwell Smith. See his *Toward a World Theology* and *Faith and Belief* for fascinating studies of the interactions and transformations of theological traditions.

Comparative theology arises out of the encounter of one religion with another and is widely practiced today in the context of religious studies. Of course, comparative theology is not new. Thinkers in the ancient Near East were fascinated to correlate the Greek, Roman, and, later, Indian pantheons with gods and goddesses found in other religions than the Indo-European ones. St. Paul's discussion of the Unknown God in Athens was a prototype within Christian theology, and early apologists such as Justin Martyr supposed a comparative theological context. The Hindu reaction to the rise of Buddhism, resulting in the reconstitution of the schools of Hinduism that we know now, was also based on a comparative understanding. In the first millennium of the common era, thinkers in India developed an elaborate language for debate among Hindu and Buddhist (and Jain and unorthodox) schools.[4] In China, the long-powerful influence of Buddhism, a "foreign" religion, on the native schools of Confucianism and Daoism produced a rich comparative discussion toward the end of the Dang and beginning of the Song dynasties. Randall Collins provides a fascinating detailed account, using both historical and sociological methods, of the interactions of philosophical and theological figures and schools, the interactions often being comparative as well as dialectical. His study is of crucial importance for anyone contemplating global intellectual history.[5]

Modern comparative theology began in earnest with the great nineteenth-century translation projects, such as Max Mueller's *Sacred Books of the East*. Despite many legitimate charges of orientalism against these translation projects, they were monumental works of scholarship and their legacy has been to render the major texts of the world's religions into European languages, especially English.[6] As English becomes a global language of scholarship, little excuse exists for theologians from any tradition to be involuntarily ignorant of the theologies of other religions. Thinkers such as Wilfrid Cantwell Smith and Mircea Eliade, who conceived themselves to be historians of religion, also produced important comparative reflections.[7] Nevertheless, comparative theology is still in its formative

4. This point was a trenchant theme in the Comparative Religious Ideas Project. See especially the articles by Francis X. Clooney, S.J., and Malcolm David Eckel in *The Human Condition, Ultimate Realities*, and *Religious Truth*, all ed. Neville. For a more detailed analysis of comparison from the Hindu side, see Clooney's remarkable *Hindu God, Christian God: How Reason Helps Break Down the Boundaries between Religions*.

5. See his *The Sociology of Philosophies: A Global Theory of Intellectual Change*. For Collins (and for most other intellectual historians), "philosophies" includes "theologies."

6. Of special recent influence has been Wing-tsit Chan's remarkable *A Source Book in Chinese Philosophy* as well as the publications of Wm. Theodore deBary and his colleagues at Columbia University. On the charges of orientalism, see, for instance, Talal Asad's *Genealogies of Religion* and Edward Said's *Orientalism* and *Culture and Imperialism*.

7. See esp. Eliade's monumental *A History of Religious Ideas* series of books.

stages relative to the task of establishing a publicly accepted set of comparative categories and comparative hypotheses within those categories. Because the comparative efforts in modern times have come from the West, their history rightly has been accused of Western bias. Therefore, it is necessary to attend carefully to the construction of comparative categories that are vulnerable to correction against bias and acceptable to a community of theological comparativists that includes anyone, from any tradition, who is interested in the comparisons.

A comparative category is the respect in which two or more theological ideas can be compared; without a common respect of comparison, no comparison is possible. To embellish the theory of interpretation outlined in chapter 4, a sign, or religious idea, stands for its object in some respect, as "red" stands for the barn in respect of color, "full" stands for the barn in respect of contents, and "Farmer Brown's" stands for it in respect to ownership. Two or more theological ideas can be compared if they stand for their objects in the same respect; they cannot be compared when they stand for their objects in different respects.

Comparison can best be understood as having three logical moments. First is the development of the comparative categories, the respects in which the traditions are to be compared. These categories need to be specific enough to bring the traditions into relation, but vague enough to register them in their own, possibly contradictory, terms. The process of perfecting the vague comparative categories continues right through to the end. Comparison, of course, never really ends, although a given project can present comparative hypotheses that it has tested as far as it can. The second logical moment is the specification of the vague category in terms of each of the traditions or ideas to be compared, saying how each tradition interprets its topic in the respect under comparison. The critical development of the ways the traditions specify the comparing category also continues to the end. The third moment is to make actual comparisons, hypotheses that state how the different traditions relate to one another in the terms given by the comparative category as enriched by the concrete specifications. These comparative hypotheses need to be tested from every relevant point of view, especially in light of the continuing criticism of the formulation of the categories and the specifications of the traditions in the categories' terms.

The second moment of comparison is especially important in the correction against bias and is related to the need for experts in each of the traditions or ideas compared. For this reason, the representation of a tradition in a comparison needs to be made vulnerable to at least five "sites" of phenomenological analysis. The first and perhaps easiest is to make sure that each tradition gets to speak in its own terms, an *intrinsic* representation; thus, each gets to say on its own how it specifies the comparative category. The second site to which the representation should be made vulnerable is the perspective that tradition has on the world, how the rest of the world looks to that tradition in relevant ways; this is a *perspectival* representation and is not to be confused with how that tradition looks from the perspectives of other traditions. The third site to which a representation should be made vulnerable is the expression of a tradition's ideas in a theoretical mode, elaborating the conceptual structure within the tradition itself in respect of the category of comparison, and making connections with conceptual structures that extend beyond the tradition where previous work has made that possible. This site is a *theoretical* representation for correction that recognizes that there is conceptual depth and self-consciousness within each tradition. The fourth site is the representation of each tradition in its practical consequences for religious life, an obvious corrective to allowing a tradition to bamboozle itself by its own double-consciousness (something of which theologians in nearly every tradition accuse other theologians in their tradition); this site is vulnerable to *practical* representation. The fifth site is paradoxical in comparison, namely the representation of what is *singular* in a tradition that gets lost in translation and simply cannot be compared accurately. Of course, to say exactly what this is would be impossible without already accomplishing the comparison; nevertheless, the singularity of theologies can be indicated indirectly, as a reminder of the limits of comparison.

Perhaps given comparative projects do not have to be explicit at every turn about each of these sites of phenomenological analysis: the intrinsic, perspectival, theoretical, practical, and singular. Most complicated representations of theological ideas in a comparative context touch on all. Nevertheless, insofar as care is taken to make the specifications and the comparisons that come from them unbiased and fair, the comparative argument needs to make itself vulnerable to correction in all these sites of phenomenological analysis. Needless to say, all comparison is provisional, awaiting further correction from angles not anticipated. Nevertheless, scholarly comparisons that have been fairly vetted, even though provisional, provide a language within which theology can proceed that takes into account the traditions compared, providing a basis for dialogue and further normative concerns.

Thus, three points of vulnerability exist within comparison: getting the comparative categories properly vague and unbiased, getting the specifications of them to be faithful to their differences in language and symbol systems, and getting the hypotheses that state just how the ideas compare to be fair, articulate, and stable. Many of the issues of this book bear upon the cultivation of interesting and accurate comparisons of theological ideas across traditions.[8]

Comparative theology is usefully studied in two connected ways. One is by scholars working collaboratively, each expert in the history and theology of one or more of the traditions to be compared, but not themselves committed, practicing, or representative of the traditions of their expertise. Such collaboration balances the centripetal interest in comparison with the centrifugal interest in making sure that each tradition is brought into the comparison with its own integrity.[9] The independence of the scholars in their own religious commitments, or lack of commitment, is important for making the comparative categories that result from their collaboration as unbiased as possible, for the sake of developing a public vocabulary for understanding the traditions together.

The second way to study theology comparatively is through dialogue in which the participants are representatives of the different traditions brought into comparative engagement. Unlike the previous approach, which disentangles the scholars' own religious commitments from those in their fields of expertise, the dialogical approach counts on the participants themselves to be correctives to the ways their traditions are seen by the others. Wilfrid Cantwell Smith is famous for saying that an important test of any scholar's representation of a religion is whether a participant in that religion would acknowledge and accept that representation. The dialogical approach to comparative theology institutionalizes that point by having immediate responses among the dialogue partners, who correct one another.

The dialogical approach to comparison involves the participants in a double role. On the one hand, they represent their own traditions and need to have solid understandings of them and how to present them to outsiders. On the other hand, inevitably they are innovative theologians in the process of dialogue, advancing (or perhaps diminishing) their theological tradition by bringing it into connection with others. Dialogue often poses questions to traditional theologies that had not been posed or answered before within the tradition. Dialogue changes theological traditions, hopefully enriching them but also making them vulnerable in ways for which they might not be prepared. Therefore, as a result of the dialogical encounter, theologians in

---

8. These remarks about comparison are given technical precision in my *Normative Cultures*, chaps. 1–4, and in "On Comparing Religious Ideas" by Wesley J. Wildman and myself in *Ultimate Realities*, ed. Neville, chap. 8. See also chap. 9 of that volume, "How Our Approach to Comparison Relates to Others," mainly by Wildman.

9. This was the principle behind the cross-cultural Comparative Religious Ideas Project; this book is dedicated to its members.

dialogue have a special responsibility to enhance, or perhaps to change and correct, the traditions they represent. To object to the risk of change involved in dialogue would have the unfortunate consequence of transforming what might have been a normative truth claim regarding a theological position into a sociological or historical claim about what has been believed, allowing the spirit of truth to slip away to those prepared to respond to good critical arguments.

The above remarks have already made it plain that theology, in employing religion as a primary resource domain for its development, needs to take advantage of all the modes of study of religion to be found within the broad field of religious studies. Literary and philological studies are important for the elaboration of the intrinsic site of analysis, letting theological traditions speak for themselves. Cultural, historical, sociological, and anthropological studies help to understand the world from the perspective of each tradition compared. Philosophical studies, as well as all the approaches to the theory of religion, are helpful in understanding the theoretical structure of traditions to be compared as well as the traditions' own conceptual history. The social sciences as well as practical disciplines such as jurisprudence are important for tracing out practical consequences of ideas to be compared. Noting the singularity of religious ideas is a matter of art. Although the proliferation of disciplines within religious studies is controversial and some of them might be ephemeral, if they have any purchase at all for understanding religion, theology needs to be vulnerable to what they have to teach, even in areas that are not comparative.

The focus in theology as symbolic engagement is on the truth of theological interpretations, and this means in the long run the truth of intentional engagements with religious realities. Religion is the primary source for theology because it is the institution of civilization that epitomizes practical and conceptual relations of human life to ultimate matters, to the finite/infinite contrasts that define the ultimate orientations of a society's world. The vast array of interpretations involved in coming to understand religions and their theological traditions and to appropriate them for normative theology often seem very far from engaging religious realities themselves. The previous chapter indicated how the values in the theological context require many sorts and levels of interpretation to formulate properly an intentional claim with an ultimate object. Many of those kinds of interpretation are not directly intentional of religious objects. Philologists, for instance, are concerned about uses of words, not necessarily with whether those uses are true or false of their subject matter. Anthropologists and sociologists are concerned about the formation of culture and society, not necessarily with whether those formations relate well to ultimate matters.

Many practitioners of the disciplines involved in religious studies themselves are hostile to normative religion and would be deeply embarrassed to find that their work constitutes a normative claim about ultimate matters. Such a normative claim is not really made, however, except when theology employs the understanding of religion involved as a sign, or part of a sign, for engaging the relevant ultimate reality. The theologian asserts this sign as true, and not false, and the various nontheological elements in the sign are elements in the cases to be made for the truth claim.

Science

The argument for including science within the scope of theology is merely an extension of the preceding point. The natural sciences, as well as the social sciences and now the medical sciences, examine things that have an ultimate dimension. Insofar as they do, what they know should be incorporated into theology wherever relevant, and they should be listened to as potential critics to which theology should be vulnerable for correction. In the recent history of Western culture, however, the relation between science and theology has been far from this benign and cooperative. In fact, science and theology are most frequently counterposed as antagonists.[10]

This antagonism has not always been the case. Through the medieval period in Jewish, Christian, and Islamic theology, the common supposition was that God's world as science might understand it cannot be at odds with God's nature and plan of salvation as scripture and theology might understand it. In the Muslim tradition, many of the great theologians were also outstanding scientists. Twentieth-century philosopher-scientist Alfred North Whitehead claimed that the underpinnings of modern science was the religious conviction in medieval Europe that God's creation of the universe has to be rational and therefore in principle comprehensible.[11]

However, the Protestant insistence on *sola scriptura* forced a wedge between the language of theology and that of science. Three closely connected emphases forced this wedge. First, theology came to express itself in the language of the Bible to a very great degree. Although medieval theology had provided copious interpretations of the Bible, they were often through allegory to other elements developed in theological history, including especially the philosophical constructions through which the connections with science were made. A strand of distinguished Protestant

---

10. Ian G. Barbour, in his magisterial Gifford Lectures on the topic, *Religion and Science*, famously distinguishes four kinds of relation between religion and science: conflict, independence, dialogue, and integration.

11. This was one of the main points of Whitehead's *Science and the Modern World*.

theology has centered itself on biblical language to the virtual exclusion of other vocabularies down to this day.[12] Second, one of the reasons for insisting on the Bible for theological language, over and above its use as primary witness, was the Protestant emphasis on the right of every Christian to interpret what is theologically important. With the vernacular translations of the Bible, such as Luther's, common people who could never read Augustine, Bonaventura, Thomas Aquinas, or Duns Scotus could be sufficient theologians for themselves if the Bible and its language carried everything important for theology. Third, as a consequence of the right of every Christian to be his or her own theologian, the rich language in Christianity since the first century, in which philosophy was used to interpret primary witnesses as doctrines and also give them critical systematic form, was set in a bad light. Protestant theology could attempt to skip over the nearly millennium and a half of theological development and return to the Bible alone.

The Roman Catholic Counter-Reformation was an extraordinarily complex and subtle response to the Protestant biblicizing of theology. It suffered from accepting the Lutheran claim that the dispute was about authority. Or perhaps Luther and the Reformers suffered from the Roman Catholic claim that authority rather than the best theological truth was at stake. At any rate, the Roman Catholic response was to insist on the authority of an official church theology, drawn largely from Thomas Aquinas. Although Aquinas and his medieval peers had a wonderfully rich vocabulary for registering the science of their day, that vocabulary stumbled when faced with the conceptual revolutions of early modern science. Without the freedom to innovate in ways that would depart flexibly from Aquinas, the Roman Catholic theological tradition found itself defending the kind of science that his theology and philosophy could accommodate. This was an important factor in the Roman Church's opposition to Galileo and other such controversies. As a result, the Roman Catholic as well as the Protestant theological traditions diverged farther and farther from serious conversation with the astonishing revolution in scientific thinking that emerged in the modern period.

The pivotal figures in the connection of science and theology in the modern period often were not the official representatives of the Christian and Jewish traditions in Europe. Rather, they were philosophers who saw that conceptions of God and other ultimate matters had to be revised in tandem with the ongoing revision of scientific conceptions of reality. Although some, such as Hume, concluded that it was hopeless to reconceive theological notions of God in light of the kind of skeptical thinking

---

12. The writings of Moltmann are outstanding examples.

associated with Enlightenment science, other giants of modern philosophy did develop brilliant new conceptions of God that kept tight intellectual ties with emerging science. Descartes, Hobbes, Locke, Spinoza, Leibniz, Kant, Schleiermacher, Hegel, Peirce, and Whitehead are heroes of this inventive philosophical scientific theology. All but Schleiermacher in this list were either practicing scientists or closely attuned to scientific thinking. None of these philosophers save Schleiermacher was close to being a church theologian, or in Spinoza's case an accepted thinker within the synagogue community; yet all of them were mightily influential in the theological discussions in generations subsequent to their flourishing, if not with their contemporaries.

In the Euro-American Protestant theological discussion in the twentieth century, Whitehead's followers such as John B. Cobb Jr., Schubert Ogden, Lewis S. Ford, Marjorie Suchocki, and David Griffin have made deep connections with biblical theology. Robert Mellert, Joseph Hallman, and most especially Joseph Bracken, S.J., have done much the same for making connections with Roman Catholic theology. Perhaps the most explicit author working to reconcile science and theology in just these terms has been Ian Barbour.[13] All these thinkers recognize the need to rethink and perhaps modify the fundamental conceptions of God—not the primary witnesses but the theological conceptualizing of those witnesses—to make fruitful connections with science.

Whereas most of these philosophers and philosophical theologians have taken scientific cosmology, including Darwin's evolutionary theory, and the conception of God in Christianity and Judaism to be the points of connection most needed, recent advances in biological sciences have raised issues of connection with other elements of theology. Medical technologies have raised conundrums for theological conceptions of the beginning and ending of life. Ecological science has raised critical questions about the relation of human life to the rest of nature that challenge some traditional theological conceptions about the uniqueness and privilege of humankind. The issues in both of these cases involve ethical considerations to a greater degree than the issues concerning cosmology and the conception of God.

Despite creative movements by process philosophers and their theological colleagues to reunite scientific and theological language, much of the discussion in Euro-American academic circles about science and religion takes a different form. The usual inquiry is into the question of whether science can be understood to be compatible with some previously defined conception of God that is not itself up for serious discussion.

---

13. See his *Religion and Science: Historical and Contemporary Issues.*

Possibly the best institutionalized inquiry of this sort is the elaborate collaborative work called the Divine Action Project, which ran from 1988 to 2003, and is carefully summarized by one of its participants, Wesley J. Wildman.[14] The topic of the project was whether intentional divine action can be conceived when the world entertaining that action is conceived the way contemporary science does. There was considerable debate over the scientific meaning of laws of nature, over concepts such as chaos theory and quantum theory, and over whether divine action means working through or abrogating natural laws, regularly or on special occasions. There was not much debate, however, over whether God should be conceived as other than an intentional actor, although two distinct models of a divinely acting God were discussed. The models of divinely acting divinity were personal theism, according to which God is a personal being who is complete without the world but can be changed by the world, and panentheism, defined as the view that God is an intentional being who requires the world in order to be complete and who can be changed by the world. Both models provide means to say that God is an intentional actor who acts on the world from the outside (for panentheism, the world is within God, although God's intentional action is from a part of God external to the worldly part).

The *image* of God as a personal, intentional actor is prominent in Christian biblical theology and much contemporary piety, particularly among the Evangelical community. The Divine Action Project required that image to be given fairly literal conceptual reference. The structure of the project itself was to test out whether such a straightforward conception of divine action can be made compatible with science, something like a scientific project to test a particular hypothesis. As a result, the connections drawn between science and theology were limited to a narrow segment of the (Christian) theological spectrum. For instance, that limiting structural hypothesis excludes consideration of the older classical Christian Neoplatonism (for which the divine plenitude transcends the distinction between self and other and hence cannot literally act on something else, or even think about something else as an object of intention); Thomism (for which God is the simple fullness of the Act of To Be, undividable into intender/intended or actor/world; there were Thomists in the Divine Action Project, however); and some ex nihilo theologies according to which the divine creative act precedes or itself constitutes any (intentional) divine

---

14. Wildman's summary is "The Divine Action Project, 1988–2003." The project was sponsored jointly by the Vatican Observatory and the Center for Theology and the Natural Sciences. Its major publications are *Quantum Cosmology and the Laws of Nature, Chaos and Complexity, Evolutionary and Molecular Biology, Neuroscience and the Person*, and *Quantum Mechanics*, all ed. Robert John Russell et al.

nature, creating the divine nature as it creates the world.[15] Those theories also speak of God acting in anthropomorphic terms, responding to prayer and redeeming the world, but not in the literal or metaphysical terms for describing God. Neoplatonic theories treat anthropomorphic language as true but on a lesser level of understanding than properly describes God. Thomism has a doctrine of the analogy of being, and ex nihilo theories have other interpretations of the applicability of symbols. The Divine Action Project was structured to rule these theories out of consideration. It also ruled out any innovative theory of God that might emerge from the discussion with science, such as Leibniz's, Hegel's, and Whitehead's creative ideas during the modern period (panentheism is sometimes attributed to Whitehead, although it is properly the theory of his innovative follower, Charles Hartshorne). Some participants in the Divine Action Project themselves held to views of God that could not be classified as personal theism or panentheism, even though, for the sake of the project, only those views were examined in detail.

The advantage of inquiry such as the Divine Action Project is that it clearly articulates assumptions and debates about interpretations within the self-imposed limits of specific discourses. If one accepts those assumptions, in this case about the validity of a range of interpretations of the meaning of natural law and about a limited range of conceptions of God, then the logic of the possible connections can be cleanly explored. Within those assumptions, the Divine Action Project was exquisitely vulnerable to internal correction and probably has laid out the alternative ways of thinking within those assumptions that will remain steady for the next generation. It provides an extraordinarily valuable service for those communities to whom the project's assumptions matter as deep commitments. In this sense, it is like a finite scientific experiment.

The disadvantage is that the relations between science and theology, especially when they tend to appear at first to be antagonistic, need to be understood philosophically, not only according to the paradigms of science or the paradigms of a kind of confessional theology that begins with unquestionable assumptions about divine intentional agency. Philosophy can never rest with assumptions. Although thinking is always in the middle, and hence assuming things, philosophy questions the case to be made for assumptions whenever they can be identified. Some kinds of philosophy construct theories like hypothetico-deductive models, as Plato did in

---

15. My *God the Creator* and other books defend such a creation ex nihilo theology, which comes out of the Scotist tradition. My *The Truth of Broken Symbols* presents a theory of how anthropomorphic symbols can apply to a self-naturing creator God; see also the discussion of personification in my *Religion in Late Modernity*.

the *Republic*.[16] Yet what philosophy does with the theories is not limited to exploring their implications: philosophy also inquires into whether and how their starting principles are justified. Philosophy is ineluctably dialectical in this sense, always backing up on assumptions. So to stipulate that the question of divine action as expressed in the biblical language of several Christian and many other traditions not itself be questioned when brought into larger historical and conceptual perspectives, including that of science, is to decline to ask basic philosophical questions. To do so is fine as far as it goes. But it seriously fails to make itself vulnerable at the crucial points of its stipulated assumptions. At this point, the scientific model of an intellectual experiment runs counter to the philosophic freedom of dialectic essential to theology.

The power of science to aid theology is not limited to offering some new ideas about nature. Nor is it to challenge theological positions by juxtaposing contrary conceptual paradigms that might be more attractive to intellectuals. The power of science for theology rather is to render new vantages from which theology can be made vulnerable. If a theistic theological position is mistaken in its conception of God because it assumes the creator is like a creature, which itself presupposes a different and wider ontological environment that only astrophysics, for instance, can articulate, then theology needs science to improve its assumptions about the creator. The greatest challenge that science poses to theology, which at the same time is the greatest contribution it offers theology, is to provide theology with new avenues to examine its own assumptions.

Art

Art has always had a didactic relation to theology, expressing in dance, music, poetry, theater, visual arts, architecture, and other media ideas already expressed in theology.[17] Nearly all of what we know of the theology of preliterate traditions is derived from their artistic remains. While interesting, the ways by which verbal theology is otherwise expressed in different media for those who do not follow the verbal argument is not to the point of the role in which the arts should be a component of theology.

More to the point is that the arts can engage ultimate matters in ways that independently precede and might inform verbal theology, whose loci include primary witnesses, doctrines, systems, and practical direction.

---

16. See Robert S. Brumbaugh's analysis of this in his *Plato on the One*. .

17. For a fine study of taste in expressiveness of art and music within worship, see Frank Burch Brown's *Good Taste, Bad Taste, and Christian Taste: Aesthetics in Religious Life*. Brown's judgments regarding Christian art have applications far beyond Christianity.

Jeremy S. Begbie has written a marvelous analytical study of how music, especially but not only improvisational music, structures imagination with regard to time so as to deepen and enrich many basic theological ideas.[18] This section will discuss four principal modes of art that might do this, indicating how theology needs to interpret ultimacy through them. In rough parallel with the four modes of symbolic engagement, they can be called artistic imagination, criticism, exhibitive judgment, and creative extension.

Artistic imagination is the obvious beginning point for understanding art. Chapter 3 presented a complicated scheme for understanding the role of imagination in theology and the remarks here merely extend that discussion. The original formulators of primary witnesses were poets, storytellers, and evangelists. Some were meta-poets, as it were, poetically uniting previous poetic elements, as was illustrated with St. Paul's reconstruction of sacrifice imagery out of diverse elements of Israelite and Hellenistic religions. Although the primary witnesses can also be asserted as doctrinally true, which almost always happens when the witnesses receive authoritative status as revealed scripture or the like, simply as products of imagination, artistic creations are not true in the sense of having cases made for them. They are not true as displacing something else as false. But they are valuable in the sense of gathering a human response that allows for the engagement of something real, including the realities of ultimate matters, and they might be true as assertions as well.

The arts include media of interpretation that are not verbal in a sense that nicely slides from primary image to critical assertion, to system, and so forth. The petroglyphs of the dreamtime world left by Australian aborigines and Native Americans in the Wyoming mountains, for instance, might be representations of world-defining boundaries that preceded any verbal conceptualizations. Grasping the finite/infinite contrasts they depict concerning the human place in the cosmos might have been done by meditative reflection and interpretive dance before much storytelling. Dance itself is an obviously nonverbal meaning. The Ghost Dances of the Native Americans at the end of the nineteenth century were extraordinarily powerful symbols for engaging ultimate destiny for those peoples in the face of the European invasion. Verbal interpretations of what they meant were obviously second-level interpretations of the primary engaging activity, the dancing. The dance movements associated with the blues and jazz in American culture have parallels in other artistic media for engaging life

---

18. See Begbie's *Theology, Music and Time*. See also the dissertation of Loye Ashton, *An Exploration on the Idea of Rhythm in Metaphysics and Christian Theology*, on musical rhythm and theology of the person, community, and liturgy.

filled with ultimate sorrow and hope together, but the artistic presentations are more engaging than verbal descriptions of sorrow and hope. The movement and music of dance is primary engagement, but by no means always primitive. Mikhail Baryshnikov dancing "The Young Man and Death" to Bach's *Passacaglia in C Minor* presents a more gripping engagement of death's fascination for young people than any dozen shelves of psychology books: that phenomenon is felt viscerally in his dance.[19] Beethoven's Ninth Symphony is often rightly called "sublime" in something like Kant's technical sense of engaging the unmeasurable infinite.[20] In other cultures, such as the Balinese, dance is combined with theater as well as music for profound, popularly accessible engagements of the ultimate realities that are the objects of the theatrical stories. Examples of art as imaginative engagement can be multiplied indefinitely.

An image danced, sung, drawn, or spoken is a kind of perception, if the argument of chapter 3 is correct. It is "a kind of" perception because it contains no assertion of the veridicality of the perception, which is what we usually mean by the word "perception" when we want to answer a question with a perception. An image is a perception in the sense of being a semiotically synthesized causal response in an interpreting organism to the causal impingements of the environment. Religiously important images are far more complicated than some responses that look as much physiological as conscious. Religious images are based on system upon system of interpretive responses. To perceive one's life situation as ultimately sorrowful and hopeful at once is a very high-level interpretive engagement. It is not merely to see that many people are sorrowful and hopeful: indeed, the revelatory character of art sometimes is to show people that their own situation is sorrowful and hopeful when they did not recognize it, either because of commercialized debasement of emotional sensitivities or the brutalizing effects of life itself. Without art, people cannot cry deeply for their sorrows or find hope beyond inertia. Art can reveal what is really there but impossible to engage without the images in dance, music, painting, theater, or other imagistic medium.[21] Art allows what is important in ultimate matters to be felt, to be brought almost viscerally into people's experience. Verbal arts do

---

19. My wife and I witnessed this electrifying performance in the late 1960s or early 1970s. An equally electrifying performance of the Bach *Passacaglia in C Minor* is the jazz version by flautist Hubert Laws and his group (Ron Carter, Bob James, Gene Bertoncini, Dave Friedman, Freddie Waits, Billy Cobham, and Dave Miller) on *Hubert Laws Carnegie Hall*, CTI Records, recorded at Carnegie Hall on January 12, 1973. The bass solo by Ron Carter does better by Bach than any of his children.
20. See Kant's precritical work *Observations on the Feeling of the Beautiful and the Sublime*, as well as his mature treatment of the beautiful and the sublime in *The Critique of Judgment*, part 1, books 1 and 2.
21. See Frank Burch Brown's *Religious Aesthetics: A Theological Study of Making and Meaning*.

this too, of course, although the elaborate abstractions that come into play with theological case making and the formation of doctrine and system often filter out the feeling that comes more directly in the dance and song.

Imagination is creative, inventing novel images. This is not to say, however, that art always has to be about the invention of novel forms. Western art mainly is of this sort. A history of art book charts the changes and advances in artistic styles. Yet some art keeps the same general genre and seeks to perfect it in the sense of deepening its capacities to carry over what the generic form has always carried over more or less well. Byzantine icons have had the same general style for a millennium and a half, and the "improvements" have been by way of making the connections ever richer and the intensity of the gaze deeper.[22] When art is innovative, however, it leads us to see things that were not seen before, often because the previous images precluded their perception. This brings the discussion to art as criticism.

Artistic criticism in theology, which does not mean the criticism of art, is the function art has to challenge a prevailing way of engaging the world in its ultimate dimensions. As has been said frequently here, images in their semiotic systems define cultures, and in so doing channel the ways by which the world, including its ultimate dimensions, is engaged. Irrespective of whether these ways are true in the sense of carrying across what is important in such a form that a case can be made for them, they are selective ways. Art can provide other selective ways. Without engaging another culture with different selections of ways of engaging, or without art that presents other selective ways, it is possible for a culture to think its ways are the only ones. Although intellectuals might verbalize other ways of engagement, art can make them felt viscerally.

Paul Tillich used to tell of observing fistfights in a Berlin art museum between young Nazis and the artistic youth of the Weimar culture. They were fighting about the differences between Nazi realism in art versus the modernist expressionism favored by the museum. Both sides viscerally felt the conflicting world definitions engaged in the two styles of art. Each side rebelled against the challenge the other's art presented to its own ultimate engagement of the world. The fight was not about ideology as such—they did not need paintings for that. The fight was about having to accept the quasi-perceptual evidence the other's art forced upon them.

A religious culture is possible that fails to give ultimate significance to the poverty of people in its midst. Nineteenth-century Victorian culture is

---

22. The 2nd ed. of the influential *History of Art* by H. W. Janson devotes 12 pages to Byzantine art, despite the fact it flourished for a millennium; art history of Janson's sort chronicles changes in style, not intensification.

an example. The literary art of Charles Dickens and other writers forced the perception of poverty on Victorian culture and changed it. A religious culture is possible for people in poverty who cannot imagine a world of beauty and satisfaction. Peasant cultures in Latin America are examples. A beautiful cathedral far removed from the personal living conditions of the peasants nevertheless gives them a vision of a dimension of the world otherwise denied them, and they sacrifice to support what only materially impoverishes them more.

Art as criticism often is seen as having an ethical edge to it, and indeed it does. But whether it is ethical is a matter of further judgment beyond the art. The art that gives ultimate significance to military sacrifice for the extension of empire and the Glory of X, for instance, is viewed as highly ethical by some, and as the opposite by others, or by the same people at an earlier or later time. Art only provides ways, sometimes opposing ways, of engaging what is ultimately important in defining the world, including human obligation. Artists themselves tend to be a little oblivious as to morals, to use Whitehead's phrase, or sometimes to be naively caught up in an ethical attitude defined by others. Artists as such need have little skill at judging moral rightness.

To be sure, the grounds for proper ethical criticism of artistic images in the right time and place have to do with truth. Do the images when interpreted in certain ways carry over what is important or not? Supposing that the images engage: do they do so truly in this sense? This is not always a simple question. To the extent that art is didactic for an ethical cause, as Nazi realism was, for instance, a critical ethical refutation of the allegedly ethical Nazi cause automatically rejects its didactic art. But to the extent that Nazi art does effect a genuine engagement, however misinterpreted it might be ultimately, there is something valuable in that art which needs acknowledgment. Perhaps it is only a blood-and-soil primitive identification of personal worth with a place and narrow culture, the remedy for which is to civilize it with a broader perspective. Nevertheless, that narrow engagement needs to be recognized.

Very often, the impact of critical art on a culture is to reveal a seamy underside that the official images of the culture gloss over. The discussion of sacrifice imagery in chapter 4 pointed out a seriousness of evil and sin that modern Western cultures like to trivialize by reducing it to personal responsibility. Yet art can viscerally force upon people in the modern West a sense for that seriousness. Herman Melville's *Billy Budd* is the story of the sacrifice of an innocent man because people were caught in a web of evil, and people in the nineteenth century got the point of the sacrifice imagery,

as did twentieth-century people who responded to the opera by that title by
Benjamin Britten. Mel Gibson's film *The Passion of Christ*, for all the controversy about its ideological content, was a powerful experience engaging
people with the depths of sin and evil. That its overwrought imagery
seemed sadomasochistic to some critics is only to say that sadomasochism
is another way of engaging the depths of sin and evil. And of course it
should be admitted that to vast numbers of people the biblical images of
sacrifice are as engaging now as they ever were, despite the surface elite culture that would deny them.

Art criticism, which is not the same as art as criticism, has at least two
roles. One is to exhibit just what a work of art does by way of engaging reality. The other is to ask the critical question of truth about that. This brings
the discussion to art as exhibitive.

Art as exhibitive judgment is perhaps best understood in terms of Justus
Buchler's notion of exhibitive judgment. Buchler interpreted all human
intentionality in terms of what he called "judgment."[23] Human intentionality, he said, has three main forms: saying, doing, and making. Judgment is
mainly assertive in saying, active in doing, and exhibitive in making. In his
book on poetry, he summarized these as follows:

(1) When we can be said to predicate, state, or affirm, by the use of words
or by any other means; when the underlying direction is to achieve or support belief; when it is relevant to cite evidence in behalf of our product, we
produce in the mode of assertive judgment, we judge assertively. (2) When
we can be said to do or to act; when the underlying direction is toward
effecting a result; when "bringing about" is the central trait attributable to
our produce, we produce in the mode of active judgment, we judge actively.
(3) When we contrive to make, in so far as the contrivance rather than its
role in action is what dominates and is of underlying concern; when the
process of shaping and the produce as shaped is central, we produce in the
mode of exhibitive judgment, we judge exhibitively. On the methodic level,
where (minimally) purposiveness and intention belong to judgments,
assertive judgment is exemplified by science, or more generally, inquiry
(including any discipline that makes a truth claim); active judgment, by
deliberate conduct morally assessable; exhibitive judgment, by art.[24]

---

23. Buchler's first major work was *Charles Peirce's Empiricism*, and he maintained the Peircean orientation along with his own very original contributions. He was a major American metaphysical
thinker of the last half of the twentieth century. For his theory of judgment, see his *Toward a General
Theory of Judgment* and *Nature and Judgment*.

24. *The Main of Light*, pp. 97–98.

Whereas his terminology employs greater simplifications than anything pursued in theology as symbolic reference (and he himself was hostile to theology in any normative sense, being an anti-supernaturalistic naturalist), his notion of exhibitive judgment is very suggestive for one mode of art as symbolic engagement.[25]

The primary characteristic of a work of art from the standpoint of human making is that it exhibits the structure given in its materials. The work of art might also make a truth claim, like an assertion, and it might also be an action, like propaganda. Nevertheless, as art it predominantly is the exhibition of the structure of the materials. To appreciate the work of art is for that structure to be taken into the experience of the appreciator. One of the chief functions of art criticism, as mentioned, is to lay out and interpret the structure exhibited to those who are not prepared to pick it up immediately.

The theological importance of this is that art can exhibit structures of ultimate dimensions of the world, which, once grasped, stand as proof against theological simplifications that lie about the complexities of ultimacy. For instance, some Christian theologies of conversion, especially those that guide revivalist activities, represent the character of conversion as a simple matter of will, or of getting a powerful pious feeling. These theologies are simply incredible to anyone who has carefully read a nineteenth-century novel about character, such as Dostoyevsky's *The Brothers Karamozov*. This is so despite the fact that the people in the novel are fictional. By means of fictional characters, the novelist exhibits complexities of human nature to which theological ideas are vulnerable. Or consider the exhibition of the complexities of evil in Dante's *Inferno*, Shakespeare's *Macbeth*, Melville's *Moby Dick*, Conrad's *Heart of Darkness*, or Golding's *Lord of the Flies*. Any of these stands as a refutation to any Enlightenment restriction of evil to the personal responsibility of conscious judgment. One might say that actual history displays the seriousness and complexity of evil better than any fictional account, as for instance in the exploitation of child labor in nineteenth-century England, or the Nazi Holocaust. Yet it is possible to misread history simplistically and ideologically, even in theology, if there are no exhibitive works of art to break that mold. Dickens's *David Copperfield* and Wiesel's *Night* exhibit a devastatingly critical level of truth

---

25. Buchler was one of the Columbia University naturalists in mid-twentieth century of Jewish birth who reacted very strongly against Jewish piety and its theological beliefs; his generation differed from the previous one dominated by John Dewey who, though a naturalist, was never hostile to theology. Buchler and I were colleagues at the State University of New York at Stony Brook for the last years of his life and, despite his views on religion, learned much from each other, me more from him than the other way around.

about those conditions even though, in the former case, the story is fictional; in the latter case, it is the art with which Wiesel tells his own story that makes it speak for the whole situation.

Here is the place to acknowledge the danger in theology when the rich symbols of primary witness are interpreted doctrinally and probated with cases that lead to dialectical systematic expressions. The temptation is always to simplify, to reduce ambiguity, and to be clear about what is being denied. Often the primary witnesses are as messy as the confluence of symbolic sacrifice networks discussed earlier, and the doctrinal restatement of Christian atonement theology leaves out the truth of the mess. Ideally, of course, the elaborate theory of critical interpretation discussed in the previous chapter will prevent such falsifying simplifications. The nuances of different meaning networks will be noticed, the different modes of reference subtly recorded, and the interactions of the multitude of purposes defining the interpreting context will be laid out in order to identify just what is true and false in what might be asserted. Nevertheless, that often has not happened. "One idea" theologies subvert the depths and riches of the primary witnesses. Art, which can be engaged at any level of theology, is a powerful corrective to theological mis-simplification.

The examples of the exhibitive power of art discussed here have been literary, and indeed, the literary arts are easiest to relate to literary theology, especially at the systematic level where theology seeks out correction. Nonverbal arts can just as well exhibit complexities of ultimacy to which theology needs to be vulnerable. Dance as much as prayer can exhibit how human beings stand in relation to an infinite creator or to a hidden Dao. Images of fecundity and human sexuality are among the most important finite/infinite contrasts in most cultures: Elvis Presley's sexual dance and music, with the whole of the rock-and-roll culture, was a far more powerful and universally effective No! to a blindly constricted theology of sexuality than Karl Barth's politico-theological objections to the Nazi kidnapping of German Christianity.[26] To be sure, some conservative theologians in all traditions object strenuously to the sexualization of popular culture, and their arguments have to do with moral standards for sexual expression and the defense of discipline against the powers of sexual license that are forces of nature. Morals and discipline are essential components of civilized life

---

26. Concerning Presley, it should be acknowledged that his music built on traditions of African-American music and dance, much of which was as sexual as Presley's. He gave it form, however, that reached far beyond the African-American ethnic culture to constitute a threat to conservative Buddhism and Islam as well as to the Christianity in reference to which African-American music defined itself. On Barth, see Rolf Ahler's *The Community of Freedom.* My reference is to the Barmen Declaration.

and have an ultimate dimension defining the world. The critical force of the artistic exhibition of sexuality in music and dance, nevertheless, is to show the vitality of primal sexuality and its real roles in the constitution of the human spirit, however those might need to be channeled for the sake of civilization. The pain of the theological culture that was offended by the open display of sexuality in music and dance came in part from the fact it was repressing and denying sexuality rather than recognizing and civilizing it. Moreover, the carnival of sexuality, particularly in expressions that reveal its character as a natural force, an intimate part of the cosmos, overturns theological authority structures. Exhibitive art does that frequently.

The exhibitive role of art is far more complex than can be explored here. Important issues concern the differences between enacting the art, for instance, by actually dancing, and participating as an observer. Is reading a novel merely observing the work of art, or is it enacting? Is the enacting of music in the performers or in the listeners? Art criticism helps theology sort these issues in individual cases, interpreting the exhibited reality in language that connects with theology.

Creative extension is the fourth mode of art's contribution to theology, and the point about it is very simple. A given expression of a theological point, verbal or otherwise, can be supplemented and extended to new meanings by additional artistic expressions. The obvious example is putting a poem to music. The music does not express the same thing as the poem. Rather, it adds a new dimension of meaning connected to and in addition to the poem. Most religions have liturgical celebrations of some sort. The verbal text is one thing. Art adds to it when the text is chanted or sung. Art adds more when the vestments of the participants themselves have theological meaning. The movement of the liturgy can be choreographed, adding the dimension of dance. The liturgy can take place in a symbolically significant architectural space. The space can be decorated with tapestries, paintings, and other visual arts, as well as stained glass. Memorabilia used in the liturgy and decorating the space can give a historical dimension to the liturgy. And so forth. In a quite literal sense, the arts can pile on networks of meaning that resonate with one another, forming a whole symbolic experience that is far richer than any one theological expression. Some theologians, for instance, the early Calvinist reformers, might want to minimize the nonverbal artistry in liturgical expressions of theology. Nevertheless, this does not lead to clarity, as if the other artistic expressions muddied verbal precision. It actually reduces the full liturgy to only its verbal component. The creative extension of theology made possible by the arts is not to provide alternative ways of expressing what theological words do. Rather, it is to amplify the verbal expressions with what can be expressed through the arts, including poetry and imaginative literature. Theological analysis of this has a much richer resource than theological analysis of merely verbal theology alone.

Practical Normative Disciplines

The fourth domain to which dialectical systematic theology should make itself vulnerable, and therefore include within the scope of theology, is what can be called practical normative disciplines. By this is not meant practical academic disciplines, except indirectly, but rather the organized or institutionalized practices within a society that aim to accomplish some essential social function. Consider some examples.

To support human life with food and shelter is an essential social function, and every society has an economy. Economics is the practical discipline of economic life, although the term is used only in scientific cultures. Economics is not only the pursuit of means that accomplish economic ends, although surely it is that. It is also normed by finite/infinite contrasts that define the world with respect to human relations with nature from which a living is worked; different cultures articulate this differently. Should human beings subordinate nature to economic ends if they can, or confine their economic activity to processes that reinforce a natural ecology? What sacrifices are to be made for economic goals—human sacrifice in fertility rites, the bondage of one class in society to support the rest, the sacrifice of leisure for enjoying the arts and religion? Should economics be a tool of politics, or vice versa?[27] Economics has an ultimate dimension insofar as its goals and practices are oriented by the culture's finite/infinite world-defining contrasts in respect to nature, humanity, and the purposes of human life.

The practice of law functions in society to articulate and enforce justice; societies differ in their conceptions and institutions of law. Yet justice itself, however conceived, is a world-defining boundary notion, an ultimate matter. Politics is the function of distributing and guiding power in a society to produce a community that reflects the society's values. Societies differ regarding their basic values and institutions of managing them. Yet that societies be organized with regard to power and management is an ultimate matter, for which societies have finite/infinite contrasts. Ethics is the institutionalized function of articulating, judging, and developing goodness and virtue within a society, and opposing their opposites. Societies differ in their senses of goodness and virtue, yet the having of some sense of

---

27. These issues are raised in interesting ways in Jared Diamond's *Guns, Germs, and Steel*.

goodness and virtue is a world-defining quality. Societies have images of finite/infinite contrasts that define obligation and its general content. Education is a social function, embodied in the sciences and much else besides, whereby past experience, especially cultural tradition, is appropriated and inquiry into the unknown is conducted. Societies differ not only in what they know, but in what they count as knowledge. Yet in all societies knowing is something that defines the human world and is given orientation by some finite/infinite contrast or other. Religion itself is a practical normative discipline by which a society patterns its institutions and behavior to relate to ultimate matters.

The disciplines listed here, economics, law, politics, ethics, education, and religion, are just a sample and themselves are very general. Economics includes food production, monetary exchange, the cultural transformations that go with trade, the support of building and architecture, roads and transportation, means of communication, and even the promotion of physical and mental health. In highly technological societies, these tend to be sorted out rather than blended together. Law includes not only institutions for the determination and administration of justice but for the promotion of the understanding of justice in education. Politics concerns local, regional, and global government, issues of war and peace, management of economic issues such as poverty and wealth that affect social structures, and many other things, perhaps even including the directions to be taken with regard to the promotion of physical and mental health. Ethics is institutionalized in educational institutions, in pro bona publica organizations, cultural pressure groups, and religious organizations, among others. Public media are powerful definers of ethical thought and criticism. Education itself is a function of more than educational institutions. The sciences are closely tied to government and industry in technological societies. The arts educate as much as science, and the search for wisdom is often institutionalized as a high-level activity that cannot be institutionalized except among elites! Religion is even more complex than this book lets on. This list can be expanded greatly to take into account differences in various societies with regard to how the practice of living is institutionalized.

The practical normative disciplines all have a religious dimension in the sense that they take their ultimate orientation from the world-defining boundary images that are constituted by a culture's finite/infinite contrasts. Perhaps it is paradoxical to speak of the religious dimension of these practical disciplines, because so often in late-modern cultures people identified with practical normative disciplines take themselves to be explicitly non-ultimate. Even if they are also religious and recognize ultimate matters in the religious institutions of their lives, they often think of themselves as dealing with the down-to-earth practical matters far removed from ultimate considerations. Practice is so often contrasted with the "theoretical" interests that would articulate a culture's sacred canopy. The day-to-day issues of practice might very well be light-years from religious considerations. Nevertheless, those practical activities, organized in disciplined ways and responsive to the vagaries of circumstance, have their overall social function because the sacred canopy defines human life as needing them. To put the matter the other way, because human life needs those normative practical disciplines, the sacred canopy has basic symbols that give them orientation.

One critical force of the practical normative disciplines for dialectical systematic theory in theology is that they can reveal the rude impracticality of biased theology. If theology tells you that God or the Dao will provide, the economic critic will say that this is false unless someone goes to work. If theology tells you that violence against human beings is always wrong, the politician will point out the barbarians coming over the hill to kill your children. If theology tells you to trust your sentiment, the law will point out the prevalence of bloodthirsty sentiment. And so on. The practical normative disciplines do not have an authoritative standing by themselves to dictate norms on an ultimate level. Theology might answer the above objections with a defense of subsistence living, an acceptance of death at the hands of an aggressor, and the willing destruction of social habits of goodness and virtue. The determination and criticism of the boundary conditions is itself a dialectical matter. Nevertheless, the practical normative conditions can present a realism to theology that theology's own dialectics might have ignored. The practical disciplines can say what happens when this is done, or that.

Another and more important critical force of the practical normative disciplines for theology, however, is that they provide a significant part of the ultimate field within which theology's primal witnesses, doctrines, and dialectical systems are tested. Many internal correctives for theology have been discussed here. The encompassing test still is how theology guides life in relation to the ultimate. Where is life? Practical life is in economic life, legal life, political life, ethical life, educational life, religious life, and other such social functions. Religion is not contained only within the institutions of religious practice: it is in the religious dimensions of all social practices epitomized by these normative disciplines. These practical domains provide the field in which the differences that theology makes to living before the ultimate can be discerned and judged.

The practical normative disciplines, therefore, necessarily should be included within the scope of theology, not only for their correction regarding realism in ultimate matters, but because they provide the terms within which theology can read its own successes and failures, truths and errors. Having made this point, which will be expanded in the last two chapters of this book, the discussion can now turn to the nature of dialectical systematic theory itself.

Before that, however, something must be said about why this chapter has treated religion, science, art, and practical normative disciplines but not the humanities. Are not the humanities also important resources for theology? Indeed, have they not been recognized as such for a long time? In fact, they have already been integrated into the argument here. In the Western academic curriculum and intellectual culture, the humanities divide into two sorts of emphases. One is the emphasis on normative matters, in ethics, philosophy, and, most particularly for the present interest, theology. Philosophy and ethics are obvious elements of theology. The other emphasis is on disciplined ways of appreciating culture, of apprehending the depths of literature and the arts, of grasping the complexities of meaning in social roles, of philosophical reflection on the assumptions of culture. If culture is not appreciated in these sophisticated ways, it is not fully possessed. The humanities in this sense are disciplines for coming into rich possession of culture. Surely, theology needs to be disciplined in appreciating the subtleties of languages and literatures, of comparative cultures, of the arts—the role of criticism in the arts has already been discussed.

The humanities are also needed to appreciate the significance of the sciences as cultural enterprises. The practice of science in a high civilization needs to take place within a sophisticated humanistic appreciation of its significance. The same thing is true with regard to the practical normative disciplines: without a humanistic appreciation of their cultural significance, they are blind. Theology needs to employ such a sophisticated humanistic appreciation of all its resources. The humanities are not separate resources for theology, like the sciences and arts: they are the cultural paradigm of theology itself in its engagement of those others.

This discussion of religion, the sciences, the arts, and the practical normative disciplines as instrumentally important to defining theology's content and scope should not obscure the more basic point that these are all important because they mediate engagement of ultimate matters. Theologians need not think of themselves as practitioners of all these disciplines, nor insinuate to the real practitioners that they are closet theologians, except to the extent needed for both sides to learn from one another. These disciplines are important for theology because they do reflect the ultimate in various ways having to do with how they are given orientation by finite/infinite contrasts. How all these various reflections of the ultimate bear upon one another is the question for systematic theology.

CHAPTER 6

Dialectical Systematic Theology

Systematic theology differs from doctrines and their defense by virtue of its concern for the proper form of theory. Theory is the mode of thought in which not only the primary assertions are made coherent and the cases made for them brought into view. Theory also reviews, funds, and makes itself vulnerable to its own critical testing. "Theory," deriving from the Greek "theoria" and with cognates in many languages, has come to mean something like a vision within which all the parts of a whole can be seen together in their connections. The visual imagery goes back to the use of the term in Greek philosophy and gets some of its power from the example of geometry, a kind of "seeing with the mind's eye."[1] The emphasis on the visual, however, has led to all sorts of philosophical difficulties that David Weissman has summed up as the view that the mind is a kind of theater for watching contents.[2] Instead of being at the heart of the engagement with reality, mind is treated as a separate kind of thing within which reality is to be mirrored. Earlier chapters here have argued that mirroring is

---

1. See, for instance, Plato's *Meno*, in which Socrates teaches a slave boy to double the area of a square by constructing a square on the diagonal when the boy had originally thought to double the length of a side. Although Socrates drew figures on the ground, they of course were very inaccurate. The boy and the audience could see in their mental imagination, or mind's eye, that a square on the diagonal is the right procedure, however.

2. See Weissman's *Intuition and Ideality* for a criticism of the Western philosophic tradition as too intuitionistic, with a presentation of a theory of metaphysics as hypothesis that is similar to the one espoused in the present book. See also his companion volume, *Hypothesis and the Spiral of Reflection*.

involved only in iconic reference, and that causal engagement also requires indexical reference.

An earlier meaning of *theoria* in ancient Greece referred to a reviewing stand or high point from which a king or general could watch the troops march by and deploy. The implication here is not the unity of a visual glance but rather a position from which all the connections could be made over time. All the parts can be contemplated in turn so that the king or general can direct the forces as needed.[3] This is closer to the meaning of theory when qualified as dialectical and systematic.

The argument of this chapter has four main steps. The first is to pursue the point raised frequently before that making good cases for its truth claims pushes theology ineluctably to systematic theory, regardless of the suspicions of theory. That theory of this sort is dialectical has a special meaning for theory itself, which will be explained. The second step is to address the problem of how to connect and stabilize the wildly diverse metaphorical language of much primary witness and also the doctrinal formulations that come from that, a problem compounded by the fact that different religious traditions with seemingly unrelated symbolic networks are involved. Another way to put this problem is to focus on how to make commensurable the different languages that need to be brought together in order to make coherent cases for truth in theology. Not only diverse religions, but the sciences, arts, and normative disciplines need to be engaged with one another, each with its own language. The answer to be defended is that dialectical systematic theory in theology needs metaphysics. The third step, then, is to explain and justify a conception of metaphysics that does the job. The fourth step is to lay out some of the main connections between the levels of abstraction that stretch from creative imaginative work, as in primary witnesses, to the highest levels of the metaphysical structure of a dialectical system.

System and Dialectic: The Making of Cases

The argument has been made in many steps now that theological claims need to have cases made for them. A case needs to be made to answer each

---

3. See the development of this point in my *Normative Cultures*, pp. 3–7. The first four chapters of that book lay out the concept of theory sketched here. Chapter 6 of *The Highroad around Modernism* takes pains to redefine theory and show how it avoids the criticisms of logocentrism. My "Contextualization and the Non-obvious Meaning of Religious Symbols: New Dimensions to the Problem of Truth" provides an analysis of ways of triangulating on the assessment of systematic theological truth, with direct reference to the alternative theory of George Lindbeck.

relevant objection, and to provide considerations to consider the claim to be true. A brief review of the argument is in order here.

Strictly speaking, a purely imaginative interpretation that is not asserted of anything is only adventitiously true or false. Only potentially assertive interpretations can be true or false. But because imagination is the activity of constructing responses to the environment that enable us to engage it experientially, imaginative interpretations are constantly at work in orienting us to the world. If not asserted, they are assumed and built in to the habits of interpreters who are pursuing their own purposes. At bare minimum, the truth question for imagination is whether, when it engages the world in assumptive interpretive activity, its assumptions carry over the important elements of the object in the respects in which the interpretation assumes its signs stand for the object. If the imaginative elements do in fact engage the world, even if they carry over the wrong message about what that world is, they are valuable in the minimal sense of facilitating engagement. If they merely seem engaging and yet in fact are deflecting engagement with reality, then the imaginative elements as such are both false as they function in habitual interpretation and destroy the value they would have as engaging.

How can one tell whether genuine engagement happens? Many kinds of cases can be made. Cultural criticism, for instance, might argue that the fundamental images of a society are delusory, based on nostalgia for a world that in fact has vanished and rendering the society unknowingly disengaged from the reality it faces. Contrariwise, art criticism might argue that some new images reveal the duplicity of the old ones and provide new means of engagement. Social sciences can argue that the images that orient a society, its sacred canopy in ultimate matters, do or do not engage the realities of life. Spiritual directors can discern in individual cases whether a person is engaged or in denial. In the long run, the experience of a people tests the adequacies of its basic imagery. To make convincing cases for imagination as engagement, and primarily for core texts and motifs of primary religious witness, requires all these approaches and more.

Beyond engagement is the question whether the images that engage do so truly in the sense of carrying across to the interpreters what is important in the objects engaged in the respects the images as signs stand for the objects. To summarize the argument so far, making cases for such assertoric interpretations requires theology first to understand the complexity of the interpretation. This means the analytical grasp of the meanings involved in the signs, how they connect, and how they contradict or reinforce one another. Truth is a dyadic relation such that the interpretation is either right or wrong in receiving as carried across what the sign conveys of the object's value. The carrying across itself is a function, in part, of reference, and the modes of reference in an assertion need to be identified. This is particularly important in theology, where non-iconic indexical references are so common. Any interpretation is made within a context, which is determined by the details of a situation and the purposes involved. A vast number of practical purposes underlie most theological interpretation. An equally vast number of purposes are involved in theological assertion itself, including the purposes of making relevant cases. Only when all these are identified, or at least implicitly grasped correctly, can the interpretation itself be identified and its denial stated so that cases can begin. For every aspect of the identification of the concrete intentional interpretation, a set of cases across a relevant scope needs to be made. Then the more critical part of making cases begins with attempts to get at the value in the object independently and to assess how it is received in the interpreter. Other aspects of religious experience are brought into play, as well as other religions. The sciences, arts, and practical normative disciplines have perspectives on ultimate matters that might bear relevance. These all need to be engaged and sorted in order to make proper cases for theological assertions.

The many different kinds of argumentation, analysis, and resource domains need to be understood together with the connections analyzed and properly sorted. The history of theology displays so many instances in which the different elements within its scope have been set in opposition to each other, uncomprehendingly, that the situation in which theology is properly vulnerable to correction has rarely obtained. The opposition between science and religion discussed above is only one example. Other religions have been viewed as hostile rather than as teachers, the arts have been viewed as subversive, and the practical normative disciplines have been viewed as antireligious in the sense of denying ultimacy.

Of course, in all these instances, particular theological positions have indeed been undermined by such considerations. This is only to say, however, that theology has learned something in the process. Realistically, theologians do not often change their minds on important matters. For many theologians in all traditions, a sense of faithfulness to their tradition disposes them to not hear challenging criticisms, to avoid engagements with other religions, the sciences, arts, and the practical normative elements of secular culture. The problem is not that theologians stick with their positions in order to make the best case for them, holding out for successful defenses when the larger public thinks this a lost cause and has moved on to the next fad; all this is to the good. Many theologians want their positions to be well entrenched rather than perfectly vulnerable to correction. The theologians alongside them, however, often of a younger generation, see the point of the critical challenges and move their own theologies to learn from the challenges. Although individual theologians might not learn from the lessons discovered in attempting to make good cases for their positions, the community of theologians within which they work can so learn. Individual theologians might think the cases they make are quite good enough. Their critical followers, however, know that each new challenge requires that a new case be made. A passionate though perhaps vain hope underlying this book is that many theologians will say, "We already have always thought that theology should pay attention to the arts, sciences, and practical disciplines of life—who accuses us of failing to do so?"

The scope of theology includes all the fields and discourses that might be involved in making relevant cases for or against theological assertions.

The most obvious of these is the development of theological assertions as doctrines that can be expressed in coordinating language so that a position's assertions can be made consistent. This usually means bringing a single consistent interpretation out of the core texts and motifs of a tradition, leaving out or suppressing other possible interpretations. Scholastic systems of doctrines, which have been particularly prevalent in Buddhism, Christianity, Hinduism, and Islam, often take the form of propositional statements that can be seen to be consistent. Judaism's scholastic commentarial tradition is remarkable in comparison with other scholastic traditions because it does not insist on consistency, noting with finality that one rabbi says this, another says that; still, the language is such that inconsistency can be specified.

The most common meaning of "system" in theology, though not the best, is the assemblage of doctrines in consistent order, perhaps with ordering lines of proof within the assemblage that derive some doctrines from others. Creeds and confessions are epitomes of theological systems, although usually with an immediately practical purpose—to articulate identity and set limits to a community. People can adhere to creeds and confessions while radically disagreeing about why they accept them. If a given theologian, however, is to defend a creed or confession as true by giving reasons for its doctrines and their connections, a self-conscious system is required. In any well-developed scholastic system there are also meta-level discussions of the nature of doctrine, the relation of doctrine to the interpretation of core texts and motifs, and all the historical and philosophical considerations, such as semiotic theory, that go into making a consistent set of doctrines. Theological systems such as Nagarjuna's or Aquinas's include not only their doctrines that refer to ultimate matters but also the elaborate philosophical considerations with which their doctrines are justified. At all points, the considerations made within a theological system have a history, not only in the history of religion or doctrine intending ultimate matters, but also in the meta-level philosophical and other areas whose history might have little to do with religion as such. According to theology as symbolic engagement, the system backing up an assemblage of doctrines should include the considerations that come from the wider scope of comparative theology, sciences, arts, and practical normative disciplines.

Theology as symbolic engagement provides a wider perspective on the sense of system as an assemblage of doctrines than this, however. Doctrines usually are understood to be descriptive of the ultimate matters in their topics. In the Western theological traditions, excluding large parts of the rabbinic commentarial tradition, theological descriptions are often called "scientific" in the sense of "describing" their subject matter. This is to limit theological assertions to iconic doctrine. Theology as symbolic engagement points out that many theological assertions have important indexical reference in their truth claims, so that they are true but not descriptive. Their truth consists in carrying across what is important in the ultimate matters into the interpreters in the respects in which the interpretive assertions take their signs to stand for their logical objects. If theology constrains the reference in such assertions to be interpreted iconically or descriptively, those assertions might well be false rather than true: God is not up in the sky—up there, it's empty space, more or less. Most of the great religious traditions, for instance, affirm on the one hand that the ultimate reality—Dao, Principle, Brahman, the Emptiness of Buddha-nature, Vishnu, the monotheistic God—is not spatial or temporal, rather being the ultimate condition for space-time. They affirm on the other hand that these ultimate realities are to be "reached" by activities that are spatial and temporal, or that draw their metaphoric base from there, such as conformity (to the Dao), manifestation (of Principle), realization (of Brahman), Enlightenment (regarding Emptiness), worship (of Vishnu), or going to meet in an afterlife and heavenly place (God). Of course, these pairings are too simple as expositions of how to live before the ultimate in these traditions. But the point is made: the spatiotemporal activities of people or souls cannot be iconically true for engaging a non-spatiotemporal ultimate. They can only be indexically true in the sense that thinking of the religious quest in their terms carries across what is important to access in the ultimate realities regarding that quest. Many religions say that the non-spatiotemporal ultimate manifests itself in spatiotemporal things, such as avatars, sacred texts, sacred events, which can be engaged in space-time. But this is to say that the manifestations are indices to the non-spatiotemporal ultimates.

Religions have known about, if not admitted to, the metaphoric quality of their symbols from the very beginning of recorded theology. Without the analytical semiotic terms, they have employed those symbols indexically. The attempt to understand and make coherent the powerful engagements of ultimacy in religion by insisting that all reference is iconic instead is to strain the living, causal power of religious symbols through a fine sieve that often results in thin gruel. Some theologians would object to this interpretive point with the claim that iconic reference is precisely what they intend, and that it is their theological faith to do so. Perhaps they intend to defend a community identity that is defined by affirmation of certain doctrines in an iconic way. For instance, some Christian theologians might say that Jesus is not an index of God, as theology as symbolic engagement would have it, but literally, in some metaphysically defensible sense, the Son of God; this is what the identity-conveying creeds affirm. What does divine sonship mean, literally? If it means that Jesus was conceived with God's sperm and carries divine DNA, it makes God too finite. If it means that Jesus is an eternally generated copy of God, it asserts polytheism. The Christian tradition has backed away from these literal interpretations to creative metaphors, or has insisted that the literalisms are broken and do not apply literally, but with mystery. This is to say that the literalisms are not quite literally true but point to something beyond them; that is, the literalisms carry also an element of indexical reference that saves them from being literally false.

Theological traditions do contain systems of iconically referring doctrines, and these have been historically significant in many areas. Nevertheless, theology as symbolic engagement offers another way of assessing the consistency of theological assertions, one that does not require the consistency of descriptive language. By means of the semiotic analysis of assertion given in chapter 4, it is possible to say how theological assertions are true or false relative to the specific contexts within which they might be concretely asserted. The question of truth is always a concrete question as to whether the relevant value has been carried over into the interpreter in the specific context. Assertions that are true when made in some contexts, by people at certain stages of religious development and psychological states, might be false in other contexts for other people. Theology, if properly attentive to the semiotic structure and context, can say how and why theological interpretations are true or false. Theology can also specify the conditions under which theological assertions are consistent or inconsistent with one another. Apparently inconsistent assertions might in fact be consistent when their differing contexts are taken into account. And apparently consistent assertions might turn out to be inconsistent when the contexts are addressed.

The truly general shape of a system of assertions, then, should not be regarded as an assemblage of consistent statements. Rather, the truly general shape is whatever allows for the intricate mixture of interpretations of ultimate matters and the cases that can be made for them, taking into account their diverse contexts in which the ultimate matters are interpreted and including all the semiotic analyses required to identify them at every level and all the related tests that come from independent interpretations, comparisons in cross-cultural perspectives, critical findings in the sciences, imaginative findings in the arts, and the checks of practical normative disciplines. An assemblage of consistent statements is one species of theological system that fits under the general shape; but it assumes that no important intentional interpretations of ultimate matters refer indexically. Nearly always, that is a false assumption. If a theological system would argue (and not merely assume) that there are no significant indexical references, only iconic ones, it would have to deal with the difficulty pointed out above of finite spatiotemporal things connecting with ultimate and infinite ones. Whitehead's process theology is a significant exception to this point. By claiming that God is finite, though in a different way from other merely temporal actual occasions, Whitehead can allow his whole system to aim at literal iconic metaphysical reference with no indexical reference. Yet his theory offers no account of the existence of the world to be described by his metaphysics (a failure to apply his ontological principle to the complex of God, creativity, and creatures).

To construe a theological system as a system of doctrines accurately identifies an approach characteristic of scholastic theologies. Scholastic theologies usually have been under attack in their own time and within their own tradition for losing the richness and vitality of the relative unsystematized religious assertions in their traditional culture. Whitehead's theology, scholastic in the main, abandons metaphysics for poetry when it comes to God in the final part of *Process and Reality*. It is far better, with theology as symbolic engagement, to construe a theological system as "systematic symbolics," to use Ray L. Hart's fine phrase.[4] As systematic symbolics, theology lays out the conditions under which symbols connect interpreters with ultimate matters, coordinates these, and assesses their truth by testing cases across the entire scope of theology that bears on ultimate matters. Systematic theology, in the sense of systematic symbolics, can

---

4. See his very important book, *Unfinished Man and the Imagination*, chap. 6, esp. pp. 305–11. Hardly anything is written in Hart's book that is not affirmed in the present book's conception of theology as symbolic engagement. The chief difference, besides his being first, is that Hart argued out of the language of Continental phenomenology, whereas theology as symbolic engagement is an extension of the American pragmatic tradition.

interpret theological claims in any religious tradition, including those in the form of doctrines and systems of doctrines. But it is not limited to interpreting all theological assertions as only iconic in reference.

As described, systematic theology, for theology as symbolic engagement, is dialectical in two related senses, the second following from the first. The first is that dialectic refers to the somewhat free-floating process of making cases. Making cases does not have any single perspective or ground, but moves from ground to ground as it covers more angles of inquiry. Moreover, in making a case for a theological assertion, the assertion itself might change in meaning, reference, and context from what it seemed to be at earlier stages of its development. Dialectic is the intellectual poise with which theology keeps its balance as it moves from case to case, from one area within its scope to another. The way by which a complex set of cases is summarized and assessed is only one position within the system from which inquiry might then move on. Dialectical language is not stable and it needs always to think the argument through from the inside.

The second sense of dialectic comes from philosophy, namely, that the making of cases needs to move up to examine presuppositions as much as to move down to examine the fruitfulness of interpretations. It might seem as if the making of a case for a theological position is to embed it within a larger theory that coordinates it with corroborating evidence and shows why the alternatives to it are false. Surely that is a large part of the dialectic of case making, as will be argued in the next section. Nevertheless, any larger theory itself has presuppositions, elementary hypotheses, first principles. Dialectical systematic theology needs to examine these as well. Not to do so is to fail to make a case for the larger theory as a whole. So systematic theology, like philosophy, always backs up on itself, aiming to come clean about its presuppositions and make cases for them as valid suppositions. This can never be a complete process. On the other hand, it can deal with the presuppositions that can be identified to have alternatives.

A final point needs to be made here about dialectical systematic theory in theology, anticipating a larger discussion subsequently. A dialectical systematic theology itself can be regarded as a large, complex sign. So long as it has within it the requisite theological assertions that intentionally engage ultimate matters, plus their cases and the theories justifying those cases (for instance, semiotic theory, astrophysics, and so forth), the theology as a whole can be treated as a sign for engaging ultimate matters. In practical religious life, say, in prayer or meditation, the entire system can function as a sign interpreted to stand for the religious object in some respect. Interpreting ultimate matters in particular theological assertions, close to the language of primary witness, presupposes the system that makes its case

implicitly. Interpreting ultimate matters with the case spelled out systematically is the explicit full engagement of the religious object in that respect. In
this sense, systematic theology can be a spiritual practice for those with a
mind for it, just as much as meditating on core texts of scripture or singing
a sacred mantra.

Stability and Commensurability of Discourse

In the last pages of the previous section, the word *theory* crept back into the
discussion, having been neglected since the introduction to this chapter.
The previous section had been anxious to relativize the notion that a theological system consists of an assemblage of consistent descriptive assertions.
Rather, a theological system, most generally construed, is a mix of symbolic
engagements of ultimacy, including primary witnesses, theological assertions of the truth about them, plus the cases that can be made for them,
coordinated as those cases must be. The system, so construed, is dialectical
because the argument moves from case to case, changing the ground as it
goes. Yet there must be some high point or reviewing stand from which it
is possible to get around the system. Otherwise, the system has no stability,
even temporary stability, and its discourses might be deceptively incom-
mensurate. This section will explore this point.

The range of discourses in theology is vast, from the vivid symbols of
primary witnesses to the careful formulation of assertions to the meta-level
cases that are made for them in philosophy, comparative theology, the sciences, humanities, arts, and all the other practical fields of endeavor. What
holds these together? What prevents the metaphoric elements from brush-
ing aside demands for critical consistency? The answer is, a multi-level theory such as is being presented in this book. How is this so? What is theory
in this sense?

Plato gave the best answer in the *Republic*. Robert Brumbaugh, among
others, has pointed out that the rhetorical structure of the *Republic* follows
the figure of the Divided Line in book 6, already discussed.[5] The segments
of the line are images, common sense, theory, and dialectic. In book 1,
Socrates talks with Cephalus and his son Polemarchus about justice, and
they argue by quoting the poets. They give up their argument when
Socrates points out that it leads to absurdity in common sense: although the
poets say that justice is giving a person his due, you wouldn't return a person's knife if he asked for it back so he could murder someone. In book 2,

---

5. *Republic* 509b and following. See Brumbaugh's *Platonic Studies in Greek Philosophy*.

Socrates talks mainly with Thrasymachus, a sophistical lawyer, whose common sense experience has taught him that justice is merely the interest of the stronger party, and that injustice pays. Because he has no formal theory for defining his terms (justice means opposite things in the previous sentence), Thrasymachus is led around in circles by Socrates to contradict himself. In books 3–5, Socrates talks with Glaucon and Adeimantus (Plato's half brothers), who are very good at theory, proposing that Thrasymacus is right in practice because the true theory of human nature is that it is basically aggressive, and they spell out a theory of society based on the aggressive struggle for power in which talk of justice is merely self-serving ideology. After pursuing the implications of this hypothesis for a while, Socrates makes a counterproposal, namely, that human nature is appetitive, and develops a theory of society based on production and consumption of what satisfies appetite, tracing out social expansion to need an army and specialized governors. Glaucon and Adeimantus, though whizzes at contemplating the implications of hypothetico-deductive theories, are not very good at dialectic, and Socrates leads them around to entertain variations on the appetitive theory, namely, that human nature is aggressive and rational as well as appetitive, and various other theories of the organization of society (in book 8, the model for society is based on social classes distinguished as aristocrats, military folk, oligarchs, and plebes—democrats). Plato's point about dialectic is that different theories allow different elements to be lifted up for consideration and each obscures others. The dialectical truth lies not in any one theory but in seeing what virtues each has in some context or other. Of course, there is more to Plato's theory of dialectic than this, but this is the main rhetorical plot of the *Republic*.

The value of a theory in the *Republic* is to provide a conceptual form for organizing phenomena that allows for expansion to new phenomena with some logical predictive force. If Thrasymachus had had a theory behind his remarks about justice, he would not have been led by Socrates, who used a ridiculously specious logical argument, to affirm that justice is the interest of the weaker after having said it is the interest of the stronger. He would not have said that injustice pays, meaning the practical denial of what is recognized as truly just and not the interest of anybody, and then be forced to admit that justice rather than injustice pays. Glaucon and Adeimantus were able to stabilize Thrasymachus's discourse with their theory of society based on the premise that human nature is fundamentally aggressive. Socrates then was able to spell out a beautifully elaborate conception of a society of three functional social classes based on fulfilling three basic character types, deriving from the premise that human nature is fundamentally appetitive, and derivatively aggressive and rational.[6] For Plato, theories are abstract conceptual structures that can be understood clearly in themselves, like mathematics, and that can be used to understand phenomena and their connections. We today might call theories hypothetical-deductive systems, or models. When we build a conceptual model, we know what we put into its parts and how they connect. If that model can be related to phenomena, the model's connections sort the connections in the phenomena.

In theology, theories are called in to stabilize discussions. Arguments about the authority of certain scriptures, for instance, are stabilized if the discussants can agree on a theory of authority. Arguments about how theological assertions refer to their objects can be stabilized if a semiotic theory of reference can be developed and agreed upon as being adequate to the debate. Arguments about what to say theologically about other religions and how to understand what they say about one's own can be stabilized by a theory of comparison and a discourse of actual comparison based on the theory. Arguments about the bearing of the sciences, arts, and normative practical discourses on theology are stabilized by theories that connect them with ultimate matters. The argument of this book has appealed to many theories of this sort.

With regard to the problem of stabilizing and coordinating all the discourses in dialectical systematic theology, a more comprehensive theory is required that encompasses the entire scope of theology. The traditional name in Western philosophy for this theory is "metaphysics," and the next section shall detail a "theory of metaphysics" that serves the purpose and is defensible in today's intellectual context. Here it is important to note something of the scope of metaphysics as the theory stabilizing and coordinating systematic theology.

Alfred North Whitehead defined metaphysics as a system of categories and principles according to which all the elements of civilized experience can be registered as instances.[7] Although he should have recognized "uncivilized experience" too, he had in mind that the great institutions of civilization epitomized the content of experience. Those institutions, for him, included philosophy, science, religion, morality, and the arts and letters.[8] Implicit in his definition is that all other theories of things, in science,

---

6. Actually, Socrates slips in the premises that human nature involves three basic faculties—appetite, aggression, and reason—that equally fundamental and universal in individuals, but differently balanced. Glaucon and Adeimantus are unaware that he has changed the basic hypothesis from which they started.

7. See the extraordinary first chapter of *Process and Reality*, the best image of metaphysics in the twentieth century.

8. For the best analysis of Whitehead's theory of civilization and its epitomes in science, religion, and the rest, see David L. Hall's *The Civilization of Experience*.

philosophy, and the rest, be fitted under the categories and principles of metaphysics as less general instances. The next section will spell this out in more detail. For Whitehead, the metaphysical categories and principles need to be (1) consistent with one another in the sense of not being contradictory; (2) coherent in the sense of being indefinable without one another; (3) applicable to the things that fall under the metaphysical system; and (4) adequate to anything that might be real in experience.[9] Such a metaphysics would be able to embrace and sort all the elements in theological discourse. Metaphysics attempts to have its reference as iconic as possible, not indexical, though it embraces and sorts indexical references. Yet until its presuppositions are fully justified, it might have indexical elements that are also not fully iconic.

The most important trait for a metaphysics that can stabilize and make commensurate theological discourse is its treatment of ultimate matters and their relation to human endeavor, including theology. Metaphysics cannot be only an elaborate epistemology or phenomenology of theology: it must deal with the ultimate references of theology too. Thus, metaphysics must model ultimate realities and ultimate concerns as well as the rest of experience. Metaphysical systems have long played roles modeling ultimacy in theology in all the great literate traditions. Daoism, for instance, models the Dao in terms of the duality of the Dao that cannot be named and the Dao that can. Confucianism has the model of Heaven and Earth, made sharp in Neo-Confucianism as Principle and Material Force, respectively. Buddhisms of all sorts have models of causation or *pratityasamutpada* that show how no ontological ultimates are possible (in competitive senses of impossibility) and that articulate the significance of this for the ultimate concern with suffering. Hinduism has many models of gods as creators and saviors, some developed with very great metaphysical abstraction, such as the Advaita and Vishistadvaita models of Samkara and Ramanuja, respectively. Christianity and Islam, and to a lesser extent Judaism, have organized theological systems around Neoplatonic, creation ex nihilo, and Aristotelian Fullness-of-Act models. Many Jewish and Christian theologians today employ Whitehead's model.

Theological argumentation that is not backed by a metaphysics easily descends into chaos. Christian theologians, for instance, sometimes speak as if God were a being alongside the world and in the next breath speak of God as the ground of being. Or if they do not come to such direct contradiction, they say things that presuppose that God is a being, and then say things that presuppose that God cannot be a being but is the ground of

---

9. See *Process and Reality*, chap. 1.

being itself. Another instability in theology is that, without an adequate metaphysics, options that should be considered are neglected; cases that should be made ignored.

For theology as symbolic engagement, metaphysics is necessary in a special way.

Most core texts and motifs of religious traditions arose against a background of ancient cultures that are different from the background of contemporary cultures. The imaginative worlds are different. Hermeneutics in the classical European sense can spell out how these worlds differ. Normative theology, however, asks whether the ancient symbols can be used in contemporary interpretations of ultimate matters. Therefore, something, metaphysics, needs to be able to represent how both ancient and modern cultures can be connected normatively to what is real. Metaphysics needs to be able to say how the ancient cultures were right, not just meaningful but right, in their contexts, and how something from those cultures, properly modified, might be right in contemporary cultures. Only metaphysics can formulate the generality of comparison needed for making this connection.

For some theologians, such as Barth, narrative is proposed as the most encompassing way to provide the stabilizing connections in a theological system. Narrative in this sense is not a simple story but a very complex one that includes metaphysical discussions within it. Narratives have a compelling force for most people, far more compelling than the kind of metaphysics advocated for theology as symbolic engagement. Theology as symbolic engagement can allow for and accept any narrative as far as it goes. What metaphysics asks of narrative in a critical vein is what the story leaves out. Just as Barth's story of Christian redemption left out the Buddhists and nearly all other religions save Judaism, any story gains its coherence by a storyline that eliminates other stories. Yet every person in a given narrative also plays roles in other narratives. Every event plays roles in many narratives. As the Annales school of historiography has shown, narrative falsifies by suppressing or marginalizing elements that do not fit the story. Metaphysics systematically asks about what a narrative leaves out in order to achieve its narrative coherence.

Narrative is particularly important in West Asian religions for articulating identity for communities and individuals. They take themselves to be defined in large part by the roles they play in the narratives. Insofar as theologians are concerned with identity, they are likely to be allergic to a larger metaphysical enframing of their identity narrative. With regard to the question of truth, however, that is, whether such and such is a worthy identity in light of the ultimate, narratives have strict limits of usefulness. The

Exodus story, for instance, so important for defining the covenant identity of Israel, is strongly biased against the Egyptians and Canaanites who had their own identities in relation to ultimate matters. The religious identity of Israel was in direct competition with the religious identities of the others, and has continued to be so down to the present day with the descendents of those in the original narrative. For many centuries, Christians delegitimated Jewish claims to be identified in the Exodus story by making that story apply to Christian messianic theology; in that version of the Christian story, say, as told by Luther, the Jews fell out of the covenant that became the reinterpreted possession of Christians. The Christian story legitimated persecution of the Jews, just as the Exodus story legitimated Israelite war against the Canaanites. The moral principles of both Judaism and Christianity are at cross-purposes to the elements in their stories that legitimate persecution and wars of conquest. Although sometimes the moral principles are limited in application to those within the respective story-given identities, they have also pressed a more generalizing agenda. The ancient rabbis said that God wept for the drowned Egyptians. Christians now like to say that God sees everyone's and every group's stories. But how can God be conceived to reconcile all those stories when so often they entail mutual destruction of identity? Hegel hoped that a meta-story could sublate the differences; yet even the meta-story left out whole peoples as well as individuals whose stories could not be shown to play roles in the meta-story. The limitation lies in the very form of narrative. Metaphysics puts narratives in a context that relativizes the legitimacy of their identity-forming functions. This is to say, religious identity includes metaphysical as well as narrative elements.

At this point, it is important to recall that the four loci of theology begin with primary witnesses, which in the West Asian religions are often significantly, though not wholly, in the form of narratives (the laws defining covenant life and the Wisdom literature of the Hebrew Bible, for instance, are not stories). As these narratives are turned into theological claims, doctrines, and systems in the other loci, they are contextualized in the ways described here as metaphysical. The narratives lose some of the immediacy of their power for defining identity. But they gain vastly in the sophistication of their roles in the formation of identity when they are read through the other theological loci. As mentioned in the preface, religious identity is careless with the truth if it aims to be the beginning of theology rather an evolving conclusion.

Metaphysics construed Whitehead's way has a tendency to be regarded as only a theory, working from the first principles and categories down to handle the phenomena. The dialectical side of metaphysics, however, requires working back up to question the first principles and categories.[10] Why should we presuppose these? How can there be the plurality of the categories and principles? Why these and not others? What is the unity of them? All the great metaphysical traditions have strategies for answering these dialectical questions, which have to do with the problem of the one and the many. The problem of the one and the many is the locus for the examination of ultimate presuppositions in metaphysics.[11]

Metaphysical systems, stated in terms of the first principles and categories, are extremely abstract. Yet they can serve as signs connecting the metaphysician to ultimate realities and thus be means of spiritual life. Metaphysical systems, taken as inclusive of what is conceived to fall within and be ordered by them, are extremely concrete. In this concrete sense, they also can be taken as signs for engaging ultimate realities.

Metaphysics

The advocacy of metaphysics for the theoretical backbone in dialectical systematic theology requires two special cases to be made in this day when metaphysics is in disfavor with so many thinkers.

The first case is in response to the supposed Kantian refutation of the possibility of metaphysics. Kant had identified metaphysics as the attempt to determine things in themselves by a priori synthetic reasoning. That the reasoning is supposed to be a priori means that it is known to be true without consulting anything given in experience; that it is supposed to be synthetic means that it claims something that is not true merely by definition. Kant thought to refute metaphysics in this sense by his argument that the only a priori synthetic knowledge we have is of the conditions for the possibility of experience, not of things in themselves. Metaphysics, he claimed, therefore at best could offer regulative ideals for ordering experience, not knowledge of things in themselves.[12]

---

10. This is the burden of argument in my *Creativity and God*, which claims that Whitehead should have pushed his ontological principle to demand an explanation for why there is a system of first principles. That principle states that any complex thing needs to be explained by reference to a decision or set of decisions that determine its elements to be their way rather than some other or none. He does not ask how or why there should be the complex set of first principles.

11. Besides being the heritage of Western philosophy, from Parmenides, Heraclitus, Plato, Aristotle, and Plotinus down to Hegel in the modern era, it was the common lesson of my extremely varied teachers at Yale in graduate school, including Paul Weiss, Wilfrid Sellars, F. S. C. Northop, Brand Blanshard, Richard J. Bernstein, Robert S. Brumbaugh, and John E. Smith. It is, of course, the problematic in Indian philosophy that sets the Vedantic schools over against the other orthodox schools. The problem of the one and the many controls Chinese philosophy from the opening lines of the Daodejing through the reconstruction of Neo-Confucianism in Zhou Dunyi.

12. All this is the argument of *Critique of Pure Reason*.

There are hosts of difficulties with Kant's argument. His whole transcendental argument justifying his system of conditions for the possibility
of experience rests on the premise that we have a priori synthetic knowledge in science and mathematics. His example of the former, that every
alteration has a cause, has been rendered debatable if not moot by the scientific adoption of statistical probabilities for understanding natural law.[13]
His example of the latter, Euclidean geometry, has been complicated by the
invention of non-Euclidean geometries, complicated twice over by finding
non-Euclidean geometries to be applicable more generally than the
Euclidean. His arithmetical example, that $5 + 7 = 12$, has been contested as
a synthetic judgment, though the debate here is not conclusive. Overall, the
sharp distinction Kant draws between things in themselves and things as
experienced rests on a Cartesian representationalist theory of knowledge
that has been roundly criticized; naturalisms of all sorts have provided
models for real things that can be engaged by knowers in ways that do not
allow the in-itself versus for-a-knower distinction to be sharp. And then
Hegel, followed by many others, pointed out that the kind of reasoning
Kant used in the *Critiques* is not allowed by the *Critiques* and itself constitutes a kind of metaphysics—saying what is really real about knowledge
and its relation to reality.

It might be said that Kant's arguments against metaphysics as leading to
antinomies is somewhat independent of his transcendental argument.[14]
Antinomies consist of a thesis and its antithesis that can both be proved
valid with no way to choose between them. Kant said there are four such
that define metaphysics, and he derived them from the titles for his lists of
categories: quantity, quality, relation, and modality. (The antinomies argument is thus highly dependent on the transcendental deduction for its
architectonic.) His first antinomy was that it can be proved both that "the
world has a beginning in time, and is also limited as regards space" and "the
world has no beginning, and no limits in space; it is infinite as regards both
time and space." His proofs, however, assume very specific conditions for
defining the terms; for instance, he says that a beginning in time presupposes a previous time before the world began, which is simply not true for
big bang theory (and many other theories of creation) that say that time
itself comes into being with motion. Kant's second antinomy is that it can be
proved that there are simples and it can be proved that there cannot be simples. This is a false opposition, however; Whitehead, for instance, argued

---

13. See Ian Barbour's discussion of the abandonment of Kantian determinism in his *Religion and
Science*, chap. 7.

14. See his *Critique of Pure Reason*, B433–595.

that actual occasions are in some respects simple, because they come to be as a unitary whole with space-time extension, and in other respects complex, because they contain and integrate other prehended things. The third antinomy argues on the one hand that there is freedom in addition to deterministic causation and on the other hand that there is no freedom. Kant's arguments here define freedom as an absolute beginning of a natural process, and many conceptions of freedom are possible that do not have to assume that. Whitehead's, for example, is based on novelty in actual occasions that is not absolute but an addition to antecedent conditions. The fourth antinomy is that, on the one hand, there is a necessary being and, on the other hand, there cannot be. Kant's argument is that God must be either inside the world of appearances or outside, and in either case must be temporally related to appearances. But there are conceptions of God that reject the characterization that God is a necessary being. Moreover, God can be conceived to create time and space as part of the world, and therefore is neither in the world nor in some other place outside the world. All these antinomies assume the setup of the problem that derives from Kant's transcendental deduction. Metaphysical theories that do not fall prey to Kant's antinomies simply have different hypotheses defining the issues. Whereas he might find antinomies in a particular metaphysics, that does not refute other metaphysical theories that define the issues differently.

A more general and decisive argument against Kant's strictures against metaphysics is related to the last point, namely, that metaphysics should be regarded as the construction of an hypothesis about reality with the kind of generality that Whitehead or Peirce prescribed. Of course, not all metaphysicians thought of their systems as hypotheses. Descartes, Leibniz, and Spinoza did not, although Plato and Aristotle did, and probably also Nagarjuna and Vasubandu (although the technical language of hypothesis would have been alien to them). Nevertheless, all the great metaphysical systems can be treated as hypotheses and engaged to be improved upon. Kant had said that metaphysics cannot be hypothetical because some certain, foundational cognition is required to determine the conditions under which hypotheses can be true.[15] But to the contrary, all that is needed is a higher-level hypothesis that explains how hypotheses might be true, an hypothesis that itself is vulnerable to correction in turn. Kant's criticism of metaphysics simply does not apply to metaphysics as hypothetical, which is what it has been in the pragmatic tradition for a century and a half and in the process philosophy tradition for almost a century.[16]

---

15. See his *Critique of Pure Reason*, B797ff.
16. For an expansion of this point and a more detailed defense of metaphysics, see my *The Highroad around Modernism*, chaps. 1 and 6, esp. pp. 27–29, 138–39.

A second case needs to be made against the criticism coming from post-modernists that metaphysics is necessarily a logocentric distortion of that to which it is supposed to apply.[17] Any metaphysics has a logical structure with categories that register some things as important and others as not so important, and that might miss registering some things altogether. The result is the marginalization of the things that do not count within the system, which can have great social as well as intellectual consequences. An example would be Hegel's claim that those peoples and cultures that do not contribute to the dialectic of history do not count; although they were or are actual, it is as if they did not exist at all, for all the difference they make to the development of the dialectic.[18] This postmodern argument is a powerful criticism, much more serious than Kant's.

To answer it requires detailing more of the nature of metaphysics as hypothetical. The general answer is that, if a metaphysical system marginalizes something important, then that is a flaw in the system, which should be amended. Precisely because such distortions are flaws, the hypothetical character of the system requires it to be amended. Yet metaphysics should not always be in such a defensive posture if it is to be useful in theology or elsewhere. It should have safeguards built into its procedures.

Charles Peirce, in his essay "A Neglected Argument for the Reality of God," outlined the logic of hypothesis making, involving three steps that he called "abduction," "deduction," and "induction."[19] Abduction is the musing over a problem to be understood or explained and the "guessing" at an hypothesis that would explain it. This is what Peirce called an "argument," because it reaches a conclusion, but not an "argumentation," which would reach a conclusion according to a rule. Aristotle called this the "wit of hitting upon the third term" that makes the connection sought.

After the abductive guess, deduction makes two moves on the hypothesis. In Peirce's paper, the problem to be solved is how the universe can have such different things in it and still be unified, and the abductive guess, which Peirce claims is made in all cultures, is that God the creator makes it that way. First, deduction reconstructs the hypothesis in clear terms, in well-formed formulas, as logicians say, in term of which logical connections can be drawn; this too is abductive, a work of imagination. (Peirce claims that at this point, different theologians make the vague notion of God specific in radically different ways, and in fact nearly always so limit the idea that it becomes contradictory to other important considerations. For him,

---

17. See David Weissman's potent response in *Truth's Debt to Value*. These issues are discussed with the appropriate texts in my *Normative Cultures*, chaps. 1, 2, and 4.
18. See his statement in *Logic of Hegel*, pp. 10ff., and in *The Philosophy of History*, 10ff.
19. In CP 6.452–93.

the vague guess of divine creation is vaguely right, although the specific renderings of this in terms of theological systems all have something wrong with them.) The next part of deduction is demonstration, in which logical implications and consequences for experience are drawn from the logically specified hypothesis. These consequences provide the categories for empirical experimentation. This is argumentation and proceeds according to logical rules.

The third stage in the development of an hypothesis, induction, tests whether the experiential phenomena support the hypothesis or not. But before that judgment is made, which Peirce called "probation," the categories for classifying the phenomena that derive demonstratively from the hypothesis need to be tested. This is the crucial point for answering the postmodernists' objections to metaphysics. They point out, rightly, that if the theory or hypothesis dictates the terms in which phenomena are recognized, then those phenomena not recognized by the hypothesis are marginalized or neglected, or are assigned improper importance. Peirce's corrective is to examine the theoretical constructs for classifying phenomena to see whether they do distort or neglect the phenomena before using them to sum up whether the phenomena support the theoretical hypothesis.

The importance of testing the theoretical categories against the phenomena before the phenomena are classified as supporting or rejecting the theoretical hypothesis cannot be overestimated. The previous chapter pointed out five "sites of phenomenological analysis" that methodically systematize the probation of comparative categories as specified by the things they compare. Those same sites generalize as a method for criticizing theoretical categories derived from an explanatory hypothesis. The *intrinsic* site is to allow the phenomena to be represented on their own terms. The *perspectival* site is to make sure that the phenomenon's own perspective on the rest of the world is registered in the theoretical description. This urges that connections with other phenomena be registered that the theoretical construct might have missed. The *theoretical* site is to bring in other theories than the hypothesis in question to understand the phenomena and square the hypothetical description with that. The *practical* site is to check out the practical implications of the phenomena in the larger environment and see whether the theoretical descriptive category registers that. And then the *singular* site is to identify those elements of the phenomena that cannot be registered in any other theoretical terms, and control for the effects of this within the explanatory hypothesis. If all of these sites are methodically explored, the development of a metaphysical hypothesis makes itself vulnerable for just about any kind of correction, and thus stands a good chance of getting around the postmodernists' logocentrism objection. Any concrete objection to a metaphysical hypothesis on the ground that it misses or distorts something triggers a criticism and revision of the hypothesis.

Merely being open to correction, however, does not guarantee fairness, neutrality, and adequacy to all the phenomena. Bias is often dumb: no one notices. Unless there is reason to think something is missed or distorted, the fault does not register. Peirce put the point this way, in reaction to Descartes. He called Descartes' celebrated "methodical doubt" mere "paper doubt."[20] You can in principle doubt everything on paper. But you cannot actually doubt everything. There are some things we simply do not know how to doubt, often because we are unaware of believing them. This is often the case with theoretical presuppositions, which is why dialectic is required to hunt these out. Also, it is often the fate of phenomena that have no voice in a given culture, that are not registered well in the culture's semiotic system. In the latter instance, part of the function of methodical inquiry is to construct standpoints from which new criticisms can be made. Much of the constructive part of theorizing is not merely trying to save what we already know by hitting upon a unifying third term, but also attempting to stand outside the culture and its hypotheses as constructed to find new angles of vision.

Metaphysics as hypothesis attempts always to stand outside itself in order to get an external critical angle. This is a necessary part of metaphysical vulnerability, and of making a case for a metaphysical system. Of course, this is a circular move, because as soon as the metaphysical system gets an external vantage on itself, it incorporates that vantage point within itself, perhaps with serious modifications to its previous categories and principles. With a metaphysical system that functions in systematic theology in ways that require comparisons with other religions and other metaphysical systems and draw lessons from the sciences, arts, and normative practical disciplines, an extraordinary degree of external cross-checking is already built in. Nevertheless, a metaphysical system is never finished. It is always a fallible hypothesis that should seek its own correction and be vulnerable to unexpected criticisms.

To function within a dialectical theological system, a metaphysical theory, the grand hypothesis, does not have to be finished. Nor does it have to be overly tentative. If the hypothesis can make cases for itself with reference to all of the elements it integrates and in relation to all the standard issues in metaphysics raised by alternative metaphysical hypotheses and critics, it has a functional steadiness. Although it might be required to change in the future, it is stable in the sense of having been corrected through all the

---

20. CP 6.498.

checkpoints that are available, at least within the limits of metaphysical and theological energy. Like theology in general, metaphysics always arises from particular starting points, bearing a history no matter how carefully expanded to be fair and inclusive. Having steadied itself through that process, metaphysics can function to provide the theoretical connections required in systematic theology as defined here, systematic symbolics.

At the end of the previous section, it was remarked that the dialectical center point for metaphysics examining its own presuppositions is the problem of the one and the many. The remark needs expansion. The foregoing paragraphs have noted how a metaphysical system, as a comprehensive hypothesis, needs to develop as many external checks as possible in the form of the sites of phenomenological analysis, to correct its categories in their applicability and adequacy to the world of things embraced within the hypothesis. That is one sense of dialectic. The other sense of dialectic described earlier is the relentless search to identify, expose, and critically make cases for the suppositions of the metaphysical hypothesis itself. It might be enough in a scientific hypothesis merely to "posit" the hypothesis and see experimentally how much and how well it explains. In philosophy, however, there is an equal and necessary drive to work up as well as down, to justify the ultimate presuppositions as much as possible. Such a justification itself would be another or an enlarged hypothesis, to be sure, but one whose motive is to explain phenomena and to explore and justify the ultimate presuppositions.

If the ultimate presuppositions in metaphysics were only those concerning the nature of hypotheses and explanation, the topic area for this kind of dialectic might be epistemology. Much of modern Western philosophy has taken this to be the case. But the problem is deeper. What is philosophical intelligibility? How is the world ultimately intelligible? When pressed, this comes down to how diversity in the world can be acknowledged so that determinate things can be related to one another. On the one hand, they have to be in some kind of unity in order to be related. On the other hand, they have to be distinct enough from one another so as not to collapse into each other. This is the metaphysical problem of the one and the many. At the beginning of Western philosophy, Heraclitus observed the manyness of things and showed that sheer diversity means that things do not have enough stable identity even to be different from one another. Parmenides, on the other hand, said that the obvious unity of things means that there cannot be real diversity and change. Subsequent philosophy in the West refused to accept these two failures to hold unity and diversity together, and the great metaphysical systems took their defining shapes from the ways they addressed the problem of the one and the many. The great metaphysical systems in Daoist and Confucian thinking, in Buddhism and Hinduisms of all sorts, as well as in Islamic thinking also can be viewed as fundamentally shaped around approaches to the problem of the one and the many. Without some solution to that problem, a metaphysical system has nothing to say about what intelligibility really is.

The problem of the one and the many can be construed extremely abstractly. The civilized traditions, however, have given the many some content as well. The multiplicity in the world exhibits unity in each of the various things, and also goodness, beauty, and truth have senses of being intelligible in their ways. The European medieval thinkers called unity, goodness, beauty, and truth "transcendentals," traits exhibited in everything. For them, a solution to the problem of the one and the many would have to be able to discuss the unity and multiplicity in individual integrity as well as moral and aesthetic value, and intelligibility. The suppositions about ultimate intelligibility in metaphysics needs to be able to give an account of all these, however they are represented.

A grave danger in the pragmatic approach to metaphysics as hypothesis is its association with modern European science. The rhetoric of "hypothesis" comes from science, and the pragmatists Peirce and Dewey were explicit about that. The hypotheses of modern science began with the paradigms of mathematical explanation in mathematical physics, and extended those paradigms through chemistry, biology, and now many new sciences. This has been an extraordinary achievement of human civilization. But it has also had a dark side. Mathematical hypotheses do not register value, only form prescinded or abstracted from value.

To be sure, mathematics itself has great beauty, as does mathematical science. An elegant experiment is a work of art. Mathematicians and scientists themselves appreciate this value. As people immersed in life, mathematicians and scientists, like everyone else, appreciate the diversities of values and strive to correct their understanding of what makes life valuable. Human experience is immersed in a value-laden imaginative perception of the world and human purposes, as much for mathematicians and scientists as for others. Yet mathematical science as such does not register the values in what it knows. It registers only the mathematical relations among its elements. If the value of something is independently identified, mathematical science can indicate how it is related to other things and how its own valuable structure is composed. But it does not register the value itself, only the form of what some other knowledge identifies as value.

The problem is that mathematical science has been taken to be paradigmatic of knowing as such. The science is a great achievement for what it does as science. It is a great danger when its form of knowledge is generalized to be the form of all knowledge. To a very great degree, this is what has happened in European modernity. Other forms of knowing were relegated to subjective status or to the status of being incompletely transformed to scientific thinking. The values of things, though recognized in common experience, were not registered in what counts as objective knowledge. They tended to be spoken of only in terms of subjective valuation on the part of interpreters, which is then construed as projection. The fault lay not in the science per se. It lay rather in the cultural consequences of science taken to be the paradigm of knowing. Kant's *Critique of Pure Reason* made that paradigm official.

Here is history's greatest monument to the evil of logocentrism—all value components were systematically excluded from consideration as objective scientific realities, not by scientists per se, to be sure, but by the social forces making scientific knowing paradigmatic. Moral and aesthetic values were re-construed as human projections onto a world of entities whose only characters are those articulated by mathematical relations. Although Plato had hoped that a definition of the Good could be given in mathematical terms of harmony and proportion, this never played out in actual mathematics. Scientists sometimes recognize an aesthetic beauty to what they know through the complexities of mathematics, but this personal appreciation has not been effective to cause the social and cultural processes to give objectivity to the moral and political values in human affairs, or even to assigning objective value to nature in ecological systems. The Romantics have protested against this cultural effect of science for two centuries, and they have been right. Modern science as a cultural phenomenon, insofar as its mathematical paradigm of intelligibility distinguishes objective fact from value, which must then be only subjective, has been a perniciously failed project in its cultural consequences. The alienation of human life with its necessary values from nature, the technologizing of engagement, and the cultural reduction of the self to willfulness, all have resulted from the cultural dominance of the scientific paradigm that separates fact from value and dismisses or subjectivizes the latter.[21] Of course, few people want to give up on the advances of modern science in its technologies and sheer knowledge. Nevertheless, the cost in alienation has been immeasurable.

The lesson is that the mathematization of modern science was not only the articulation of its own discipline but also was a cultural project. That

---

21. This is a common theme in Continental philosophy. For an excellent review of the literature and arguments, see David Strong's *Crazy Mountains: Learning from Wilderness to Weigh Technology*. See also David Rothenberg's *Hand's End*. See as well my essay on the richness of nature in *The Highroad around Modernism*, chap. 12, which begins by citing a passage from Leonardo da Vinci making the point in 1494.

cultural project functioned as an implicit metaphysics for the culture of the European Enlightenment and it did not examine its presuppositions dialectically. If it had, it would have seen that its supposed solutions to the problem of the one and the many so separated what it admitted as real from value that it would have had to reconsider its project. Although such philosophical considerations are not part of the practice of science itself, they are intrinsic to science as a cultural project. Perhaps the centuries of alienating modern science were necessary for science to learn from experience. Perhaps now science can be reinterpreted within a more comprehensive metaphysics. A new metaphysics that would integrate science and the elements of value it has dismissed or obscured would require a major paradigm shift in the sciences themselves. And it would anticipate a major alteration of the culture of late modernity. The postmodern critique of logocentrism is the latest in the Romantic reactions to the systematic failure of scientific hypotheses properly to register value, but it does not supply a metaphysics that would allow the truth of science to be integrated with the truth about value.

Because the problem of the one and the many deals with ultimate suppositions, it has always been at the heart of theology in its systematic modes. It might be argued that the problem of the one and the many is really a set of local problems, specific manys that need a unity, and specific kinds of intelligibility defined by each of the local solutions. By making the problem of the one and the many a piecemeal affair, it might be thought that its ways of defining intelligibility do not say much about truly ultimate presuppositions about intelligibility. Yet this is insufficient, because the issues in local problems hang on the problems of unity and diversity at the most abstract level. Of course, there are local problems of how to achieve unity and enhance diversity, but those are not the problem of the one and the many. The problem of the one and the many is how to conceive unity and diversity per se, whatever their local expressions. The elements involved in any solution to the problem of the one and the many are ultimate matters. To go from primary religious witnesses to the dialectical metaphysics of ultimate presuppositions is a long, tortuous, and difficult road. But people in all the great theological traditions have traveled it, just as it has been refused by people in those traditions. It can be traveled in contemporary systematic theology by means of theology as symbolic engagement.

Levels of Abstraction

Since the beginning of this book, the argument has tracked two related sets of four categories. The first is the four modes of symbolic engagement:

imagination, assertion, dialectical systematic theorizing, and practical reason. The second is the four loci of theology: primary witness, doctrine, theological systems, and practical religious exercises for individual and communal behavior. Although all the modes of symbolic engagement are involved in each theological locus, they predominate in the order of those respective lists. Imagination predominates in primary witness, assertion in doctrine, theorizing in theological systems, and practical reason in religious practice. I will discuss practical reason and religious practice in detail in the next two chapters.

All the symbolic engagements are made by interpretation. Imagination, even at its most primitive levels, functions to provide signs by which the world is taken in. Assertion makes intentional interpretations with truth claims about the religious object engaged in the interpretation and supposes cases to support the truth claims. Dialectical systematic theorizing contains interpretations of many sorts within it, but the result is a theory that itself comprehensively serves as a sign for engaging the religious object. Practical reason guides life to interpret the religious object. At each mode of symbolic engagement, there can be intentional interpretive engagements of ultimate matters, as we have seen in this and earlier chapters.

This last point is important to stress, because many people believe that, among the loci of theology, the concrete engagement is at the level of activity shaped mainly by the primary witnesses expressed in core texts and motifs, and in religious practice. They believe that as one moves more abstractly to carefully formulated doctrine, and then even more abstractly into theological systems whose unifying thread is metaphysics, one moves away from concrete engagements with ultimate matters. The semiotic theory in theology as symbolic engagement demonstrates that this need not be so. One can engage concrete realities with abstractions as well as with raw deliverances of imagination. The symbols close to primary witness and raw imagination are perhaps more vivid and resonating than both the abstractions in doctrine that leave out so much and the abstractions in dialectical systematic theory that put in so much as to blunt sharp emotional focus. The primary witnesses expressed in core texts and motifs might be available to many more people than doctrines and systems; most people would not attempt to engage ultimate matters with doctrines or systems, but with the prayers and liturgies expressive of the core motifs. Nevertheless, no level of abstraction is any less engaging in principle than any other for people prepared to interpret ultimate realities at that level. That many theologians choose not to develop metaphysical abstractions that are signs for engaging ultimate matters does not detract from the value of doing so.

   In point of fact, the great theological traditions, if not the popular religions associated with them, all have representations of ultimate ontological realities that lie along a spectrum from very concrete, usually anthropomorphic images, to highly abstract, transcendent conceptions that often are self-breaking or apophatic. The case of Christianity has already been discussed in some detail. The language of much of the Bible is anthropomorphic, and this has been laid down upon, and in the New Testament developed in terms of, the general conception in the Hellenistic world of the High God. The theological tradition has elaborated major metaphysical conceptions, such as in Neoplatonism, creation ex nihilo theory, and Thomism, that render the High God that was affirmed with such clarity in the patristic discussions. Yet these same metaphysical conceptions have been connected to the more anthropomorphic biblical language too. Islam has the vivid concrete imagery of the Qur'an that has been conjoined with conceptions of Allah that transcend even the Ninety-nine Names. Popular Hindu sects worship gods on every street corner while the theologians in the orthodox and heterodox schools think in highly abstract terms, the best known of which is the theology of Advaita Vedanta.[22] Buddhism in some of its forms denies any ontological realities and yet personifies them in devotion to Avaloketishvara (Guanyin) and other bodhisattvas and coming Buddhas. Buddhist notions of emptiness and nirvana, while perhaps not intended to interpret ontological realities, are extraordinarily abstract in the Madhyamika and Yogacara theological systems. Chinese religions need to be considered together, for reasons peculiar to that situation.[23] Both Daoism and Confucianism, in their philosophical representations, employ a very abstract language such as Dao, Heaven and Earth, Principle, and Material Force. Yet in their practice, they employ shamanistic or Buddhistic (deriving from Hindu) imagery of a world filled with spirits and deities. Medieval Daoism developed a full panoply of representations of ultimate realities across the spectrum from anthropomorphic to transcendently abstract.[24]
   Religions differ with regard to where the center of gravity falls for the rhetoric of their core texts and motifs that symbolically shape daily light

---

22. See, first, Diana Eck's *Encountering God* for a phenomenology of the point in India, and then her *A New Religious America*, which makes a surprisingly similar point for the United States.

23. In the Comparative Religious Ideas Project, Livia Kohn insisted that we consider not Confucianism, Daoism, Buddhism, and shamanism, but "Chinese religion," which unites all these. She is right, even though the textual traditions are somewhat distinct.

24. See Livia Kohn's anthology of relevant texts, *The Taoist Experience*. See also her textual analysis, *Taoist Mystical Philosophy: The Scripture of Western Ascension*. Then see her interpretive book, *Early Chinese Mysticism*, and also her edited practical reason volume, *Taoist Meditation and Longevity Techniques*. For a fascinating history of Daoism that integrates the philosophical and the devotional elements, see James Miller's *Daoism*.

and thought. The West Asian religions set their rhetoric at the anthropomorphic end of the spectrum, despite having transcendently abstract representations early on. The East Asian religions set their rhetoric at the abstract
end, despite having anthropomorphic notions in their practice and history.
Shangdi, the pre-Confucian High God of China, was originally a storm god,
like Yahweh. Traces of anthropomorphism remain in Confucianism's focus
on the mandate (or will) of Heaven.

An hypothesis for understanding this common spectrum of images or
conceptions of ultimate realities is the following.[25] On the one hand, the
shaping of the ultimate religious quest comes from the very particular personal and communal engagements with ultimate matters, particularly in
sickness, death, feeding the community, rites of passage, natural and historical disasters. Songs of joy and prayers for deliverance tend to reflect the intimate character of personal life, and the symbols for the ultimate realities to
which (or to whom) they are directed tend to be personal too. The demons
of evil and deities of enlightenment are not exactly human, but human
enough to be engaged as persons. Even in religious traditions with very clear
transcendently abstract representations of ultimate realities, devotional life
usually personifies the object of devotion, as in the cult of Guanyin.[26]

On the other hand, theologians know the difference between ultimate
matters and the proximate ones and naturally work to de-relativize the
commitments in anthropomorphic language, leading to transcendently
abstract conceptions. Two motives push this work. One is the critique of
idolatry, strongest in Islam but strongly present in the other religions. Any
religious object identified within a context or environment is not as ultimate as the context or environment plus the religious object. In those theological situations in which major religions formed themselves in encounters
with other religions, the comparative theology involved in articulating differences implicitly developed comparative categories that were more
abstract than, and inclusive of, the representations previously thought ultimate but now recognized as penultimate.

The other motive pushing toward theological abstraction in representations of ultimacy is the recognition that the intelligibility of conceptions of
ultimate things needs to present a treatment of the problem of the one and
the many. Theologies of a celebratory sort, or those concerned mainly with
identity, might not be concerned with truth about intelligibility. But insofar as they are, an approach to dialectic is a step forward. In order to be
properly dialectical, looking up at presuppositions rather than only down to

---

25. See the elaboration of this hypothesis in *Ultimate Realities*, chap. 7, by Wesley Wildman and me.
26. On personification in prayer, where one knows the object is not much like a person, see James
Carse's *The Silence of God*.

implications, theology turns metaphysical. Metaphysics is self-referentially responsible regarding presuppositions only when it presents itself in the language of the one and the many. As argued earlier, the great metaphysical systems functioning in theology take their shape from how they address the one and the many.

A tension exists in theology, then, between ontological ultimacy, which leads theology toward abstractions and the one and the many, and the anthropological ultimacy of the religious quest and life. From any place on the spectrum, there will be pressures to move as well to the other places, for anthropological or ontological reasons. Understanding how religions have lived with theological systems requires tracing out this point in the various instances.

Theology as symbolic engagement is thus ready to look at the spectrum of treatments of ultimacy in the following way. Theology presses toward the abstract end of the spectrum as it attempts to be literal or mainly iconic in its references to ultimate matters. The need to be as iconic or literal as possible comes from the fact that systematic theology needs to make cases for theological assertions and also to assess and connect the cases, developing language that moves as neutrally and meaningfully as possible across many fields of discourse, including all levels of religious language, comparative religions, the sciences, arts, and practical normative disciplines.

Theology, on the other hand, treats the anthropomorphic symbols of ultimate matters as referring indexically, in large part. The anthropomorphic imagery is to be understood in theology, regarding its truth, in terms of how it carries over what is important in the religious object into the interpreter in the respect in which the imagery stands for the object. If the reference involves significant non-iconic indexicality, then theology might say that interpretations using it are true in specified contexts without saying that the object is like what the symbols say. Christian theology, for instance, can affirm that God is not a person who looks out intentionally upon a world, while affirming also that in some contexts it is far better to symbolize God as such a person than to cry to the Act of *Esse*. Neo-Confucian thought can affirm that ultimate Principle is indeterminate save insofar as it is embodied, while also affirming that one's greatest obligation is to discover the mandate of Heaven for oneself.[27] With care, a dialectical systematic theory can lay out the varying conditions under which it is appropriate to engage ultimate matters with representations all along the spectrum from the most anthropomorphic to the most transcendently apophatic.

---

27. On this existential component of Confucianism, see Tu Weiming's *Humanity and Self-Cultivation* and *Confucian Thought: Selfhood as Creative Transformation*.

CHAPTER 7

Practical Theology in Religious Life

—⟨⟨⟩⟩—

Practical Reason and Ritual

Practical reason is the thoughtful guidance of life. Three grand traditions of practical reason help understand its richness: the Aristotelian, the Platonic, and the Confucian.[1]

Aristotle emphasized the involvement of practical reason in direct action itself.[2] Consider the following "practical syllogism": major premise—"white meat (of a chicken) is good for a fever"; minor premise—"Socrates has a fever"; conclusion—the act of giving Socrates white meat. Of course, the conclusion can be represented in an imperative proposition—"give Socrates white meat." Sometimes for Aristotle, practical syllogisms are only representations of conditions and imperative actions. The core of his idea, however, is that practical reasoning is directly connected with action itself. The pragmatic approach to symbolic *engagement* adopts this core Aristotelian point.[3] For Aristotle, one learns practical reasoning and rationally guided behavior by profound acculturation with the best in one's society,

---

1. Of course much also is to be learned from Jewish and Islamic legal traditions, although that is another project.

2. See his *Nichomachean Ethics*, book 6.

3. See Richard J. Bernstein's *Praxis and Action*, which draws out this Aristotelian theme in discussing Hegel and Marx, Kierkegaard and Sartre, Peirce and Dewey, and major figures in analytic philosophy. The idea is important in theology through the work of "practical theologians." See Don S. Browning's *A Fundamental Practical Theology*.

especially by following good role models who can teach the knack of hitting upon the mean between excessive and defective behavior. Alasdair MacIntyre has brought this Aristotelian approach to practical reason to the center of contemporary social and political thought.[4]

The drawback to the Aristotelian account is that theoretical reason is regarded as a higher form of reason and the good life than practical reason, and that practical reason can be complete in its way without theory. For Aristotle, only those seeking philosophic virtue need to stretch to theoretical reason whose excellence is that it is *not* practical. Theory is good for Aristotle precisely because it is not for the sake of anything beyond itself. Aristotle's argument is worth quoting, because his position on the inferiority of practical reason to theoretical, and of inquiry to contemplation, is frequently missed.

> If happiness is activity in accordance with virtue, it is reasonable that it should be in accordance with the highest virtue; and this will be that of the best thing in us. Whether it be reason or something else that is this element which is thought to be our natural ruler and guide and to take thought of things noble and divine, whether it be itself also divine or only the most divine element in us, the activity of this in accordance with its proper virtue will be perfect happiness. That this activity is contemplative we have already said. . . . For, firstly, this activity is the best (since not only is reason the best thing in us, but the objects of reason are the best of knowable objects); and, secondly, it is the most continuous, since we can contemplate truth more continuously than we can *do* anything. And we think happiness has pleasure mingled with it, but the activity of philosophic wisdom is admittedly the pleasantest of virtuous activities; at all events the pursuit of it is thought to offer pleasures marvelous for their purity and their enduringness, and it is to be expected that those who know will pass their time more pleasantly than those who inquire. And the self-sufficiency that is spoken of must belong most to the contemplative activity. For while a philosopher, as well as a just man or one possessing any other virtue, needs the necessaries of life, when they are sufficiently equipped with things of that sort the just man needs people towards whom and with whom he shall act justly, and the temperate man, the brave man, and each of the others is in the same case, but the philosopher, even when by himself, can contemplate truth, and the better the wiser he is; he can perhaps do so better if he has fellow-workers, but still he is the most self-sufficient. And this activity

---

4. See MacIntyre's *After Virtue*.

alone would seem to be loved for its own sake; for nothing arises from it apart from the contemplating, while from practical activities we gain more or less apart from the action.[5]

The practical downside of Aristotle's theory is its difficulty in determining the best in one's society, in identifying the right role models, particularly in times of social upheaval. When tradition itself is suspect, Aristotle's practical reason is rudderless.

Theology as symbolic engagement is firmly committed to embedding theory of the most critical and systematic sort in practical theology as it guides life. The previous two chapters have detailed a rich scope for systematic theology that stretches customary thinking about theology. Even the theories in the sciences are relevant in theology for preparing for the guidance of religious life. To find the base for this, we look beyond Aristotle to Plato.

Plato's Divided Line was described earlier as having four segments, each of which involves a typical kind of thinking. In the first, the imagination of the poets is filled with arresting images and phrases, but without a solid, commonsense context. At the beginning of the *Republic*, Cephalus and Polemarchus quote a poet to the effect that "justice is giving everyone their due." They cannot defend the phrase, even though later in the *Republic* it is given solid justification, with an understanding of what is due to people and under what circumstances. The second segment is the commonsense world typified by Thrasymacus, the successful, sophistical lawyer who has made a fortune by making the worse argument appear the stronger. This is something like Aristotle's sense of inherited culture, but without Aristotle's confidence in identifying what is excellent and best in the culture. Plato took Greek culture's aristocratic ideals to be deeply threatened by sophistical relativism. Thrasymachus's practical reason might work well in the context of the courtroom to which it was acculturated, but he was led in circles by Socrates' specious, weak arguments because he had no theoretical grasp of his notions. The *Republic* later would justify his claim that injustice pays

---

5. Aristotle's *Nichomachean Ethics* 10.7.1177a12–1177b4. Aristotle goes on to say in the same chapter: "But such a life would be too high for man; for it is not in so far as he is man that he will live so, but in so far as something divine is present in him; and by so much as this is superior to our composite nature is its activity superior to that which is the exercise of the other kind of virtue. If reason is divine, then, in comparison with man, the life according to it is divine in comparison with human life. But we must not follow those who advise us, being men, to think of human things and, being mortal, of mortal things, but must, so far as we can, make ourselves immortal, and strain every nerve to live in accordance with the best thing in us; for even if it be small in bulk, much more does it in power and worth surpass everything. This would seem, too, to be each man himself, since it is the authoritative and better part of him. It would be strange, then, if he were to choose not the life of his self but that of something else. And what we said before will apply now; that which is proper to each thing is by nature best and most pleasant for each thing; for man, therefore, the life according to reason is best and pleasantest, since reason more than anything else *is* man. This life therefore is also the happiest" (1177b26–1178a9).

as a condition within a degenerating unjust society; it would also justify his claim that justice is the interest of the stronger by defining human strength as excellence in the harmonized virtues of reason, spirit, and appetite. Socrates, better than Thrasymachus, was able to make the worse argument appear the better. Theory, in the third segment for Plato, is the construction and analysis of ideas arranged in something like hypothetico-deductive systems. Like imagination in the first segment of the line, theorizing is a constructive human activity; like common sense in the second, theorizing encounters objective reality in the structural forms of the ideas it analyzes. Plato's famous "ideas," however constructed, have a logical structure that is just seen. Plato's favorite examples of theory are from mathematics, although in the *Republic* the examples are theories of the origin and structure of political society.

Like Aristotle, Plato acknowledges the delight and intrinsic interest in theoretical thinking, pleasurable for its own sake. But unlike Aristotle, Plato promotes dialectic, the thinking characteristic of the fourth segment of the Divided Line. Dialectic is the play with theories that moves in two directions. One is to move down to the concrete world otherwise engaged by common sense to employ the various theories to see which phenomena they enlighten and which they hide or do not recognize; the *Republic* tests several theories of society and government this way. The other is to move upward to hunt for the presuppositions of the theories, especially for the nature of the Good itself that makes formal theories coherent; Plato's dialogue *Parmenides* is the most extensive treatment of this sense of dialectic.

The main point of the *Republic* is that theories and skill at their judicious employment are what make thinking excellent at the guidance of life. Although Plato said there is true delight in playing with theories speculatively and dialectically, their true function is to bring excellence to guiding personal life and statesmanlike guidance to the state. In the famous Allegory of the Cave, commonsense people, chained to watch shadows cast on a cave wall and made to guess what they mean, are unchained and dragged up to the light where they see things as they really are—theoretical ideas and their proper use. They did not want to leave the cave, but once they do, they are so enthralled by the light and beauty of theoretical forms that they want to stay on the surface. So they have to be dragged back down into the cave to explain things to those still chained, to lead them. For Plato, the mere enjoyment of theoretical and dialectical understanding is irresponsible if it is not also dedicated to the tasks of guidance, to practical reason.[6]

---

6. The Allegory of the Cave begins in book 7 of the *Republic* at 514 and goes through 521, leading to the discussion of the ideal curriculum for the training of philosophers for guiding the city. All this because theory needs to be internalized, understood dialectically, and then learned to be applied practically.

Whereas Aristotle thought that theoretical reason is above practical reason precisely because it serves no end other than itself, Plato thought that theoretical and dialectical reason are instrumental to practical reason in a larger sense of guiding life, including deliberating about the goals of life.

So for Plato, in contrast to Aristotle, practical reason requires a kind of elite education that is heavy on theory and dialectic. In the ideal curriculum Socrates describes in the *Republic*, candidates for political leadership are made to study for years in school, with special concentrations on mathematics and science. Then they spend five more years studying philosophical dialectic. Finally, they are sent off to the provinces, where they cannot do much damage, for fifteen years to practice political leadership as they learn the art of timing, which means among other things knowing when to analyze the situation with which theories. Then they have the proper education in theory and practice that would justify bringing them back to the capital to exercise important leadership.[7] The *Republic* parallels the discussion of social government with the discussion of the "government" of the individual person, and ends with the moral that the most important thing an individual can do is to find the education that will provide the expertise for mixing the particular set of circumstances and talents of the individual's life. For Plato, practical reason is inclusive of and higher and more important than theoretical reason; it is dialectic aimed at the guidance of personal and social life. The pragmatists fully adopted Plato's theory in this regard, although with a different ontology of the "forms."

Aristotle and Plato disagreed about practical reason on many accounts, not least about their fundamental images of the world. For Aristotle, the world is made of substances that are in process of actualizing their potential with the goal of becoming complete. The actuality emerging in the present is always dependent on the actuality in the past, and the act in substances also defines what would complete them. Goodness for Aristotle is structural wholeness or the full actualization of potentials. The virtues of practical reason, therefore, need to find their sources in the past that also defines their goals—deliberation is about means, not ends, said Aristotle. Of course, Aristotle did not believe that the past contains only goodness so that blind acculturation is the way to moral virtue; discriminations need to be made. Yet the discriminations need to be learned from the sources of the best that must be found in the past somewhere.

Plato by contrast saw the world as a maelstrom of processes intersecting temporarily to form larger harmonies such as healthy individuals and societies, but constantly under threat of becoming unglued. Because concrete

7. See the *Republic* 7.521–40.

affairs are always in process, nothing has a truly stable identity or "being" for Plato. Concrete things are always "becoming" something else. The only things that have such stable identity are ideas that simply are what they are. Human life needs to find the ideas that cut the processes of life at their natural joints, allowing for temporary knowledge and some control. Structures of concrete reality are only temporary states of affairs when the ideas people can contemplate theoretically manage to stick for a while. One of the main themes of the *Republic* is that even the best of societies will decay because of theoretically unaccounted-for events—a misalignment of stars, for instance.[8] Therefore, practical reason's guidance cannot look only to the past. The statesman must be somewhat above the law of the constitution and look to transcendent principles of theory and harmony that allow for radical adjustments to take account of changing circumstances.

Both the Aristotelian and Platonic images of the world and corresponding conceptions of practical reason differ from the Confucian image. Ancient Chinese cosmology generally imagines the world as a connected field of energy (*qi*) shaped by constellations of yin-yang vibratory patterns. These constellations are patterns of change rather than essences of substance, and they echo one another, large and small, here and there, throughout the cosmos; the sixty-four hexagrams of the Yijing constitute a "table of elements" of change patterns.[9] The human core of thinking and acting should be in harmony with the things perceived and acted upon. The problem of knowledge in ancient Confucianism is to improve the ways by which the heart echoes and defers in action to the characters of the things, especially people, in the environment. The phrase "rectification of names," a Confucian epistemological slogan, refers to the project of learning how correctly to identify the nature and worth of things in order to behave correctly toward them.[10] The interactive continuities of thought and action with the "ten thousand things" are very directly in line with the pragmatic theory of engagement, right down to the recognition that what is most important to get in knowledge is an appreciation of the worths of things.[11] Daoism does not differ from Confucianism in this point. Because all knowing is a form of acting toward things, covertly if not overtly, all thinking is imagined as practical reason.

---

8. *Republic* 8.546.

9. See the three essays by Livia Kohn and James Miller in the Comparative Religious Ideas Project volumes *The Human Condition, Ultimate Realities,* and *Religious Truth,* ed. Neville. For the point about yin-yang being vibratory patterns of *qi,* see my Foreword to Sophia Delza's *T'ai-Chi Ch'uan.*

10. For a general review of the themes of Confucianism, see John H. Berthrong's *Transformations of the Confucian Way.*

11. This is a main point of Warren Frisina's *The Unity of Knowledge and Action.*

Confucianism and Daoism agree that human problems in family life, politics, religion, or wherever are functions of disharmony. To be in harmony, the patterns of changes need to reinforce one another. Disharmony of the body, resulting in illness, is when the organ systems do not work together. Disharmony in the state is when the various offices and social classes do not work together. Disharmony in the family is when harmonizing love is not conveyed through the playing of roles. Disharmony in knowledge is when the knower is not sufficiently developed to perceive the environment correctly or is not sufficiently developed to carry out inner intentions into effective action. Sufficient development of the self in these regards requires cultivating bodily effectiveness and grace, as in martial arts, calligraphy, singing, and dance. It also requires cultivating social relationships so that one is in a position to perceive what is going on and to carry out actions that nearly always are conjoint actions with others. And of course it involves the cultivation of erudition, analytical skills, powers of reflection, meditative stillness, and capacities to learn from others.

In this last point, Confucianism sides with Plato against Aristotle in making all kinds of theoretical knowing instrumental for practical action and behavior, and in emphasizing the ideal of harmony. Yet it is more holistic, social, and physicalistic in its understanding of human cognitively shaped engagement with the important things of the world than Plato.[12] One Confucian slogan for this is "to be one body with the world." Nothing in ancient Confucianism's texts or motifs of thought, or Daoism's either, feeds the dualism of mind versus objects that in the West found support from Aristotle's notion that the mind mirrors the forms of things in true knowledge or from Plato's of the two sides of the Divided Line into faculties of knowing and objects known for each segment.

For Confucianism, though not for Daoism, the human predicament for practical reason is deeper than restoring broken harmony. To put the point in the language of Xunzi, the great younger contemporary of Mencius, heaven and earth, that is, "nature," give human beings a bio-psychic endowment that is radically underdetermined.[13] We have all sorts of natural possibilities for physical movement, but nature does not tell us whether to stand with feet parallel (the Chinese way) or angled outward (the Western way), whether to greet people with direct eye contact or with a deferential

---

12. These points are all explored at great length in the three volumes by David Hall and Roger Ames: *Thinking through Confucius, Anticipating China,* and *Thinking from the Han.* Although Hall and Ames's interpretations are controversial in particulars, they make the case for the general interpretation of the Chinese tradition supposed here.

13. See chap. 17 of *Xunzi,* and see also Machle's interpretation of this in *Nature and Heaven in the Xunzi.*

aversion of eyes, and so forth. We have all sorts of emotional capacities for love, attraction, fear, anger, and so forth, but nature by itself does not connect these with appropriate objects. We have a natural capacity for understanding and self-control, said Xunzi, but nature by itself does not connect that with what there is to understand or with a sense of self and its responsibilities to others. Being thus radically underdetermined in natural endowment, human beings need something in addition to the contributions of "heaven and earth" in order to fulfill the natural human potential for civilized life.

The Confucian solution to this problem, detailed by Xunzi and others, is that ritual behavior needs to be added to heaven and earth's natural endowment. Ritual is behavior shaped by a semiotic system and it is learned, mainly unconsciously, the way language is learned. Elementary ritual motions teach infants how to stand and move; more complicated ones teach them how to defer to others with the right eye contact, body language, and so forth. The principal ritual acknowledged in every society is its language; language, however, is not just words but also lives within wider semiotic rituals of gesture and a sense of appropriateness of when to speak, to whom, and about what. Rituals make possible the connection of emotions with appropriate objects, shaping the conditions under which emotional responses are appropriate. Rituals articulate social roles in family, community, and government. Rituals in high-level cognition provide habits of mind that organize life around deliberation and self-control. All social habits and personal habits are to be understood as ritual. Political and religious "court and temple liturgies" are merely the explicit and conscious top tip of a pyramid of ritualized behavior learned and perfected (or not) throughout life.

Xunzi and the Confucians always understood that rituals are conventional, not given by nature. They knew that there are many styles of movement, different body postures for conveying respect or hostility, different languages, and different ways of ritually organizing society and celebrating public liturgies. They expressed this in the slogan that "the human completes heaven and earth." Civilized life, which exists as a natural potential, cannot be realized without the addition of semiotically shaped ritual behavior to nature. It might be possible to cooperate on the hunt, but friendship is impossible without the rituals of friendship. It might be possible to produce offspring, but family life is not possible without family rituals that shape care and love. A powerful headman might keep order in the clan, but political life is not possible without the rituals that distribute responsibility and authority. People might meet by accident, but without rituals of greeting that are tied to social identities, the primitive emotions of fight or flight might prohibit civilized engagement. Ritual makes civilization possible and, without ritual, that is, without semiotically shaped behavior, civilization is impossible. Just as language makes verbal communication possible without determining exactly what to say, so rituals at all levels and in all areas of life provide general forms for the dance of civilization without dictating the exact steps. The Confucians never thought of ritual as a mechanical form, a mere lockstep that might allow for a mechanical scientific understanding of human behavior. On the contrary, to be human means to learn how to inhabit the rituals, to individuate them for the circumstances and the individuated identities of the people involved. Human individuality for the Confucians is by no means exhausted by the process of individuating the ritual behaviors for life. Nevertheless, the individuation of rituals is what makes a person part of a civilized society.

Because for the Confucians rituals are conventional, it does not matter much just what conventions a society has, as long as they have some effective conventions for making civilization possible. It does not matter which language they use, as long as they have a language for social discourse. It matters not whether greetings are expressed by bows or handshakes, as long as the greeters share some effective ritual. Family life can be organized with many different patterns of social roles as long as there is some pattern that is effective for the cultivation of humaneness, love, and the learning of ritual itself. Societies are in trouble when they lack effective rituals.

Confucius agrees with Plato that life is precarious ("precarious" actually is almost a technical term for John Dewey, making this point).[14] He lived in a social condition of even greater violence and social unrest than Plato did. He and Plato also agree that the imposition of order by military means does not address the root issue and only makes things worse. They agree as well that the solution lies in education, and both were the founders of extraordinarily influential educational institutions and processes, the core of the great civilizations of East Asia and the West, respectively. Where Plato wrote dialogues, Confucius's Analects are records of his dialogues with students and officials.

The chief focus of Confucius's educational reform was the teaching of ritual. He ran a school to teach young people ritual propriety, including music and dance.[15] His underlying analysis of his social situation, however, was that it lacked the rituals for civilized life. Although the legendary civilizations of the past were rich in rituals, he thought, Confucius saw his "Warring States" period as a time when those rituals had become corrupted

14. See Dewey's *Experience and Nature*, chap. 2.
15. See Robert Eno's *The Confucian Creation of Heaven: Philosophy and the Defense of Ritual Mastery*.

or inoperative. Thus, there were no political rituals for keeping the peace and the situation had degenerated to constant strife among warlords. There were few effective rituals for economic cooperation and so poverty and thievery were rampant. Proper family rituals were lacking and so people never learned love, respect, and the other aspects of the Confucian virtue of humanity or humaneness (*ren*). Confucius's educational project was to recover the effective civilizing rituals of the legendary sage-kings and teach them to the younger generation. Although he claimed merely to be handing down those ancient traditions, most scholars now say that he was extraordinarily inventive.

The chief part of the Confucian moral project, practical reason, is thus the identification and criticism of the present situation with regard to the effectiveness of the rituals that are operating and the recovery or invention and inculcation of rituals that make civilization possible. For Confucians, practical reason is not exhausted in ritual analysis and reformation, because there are many issues of decision and policy that take place within a ritual context but are not dictated by that. Moreover, Confucianism from Mencius to the Neo-Confucians emphasized the existential project of transforming the self to become a sage, only part of which is a project in ritual improvement.[16]

Nevertheless, the focus on ritual is a primary placement of the energy of practical reason. Aristotle would applaud the Confucian recognition that moral (or immoral) behavior springs from the given patterns of society, and he understood, with Confucius, the conventional character of socialization. Plato would applaud the Confucian recognition that the criticism of the ritual situation and invention of new rituals must come from a source that transcends the situation criticized. Because of the emphasis on ritual, communitarians such as Alasdair MacIntyre often claim Confucius for Aristotelian traditional conservatism. The better judgment, however, is the Platonic one: that Confucius was a revolutionary precisely because he attacked the ritual structure of his own society with transcendent norms for better rituals. Many Chinese, of course, associate Confucius not with his revolution in ritual but with the conservative bondage to fixed and inhumane rituals that resulted at times from the uses to which his philosophy was put.

Confucius and his tradition were far slower than Plato and his tradition to delight in free speculative theorizing, and the dialectical application of

---

16. This is the main burden of Tu Weiming's brilliant early essays in *Confucian Thought* and *Humanity and Self-Cultivation*. See our continued discussion of this in his Foreword to my *Boston Confucianism*.

sciences so conceived, to the mending of rituals and other aspects of the guidance of life. No reason exists, however, why the delight in theoretical speculation and science as inquiry cannot be integrated into the Confucian conception of the well-developed person for engaging the situation with clear, complex perceptions and complicated, effective, nuanced responses. A Platonized Confucianism provides a rich model for practical reason that now can be turned to the sphere of religion.

Ritual and the Sacred Canopy

The connection between practical reason in general and ritual can now be adapted to practical reason in theology. Theology as symbolic engagement hypothesizes that the habitual social and personal patterns of religious life are those rituals that shape human life relative to the various elements of the sacred canopy. Human life has many kinds of rituals, in the rich Confucian sense, that do not have much to do with the sacred canopy, however much they might ultimately take their orientation from that. Religious rituals, however, are those that pattern life to reflect or be rightly related to the sacred canopy. This is an hypothesis about how to define patterned religious life, not an empirical observation about which social and personal rituals are regularly called religious.

The sacred canopy is the more or less coherent interweaving of the images of a given culture's finite/infinite contrasts, the boundary or world-defining conditions without which the definitions of the world as such would be missing and the activities of daily life would have no ultimate contextual orientation. The images within the sacred canopy are expressed in the core texts and motifs of religious cultures and are rehearsed in liturgies, arts, and other media. The coherence of a given sacred canopy is a matter of more or less, and because the social conditions of the culture are constantly changing, the nature of the sacred canopy's coherence itself changes, generally playing catch-up. Peter Berger has detailed many of the vicissitudes of the Christian sacred canopy in European modernity and in contemporary non-European non-modern but modernizing societies.[17]

No sure and stable way exists to identify the boundaries of a given social canopy because cultures exist within larger cultures and are constantly interacting with yet other cultures. The criticism was lodged earlier against the Yale School's theological conception of religious groups as cultural/linguistic communities with sharp boundaries—the boundaries in fact are porous and constantly shifting and overlapping. Yet the Yale School had a

---

17. See his *A Far Glory* and *Questions of Faith*.

profound point in seeing that a society takes its theological orientation from an underlying theological conceptual structure and that some of the work of theology is to see to it that the society or religious community behaves in accord with that deep structure. Expressed in the language of theology as symbolic engagement, the argument now would say that the sacred canopy is the deep structure and that practical theology interprets how the canopy should be reflected in the religious rituals patterning the community to cultivate a normative religious identity.

Discussions in the previous four chapters have detailed a fairly complex theory about how theology elaborates the primary witnesses that are expressed in sacred canopies into assertions that can be criticized and defended with good cases. Case making leads theology into the broad scope of theological resources in the study of religions, the sciences, arts, and normative practical disciplines. It also leads through the complexities of dialectical systematic theorizing. At the popular level in a religious culture, the sacred canopy might be taken pretty much in the imaginative terms of the primary witnesses to the finite/infinite contrasts expressed in the core texts and motifs. Theology as reflection on ultimate matters deepens popular imagination and gives it coherence, inner resonance, and testability, as will be argued in the concluding chapter. Assertive and systematic theology become practical theology, theology as practical reason, when they lead to the criticism and reformation of the ritual patterns of religious life and also when they guide particular religious responses.

To understand how systematic theology becomes practical requires some reflection on the locus of patterns of religious ritual. Proper systematic reflection would require a comparative study that developed a list of steady comparative categories for the elements of social patterns that are religious. Emile Durkheim proposed that such a list might come best from a study of the elementary or primitive forms of religious life rather than from the sophisticated literate religions with long theological traditions.[18] If the argument of this book so far is on the mark, however, namely that theology enriches and complicates religious reflection and its patterning of life, the opposite is likely to be the case: religions are increasingly recognizing their practical reach. Suffice it for the present purpose to discuss a variety of patterns to indicate something of the spread of practical theology's involvement in shaping life.

The most obvious religious patterns are those of direct communal worship involving recitation or chanting of scripture, prayers, perhaps sermonic commentary, music, and dance. In the West Asian religions, these tend to be

---

18. See Durkheim's *The Elementary Forms of Religion Life.*

weekly—Sunday for Christians, Friday for Muslims, and Saturday (or Friday evening, which counts as Saturday) for Jews. South and East Asian religions also have community worship at temples and shrines of various sorts, and in Western countries are coming to approximate the West Asian weekly model. For nearly all religions, family devotions are as important if not more important than community worship. In fact, only Christianity and Buddhism, believing in corporate religions that call one out of the family, give great significance to public community worship. Family devotions focus on continuity with the past, as in filial prayers to ancestors in Chinese religion and the seder in Judaism, on petitions for dealing with daily life, and on nourishing the future. Religious patterning in the domestic scene is not limited to explicit rites of worship. Stephen Prothero has argued that even the decoration of American homes in the nineteenth century became much influenced by popular Christian religious art, which had been banned by the anti-visual bias of earlier American Calvinist Christianity.[19]

Religions pattern life in ritual ways to celebrate or articulate the world-defining moments of life: birth, puberty and initiation, marriage, the production and nurture of families, catastrophic suffering, old age, sickness, and death. Religions pattern the calendar year with holidays celebrating founding, fertility, transplantation, and change, nearly always with special attention to the change of seasons as world founding. Durkheim argued, rightly, that religious patterns serve purposes other than those they seem to celebrate directly. So, for instance, in predominantly Christian or post-Christian societies, Christmas orders the retail business cycle. Religions provide the iconography for art, architecture, and adornment such as jewelry, all of which flourish in a culture with a ritual character. Religions supply the gestures, the body postures, and the words of exclamation for moments of great significance, beauty, tragedy, and crisis: "God damn! Jesus, that hurt!" Religions supply norms and tacit understanding of what the development of character should be for women and men. Hardly any social pattern or ritual exists in any society that might not be shaped in part by some reference to a feature of the sacred canopy that orients it with respect to the founding boundaries of the world, the finite/infinite contrasts.

Given the wide scope of locations for religious ritual or rituals shaped in part by religion, it is possible now to look at theology in the role of deliberately shaping the ritual patterns of society. Although most theology does not invent ritual patterns for how to live before the ultimate, it does criticize, systematize, and draw implications for consistency and new extensions

---

19. See his *American Jesus*, a study of how Christianity in general and images of Jesus in particular have been adapted for the indigenization of Christianity in America.

of how to live. Whereas popular religions might have a fairly immediate patterning based on core texts and motifs, theology, with its critical and systematic richness, asks what those primal witnesses are really about, how they stand with respect to the primal witnesses of other religions, and how their implications are affected by what is to be learned from the secular world, the sciences, arts, and normative practical disciplines. The disputes among theologies about these matters play out directly in what they recommend as practical patterns of religious life.

However those disputes turn out, theology as reflection on ultimate matters in symbolic engagement sees and attempts to articulate a connection between the ultimate realities and concerns expressed in the sacred canopy and the patterns of daily life. Despite the fact that most daily concerns are proximate ones, theology is concerned about how those proximate projects take their orientation from the world-defining finite/infinite contrasts. What should people's response be to the sheer contingent existence of the world? Gratitude? Nervousness? Ultimate cynicism that life is a joke? What should people's response be to what a religion articulates as the ground of value and obligation in the world? How should ultimate definitions of what it means to be at home in the world play out in sharing that world with other people, relating to the natural environment, and so forth?

If theology cannot draw out the implications of its critical and systematic work for how to pattern human life before ultimate matters, it has not completely understood the context of its own work. Part of the context of even the most complex systematic intentional interpretation of ultimate matters is the need to translate what is important or valuable in ultimacy, in the respects in which a theology's signs stand for them, into the practical patterns of everyday religious life. Otherwise, the theology is not true in the sense of carrying over the value in the ultimate into a human stance toward it. Theology as symbolic engagement is not true unless and until it has engaged the ultimate with symbols that transform life to embody what is ultimately important.

This last point is important but dangerous. The danger lies in the ready leap so many people, including professional theologians, are prepared to make to practical applications. They dismiss the details and complexities of theology in order to demand practical relevance. This of course misses the whole point about the critical and systematic modes of responsible theological engagement. It constitutes an anti-intellectualism that misses the Platonic contribution to understanding practice. Easy reduction of theological theory to quickly understandable practice under the demand for "practical theology" is a betrayal of the richness of symbolic engagement with which theology needs to work. Nevertheless, if that danger can be guarded against, theology in the richest sense finds its truth in carrying what is ultimately important into the ways people stand before ultimacy in daily life.

Theology and Crisis

The practical significance of theology is not only in guiding the social and personal habits that ritualize human responses to the bearing of ultimate matters on life. Theology also responds to historical crises in ultimate matters. In fact, theology as a self-conscious discipline that functions in religious communities and in academic thinking is almost exclusively the sort that addresses historical issues. In most contexts, the day-to-day monitoring of the rituals of patterned life before the ultimate is taken to be what Christians call a "pastoral" responsibility. Histories of theology rarely deal with guidance of the rituals by which people live, however much they should do so.

Wesley J. Wildman distinguishes two types of theology, or "theological literacy," as he calls it.[20] "Type A" consists of the theological knowledge that works in ordinary circumstances to express appropriate belief and guidance for individuals and communities through the difficulties of life. At the popular level, this means learning the terminology of one's religion's sacred canopy and how to keep it connected with life's issues. At a more sophisticated level of theology, the doctrinal issues are objectified and systematized, with relevant criticisms taken into account and some fairly practiced and even scientific ways of relating the sophisticated understanding of the sacred canopy to the exigencies of life.[21] "Type B" theological literacy is creative thinking that is sparked when the sacred canopy is rent or the transitions from the canopy to relevant practice are blocked or shaken apart. In the terms of the previous section, Type B theology is required when ultimate matters no longer are served by the rituals that shape human responses in continuity with the sacred canopy, and when no minor adjustments can be made by Type A thinking to let society and individuals simply get on with their lives. Wildman's description is worth quoting at length:

> The sociology of knowledge has made it abundantly clear through the work of scholars such as Peter Berger and Thomas Luckmann that humans construct their social reality. A theological interpretation of this basic result

---

20. See his "Theological Literacy: Problem and Promise."
21. Wildman does not develop the point that Type A can have extremely sophisticated versions and focuses rather on the benefits and drawbacks at the level of popular religion of making the assumptions in the sacred canopy explicit. Nevertheless, there are pastoral traditions that practice Type A theology in very sophisticated ways, for instance, in the Jesuit traditions as customarily caricatured: imaginative casuistry.

can be developed by likening cultural constructions to the earth's ozone layer. As the fragile ozone shields the earth from harmful high-energy radiation while allowing safer light to warm and power the ecosphere, so do the social constructions of human beings protect both individuals and corporate life from the harsher dimensions of reality while simultaneously allowing enough truth through to illumine and power personal and cultural creativity. Moreover, formal religions and informal religious or spiritual activities are key components in the construction of this protective cultural ozone layer. They promote engagement with the divine reality out of which emerges the complex wonder of our lives even as they protect us from the full glory of this reality. When the chaotic or the awesome breaks through into our lives, as it does often enough, the ozone thins and the socially constructed world becomes more translucent to the bright glory of God, at least for some. Such light sears and, in pain and awe, we blessedly never forget. This is as clear a fact of life as any other. I speak of this bright mystery on the other side of our protective social constructions as God, but for present purposes I could live happily enough with many accounts of it— as nature's fecund depths, as the mystic's unspeakable mystery, as the power of being itself—so long as they were properly empirical about explaining this fundamental feature of human experience. Any such account allows theology room to move, though not necessarily a particular religion's version of theology.[22]

What causes the breakthrough of the "chaotic or awesome" in our lives? What causes the rents in the sacred canopy? Life presents some undeniable facts that simply cannot be brought under the canopy in practical ways. Wildman's example was the attempt of religious people to understand the shootings at Columbine High School when a couple of students went on a murder rampage. That simply could not be comprehended within the terminology and resultant practices of Jews and Christians who tried and found wanting the traditional conceptions of God as wrathful, or forgiving, or benevolent, or disinterested, or absent. Of course, the Holocaust was the great indigestible fact for twentieth-century monotheists. When something like that happens, a crisis, theology needs to think outside the context of the germane sacred canopy and its connections to the practice of life.

Crises are of many sorts. Three can be mentioned to typify the range: crises of religious revolution, of historical disconfirmation, and of plausibility conditions.

An extraordinary crisis in the form of a religious revolution occurred in South Asia in the sixth century before the common era when Buddhism

---

22. "Theological Literacy: Problem and Promise," pp. 347–38.

arose out of the situation in which the Vedic religion of the Aryans had been imposed on the religious practices of the earlier peoples over a period of centuries. Doubtless, many causes contributed to the Buddhist crisis. The Aryan-imposed order was a rigid caste system in which the natively earlier peoples were at the bottom. The social integration of the peoples was difficult. The authority of the Vedas had ceased to be self-evident to many. The answers that religious culture gave to ordinary problems such as suffering and death seemed without persuasive fire. Buddhism arose, centered around the person of Gautama Buddha, with doctrines and practices that turned the older assumptions upside down. Buddhism embraced all castes. It rejected traditional family structure in favor of a mendicant life and monastic religious organization. It denied the classic Vedic view that the self is ultimate reality and is self-same in all individuals by claiming there is no self at all. Buddhism did all this while remaining within the mythic cosmos of the older Vedic culture.

Whatever the merits of early Buddhism on its own, the shock of its extraordinary success forced the theologians of the Vedic culture to commence Type B theology. No unified response occurred, but many divergent creative ones did. As mentioned earlier, the "six orthodox schools" emerged, each with its way of defending the authority of the Vedas and each with practical implications for ways of life; there were also many heterodox schools. The Vedas were systematically interpreted from the standpoints of each of the schools, however inconsistent with one another, and a common language was developed among the schools to express their debates.[23] Moreover, the ancient tradition was rehabilitated through classics such as the *Ramayana* and the *Mahabharata*, which provided the core texts and motifs for a revitalized Hindu practice, both popular as well as sophisticated. The Bhagavad Gita is a chapter in the *Mahabharata*.

This is not the only example of religious revolutions, of course. Second Temple Judaism went into revolution sparked by Hellenizing thought and Persian apocalyptic thinking, resulting in the creative explosion that gave rise to Rabbinic Judaism and Christianity. The destruction of the temple was a catalyst, but the revolution had been brewing before that and drew on many sources broader than the vicissitudes of temple worship. In China, the advent and spectacular success of Buddhism after the Han and through the Dang Dynasty stimulated the extraordinary invention of Neo-Confucianism in the Song. Neo-Confucianism co-opted many elements of Buddhism and Daoism, Sinified them thoroughly, and reconstructed Confucian antiquity as the source of the new Way of life.[24]

---

23. See the study by Francis X. Clooney, S.J., *Hindu God, Christian God.*
24. See Berthrong's *Transformations of the Confucian Way.*

Crises of historical disconfirmation are also potent stimuli to creative practical theology. Perhaps the most complicated was the dawning realization in the nineteenth century by Confucians that their culture was not the center of the cosmos. Having successfully absorbed and Sinified Buddhism, the Confucians, including those at the court of the emperors, had difficulty abandoning the finite/infinite contrast that China is the center (the Chinese word for China, Zhongguo, means central country). Yet China found itself caught in a web of economic and military forces whose main power centers lay elsewhere. The opium culture resulting from the trade forced upon China by the Western imperial powers showed the weakness of Confucian family culture. The Confucian institutions supporting their great love of learning simply lagged behind the West in science and technology, even though the European breakthroughs had been shared by the Jesuit missionaries in China in the sixteenth and seventeenth centuries. The tragic irony was that the rot in late nineteenth- and early twentieth-century Confucian culture was exposed by a foreign import, Marxism. In our own time, Confucians in the diaspora forced by the Communist victory in 1949, as well as a new generation of Confucian scholars in the People's Republic, are rethinking the intellectual bases of Confucianism and also, more importantly, the practical ways of life following from that. This is the most creative time in Confucianism since the rise of Neo-Confucianism.

Of course, many other examples exist of historical disconfirmation of a tradition with its sacred canopy causing a vital new creative theological energy. The Holocaust has already been mentioned. After Auschwitz, most ways of thinking of the Jews as the Chosen People and of Christians as loving people are simply impossible. Ours is an extraordinary time for Jewish and Christian theology. This is not the first time for those traditions. The ancient fall of Israel to the Assyrians and of Judea to the Babylonians signaled the weakness of Yahweh compared with the gods of those other people. The prophetic tradition creatively reconstructed Israelite religion to say that Yahweh was the God of all people, and the only God. The crucifixion of Jesus was a devastating shock to his followers, who responded by proclaiming him raised from the dead and victor over the evils of both heaven and earth. When Jesus did not return when expected, Christian theology developed a metaphysics that put the return in cosmic perspective.[25]

Although connected with both religious revolution and historical disconfirmation, theology needs creative practice in responding to crises of

---

25. Gerd Theissen's *A Theory of Primitive Christian Religion* argues for the hypothesis that both prophetic Judaism and early Christianity simply raised the ante when their projects seemed to fail, in the first instance claiming that Yahweh was not defeated but was rather the God of all nations and was using some to punish Israel. In the second instance, the humiliating crucifixion of Jesus was not defeat but the crucial winning stroke in a cosmic struggle.

plausibility. The great example is the effect of European modernity on Christian and Jewish theology. The paradigms of science, especially mathematical science, came to define plausibility, and as the Enlightenment drew out the implications for theology, much traditional theology simply made no sense. In one aspect, this was an intellectual problem, properly located in the theoretical part of dialectical systematic thinking and the cases it can or cannot make for doctrines. The more practical problem to be addressed by theology as practical reason, however, is that the new paradigms changed the ways moderns imagined their world. The image of the Earth as circling a sun in a solar system located in a spray of stars with no center competed with and displaced the biblical image of the Earth as centered beneath the stack of divine heavens and above the hells. The image of the cosmos as millions (now billions) of years old displaced the previous image of creation as taking place just several thousand years ago with countable human generations. The image of Christian culture as one among other great religious cultures, discovered by the explorers, displaced the image of Christianity as the divine success story, although that did not happen until the end of the nineteenth century.[26] The displacement of the images in the Christian sacred canopy, with its biblical core texts and liturgical motifs, has been of immense practical importance. Aided by wars among Christian nations with weapons of mass destruction, it has undermined the plausibility of Christianity for many people in the middle and lower classes as well as among the intellectual elite. The despair, anonymity, and alienation articulated by the Romantics and then again by the existentialists were, and are, powerful cultural consequences of the shift in the imaginative base of plausibility conditions. And finally, the reduction of Christian political culture from its medieval moral base, however misguided and hypocritical that might have been, to the acknowledgment that power is the only thing that counts because it serves the national will, which has no moral base but its own will, was unveiled by Nietzsche and embraced by early twenty-first-century neoconservatives. Attempts to counter the politics of naked power by coupling it with or rejecting it in the name of some premodern version of Christianity are vain. The plausibility conditions for premodern Christianity are constitutive of the imaginations only of non-modern people or of modern people who can segregate their imaginations so as to contain contradictions. Christian theology is now searching for creative new modes for understanding its sacred canopy, modifying it, and developing new institutions, strategies, and policies for coping with the fall of

---

26. Ernst Troeltsch was the pivotal figure here. See Van Harvey's *The Historian and the Believer* and Wesley Wildman's *Fidelity with Plausibility* for enlightening accounts.

Christendom into power politics and disengaged fantasy. The history for the last two centuries of Western Christian theology, both Protestant and Roman Catholic, can be read as a series of responses to the shifting conditions of plausibility as they play out in the practice of religious life. What is said of Christianity here is also true of contemporary thinkers in every other religious tradition.

All of these crises cause theology to rethink itself, with new understandings of the primary witnesses, new organizations of the sacred canopies, often new elements, or even new canopies. Doctrines (now understood within theology as symbolic engagement as systematic symbolics) need to be altered or given new kinds of cases. Dialectical systematic theology needs to analyze just what the issues are in the crisis, identify resources for dealing with that, and construct new theories that are capable of carrying over truth about ultimate matters into theoretical understanding.

But theoretical understanding is not the resting place, or even the point of spending the energy on theology in assertive and systematic modes. Rather, theology needs to employ the theoretical resources to reconstruct the practice of religious life in rituals, and also to redefine religious identity and religious projects. Theology, inclusive of all its critical and theoretical work, needs to direct responses to the crises. Theologies of other religions need to be developed for every religious community. History needs to be accepted for the lessons it teaches, and responses to the ultimate need to be reconstructed to engage those lessons. In times of crisis, theology becomes the most practical of all disciplines because it needs to guide all things as they relate to ultimate matters.

Breaking on the Infinite

Wildman makes another point that brings this chapter to its final topic. Although the language of "the social construction of reality" is a recent notion framed in the theoretical structure of sociology of knowledge, the great theologians have always known about it in some way. He applies that point to Judaism and Christianity, but it holds for the rest as well. Although theologians would call neither their core texts and motifs nor their own theological systems "hypotheses" until the late-modern period, they would recognize in some way that they are reading "signals" of divinity, to use Peter Berger's apt phrase.[27] They knew they were struggling to adapt and invent ideas to express what could not be fully grasped in those ideas. Sometimes theologians are conveniently ready to leap to "mystery" prematurely to

---

27. See *A Far Glory*.

admit the limitations of their ideas. Sometimes they are confident that their ideas build the mystery into the conceptions. In one way or another, even the most brilliant, creative, and dogmatic of theologians, East and West, admit that conceptualizing the ultimate is a task that finally has to fail.

A technically precise intellectual reason can be given for this final failure. Theology's main objects are finite/infinite contrasts. The finite side is some real part of the world; the socially constructed grasp of it defines the cultural world or sacred canopy of its culture. The infinite side is what "would be" if the finite side did not exist or function as world defining. That infinite side is literally infinite. Even with no consciousness of the somewhat arbitrary and historically conditioned character of the social construction of the finite side, the infinite side is *palpably beyond reach*. Engaging a finite/infinite contrast, we touch what cannot be touched. This is a common experience universal to all religions and popularly experienced as what Kant called the sublime. In a sublime experience, we know, we perceive, we grasp in the heart that there is something we are not comprehending.

So much for the intellectual adventures of dialectical systematic theologians who understand the apophatic moment in theology. Theology is kataphatic insofar as it explicates the finite side of a finite/infinite contrast. It is apophatic insofar as it explicates the consequences of the infinite side. Because the principal real objects of theology are finite/infinite contrasts, not one side without the other, kataphatic theology, when pushed to carry over what is important in the contrast, breaks on the infinite and assumes the form of apophatic theology. For the same reason, apophatic theology merely wallows in indefiniteness, without dialectical connections to a kataphatic theology explicating the sacred canopy whose rents allow through the glorious light of mystery.

What about this theology's guidance of practical life? Theology as kataphatic/apophatic teaches people to be thoroughly committed and invested in a way of life defined by its system, and yet to know that this is a contingent, conventionally relativized way of living before the ultimate. This is to say, practical theology teaches ultimately that people should live to mirror or image (*imago Dei*?) finite/infinite contrasts. Finitely, people with ultimate concern cannot escape engaging the habits and crises of life in committed ways. Infinitely, people with ultimate concern are reduced to awe before the infinite.

The ultimate practical import of theology in all its modes is to guide the engagement of people with ultimate matters, with ultimate realities, according to ultimate projects, and in respect of the bearings of ultimacy on all aspects of life. This ultimate practical import is very difficult to achieve, and three common ways of missing or deflecting it should be singled out for comment.

The first is that some people might have no ultimate concern at all, and theology fails its practical mission if it lets them get away with this. Paul Tillich affirmed that everyone has an ultimate concern, and he based his argument on the conception that a self by definition faces a world and finds its own centeredness, from which its subjectivity arises, in an ultimate concern. He assumed that if one has many proximate concerns, there must be some one concern that one would give up last, that one would hold on to when all other concerns are abandoned. Yet this seems to be empirically false. To use the language of modern psychology, many people have narcissistic personalities. They waffle between grandiose thoughts that the whole world revolves around them and a feeling tone of flattened affect in which nothing is important or worth an emotional response. For narcissistic people, there is no realistic coordination of self and world, and the self does not have a real center in terms of which it engages the world. So they lack ultimate concern. For many other people, the organization of concerns is a flibbertigibbet affair, with shifting patterns of priorities. This is especially common in a consumerist society where social pressures are specifically focused to determine people's priorities of concerns by market appeals. Such people are socialized into a perpetual state of immaturity, unable to center their lives in priorities that have an ultimate center.

So one of the ultimate practical tasks of theology is to guide religions into cultivating and nurturing ultimate concern. The means at theology's disposal are the creative acts of imagination, the critical development of assertions, and the dialectical systematic theorizing that add up to theological teaching. Theology fails at this part of its ultimate practical task if its teachings do not lead to ultimate concern and overcome the obstacles to having that concern. Because of the complexity of theology as described here, most modern forms of religion distinguish the theologian from the popular presenter of theological teaching. This is perfectly legitimate from a theological perspective, as long as the presenter understands the complexity of theology and does not water down or oversimplify the nature of ultimate concern in order to get a merely emotional response. The truth of the presentation depends on whether the value of having an ultimate concern, for the sake of relating to ultimate matters, is carried across into those taught.

Assuming an ultimate concern, another ultimate practical task of theology is to guide people's practical commitments to the religious issues of their watch. This is theology's kataphatic practice. However much apophatic conscience tells people that their categories for engaging the ultimate are conventional, limited, and broken when pushed to the boundary, they are the actual categories people have for engaging the ultimate. Kataphatic theology strives to repair, extend, improve, or perhaps replace sacred canopies in order to provide orientation for the affairs of life; it imagines new conceptions and systems to take into account new exigencies; it crafts ever clearer and more vivid assertions about ultimate matters and builds ever more relevant and vulnerable cases for them; it embraces ever wider and deeper perspectives from which to understand the subtleties of symbolic engagement of ultimacy in all areas. Even if these finally break on the infinite, they are the best theology can do for the moment as it seeks to guide people in engaging the ultimate in their situation. Theology's ultimate practical significance in part is to teach people with these kataphatic lessons how to express their ultimate concerns by engaging the particularities of their lives.

Religious people sometimes succumb to the temptation to try to transcend their situation. Sometimes apophatic mystical theology leads people to think they are above the fray, that the struggles of responsibility to family, friends, community, culture, and history are ultimately insignificant. Sometimes Buddhist rhetoric of non-attachment is employed to justify a kind of disengagement from the world. Yet the very point of the Buddhist notion of non-attachment is to free people from attachments to ego and a false sense of the permanence of things so that they can engage reality such as it is.[28] "Suchness" is the Buddhist word for what is real and worth engaging. Often the situations people find themselves in are terrible and very good reasons exist for wishing one lived in a different time, in a different social class, with different skills and duties. Religion sometimes fosters the fantasy that the present world is not the one to be engaged, but rather some other, perhaps future, condition. Practical theology carries across what is ultimately important when it teaches how to accept the issues at hand as the ones in which to work out ultimate matters. Nirvana is *samsara*, the wheel or daily round of life. This point has been recognized in all religions in different ways.

The third and apophatic practical task of theology is to open people in practice to the brokenness of their symbols of the ultimate. Without in the slightest negating the previous point, that people need to be engaged fully "to the death" with the issues of their situation as understood and guided by their finite theological categories, theology needs also to teach the "great

---

28. See Christopher Queen's *Engaged Buddhism* and *Engaged Buddhism in the West*. See also Park Sung-bae's *Buddhist Faith and Sudden Enlightenment*.

death" even of those religious categories and practices. Theology's instruments or signs for this apophatic practical task are all the kataphatic points made above, but interpreted dialectically to show their limits, their arbitrariness, and their ultimate inability to capture the infinite side of the finite/infinite contrasts. Even the finite side, no matter how dialectically circumspect and inclusive, has the arbitrariness of beginning with some sacred canopy or other.

Wildman suggested, in the long quotation above, that at least one of the ways theology teaches the practical apophatic lesson is in opening people to special religious experiences that break through the sacred canopy. In this he stands in a long mystical tradition that goes back in Christian thought through Berdyaev and Schelling to Boehme and Eckhart, perhaps eventually to Neoplatonism. Generally, these mystics have been marginalized by official theologians specializing in the kataphatic tasks of keeping the sacred canopy repaired and elaborating its significance in doctrine and symbol for the sake of sustaining the "orthodox" patterns or rituals of this tradition's way of relating to ultimate matters. Deep mystical experience shatters and relativizes ordinary life, even ordinary authentic religious life. Mystical experience is dangerous to orthodoxy. This point holds in every religious tradition, each of which has its experiential virtuosi in some competition with its ritual masters.

For the same reason, orthodoxy is dangerous to the practical grasp of the apophatic mystery. Orthodoxy can become so set on defending, while perhaps improving, the sacred canopy and the practical consequences of its theological elaboration that it betrays the infinite side in the finite/infinite contrasts embodied within the canopy. Many religious traditions, if not all, exhibit a kind of rough cycle of emphasis on correctness shifting to emphasis on the ecstasy of the religious heart that comes from the side of mystery. Perhaps a balance of the two sides is the most that practical theology can hope for, guiding the constant resetting of the course as one side or the other goes too far.

The ideal, however, is engaged serenity or equanimity that includes within it transformative moments of ecstasy, bliss, and self-lessness. The religious virtuosi in all traditions, the "saints," have been people who could be wholly devoted to the issues of their situation, addressing them with the theological means at their disposal, and yet serene in the knowledge that there can be other ways and that none of them contains the fullness. The Confucian scholar-official, the Daoist adept, the Buddhist bodhisattva, the Hindu master of the many yogas, the learned rabbi, the Christian saint, the Muslim warrior in the jihad of the soul, are all models of engaged serenity.

Most people known for their engaged serenity are not theologians, although a surprising number of the great theologians in various traditions are also known for that. Practical theology, the practical reasoning that attempts to carry over the religious truth about ultimate matters into people's lives, aims to teach that truth without necessarily carrying the baggage of the doctrines and systems. Without the doctrines and systems, theology has no purchase on self-criticism. It would not know whether it is telling the truth. But the truth does not always need to be conveyed with the instruments of criticism. It can have humbler forms.

Nevertheless, theology fails its ultimate practical responsibilities if it is not ready to supply the reasons and critical apparatus when the questions are raised. Engagement in the practical religious affairs of life seems easier if the infinite side of the finite/infinite contrasts is disengaged and the finite side asserted as plain, undialectical truth: theology needs to counter that disengagement with demonstrations of the brokenness of the symbols in finite/infinite contrasts. By the same token, simple serenity can drift away from engaging the ultimate in everyday matters. Theology needs to be ready to give the reasons why that is a mistake.

Late-modern societies tend to think of theology on the model of a profession, with special expertise in matters of the sort described here to be called upon when relevant. This model contains a large truth, especially with regard to the education of theologians. Yet it disguises the fact that theology in its sophisticated forms needs to be pervasive in society if individuals and communities are to be guided well in relating to ultimate matters. Theology is at the heart of liberal education.

CHAPTER 8

Truth, Scope, Publics, Tests

———ໜ———

The previous chapter discussed how theology has the practical purpose of guiding religious life. The present one argues that theology makes its case for a position in the long run by how well it does that. If truth in theology is conceived as symbolic engagement, then the assessments of that truth in each of the modes of symbolic engagement consist in making cases for whether what is important in the religious objects is carried over into the interpreter in the respects in which the symbols engage those objects. The modes of symbolic engagement distinguished are imagination, critical assertion, dialectical systematic theory, and practical reason.

The argument here has four steps. The first is to restate the senses in which theology is true, summarizing the previous argument and also introducing some new distinctions. The second is to reflect on the scope of intellectual enterprises into which theology needs to enter in order properly to express, explain, and justify its claims to truth. This is a double-sided endeavor: on the one hand, to learn from any quarter that might have something relevant to teach and, on the other hand, to make theological truth claims vulnerable so that they will be corrected if they are mistaken. The third is to consider theology as set within a larger public, or rather a set of publics, in which intellectual debate appropriate to its scope can take place. Insofar as the conception of theology as symbolic engagement defended here can be urged as a positive prescription, the publics that are not yet in existence necessary for theology's scope need to be created. The fourth step is to point out that theology's cases need to be persuasive in all the publics relevant to the theological subject matter. Not everyone in those publics needs to be interested in the theological claims, but if they are, theological cases need to be tested by what interested parties can understand and approve of them.

Chapter 7 argued that theology as practical reason needs to be able to guide religious life truly. The present chapter argues that life has a religious dimension (that is, has ultimate bearing) within all the publics organizing theology's scope, because all elements within that scope bear on the ultimate in some sense. Therefore, the "religious life" for which theology should seek guidance is not limited to people who think they are religious or practice the rituals of specific traditions. The religious life in which theology is tested in the long run includes all the publics, intellectual, practical, and creative, within which ultimacy has some bearing.

Symbolic Engagement

The primary sense of theological truth is the interpretive engagement of religious objects (something having to do with ultimacy, usually sketched in a religion's sacred canopy) by means of signs or symbols such that what is important or valuable in the engaged objects is carried over into the interpreter in the respects in which the signs or symbols stand for the objects. The previous chapters have given this formula expansive detail. The signs and symbols in the networks of their semiotic codes have extensive reference. The primary sense of theological truth, however, is when those signs and symbols, bearing their coded semiotic culture, are used to refer to the objects intentionally. This is interpretation as actual engagement of the objects.

Imagination as a mode of symbolic engagement is true in an attenuated sense compared with the modes of critical assertion, dialectical systematic theory, and practical reason. Those others are conscious of a dyadic character to truth—this and not that—and carry the implicit or explicit claim that cases can be made for the truth asserted. Imagination rather is true only in the sense that the "image" it provides by which elements in the world can be gathered in interpretive experience, allowing those elements to be engaged, in fact carries over what is important. Imagination can be employed in interpretation as an assumption without interpretation going so far as to claim that it is true. Its truth would lie in the fact that the signs and symbols by which it has successfully engaged the interpreters with the object for some purpose or other in fact carry over what is important as a subsequent assertive interpretation might determine. Imagination is a dominant mode of thought in the theological locus of primal witnesses. But it also functions in assertion when new ways of gathering things to be asserted occur—the wit to hit upon the third term, in Aristotle's phrase; and it occurs in every creative move within dialectical systematic thinking. Most importantly, imagination occurs in practical reason as ways are found to bring what is valuable in ultimate matters to make a difference to how people live with those matters.

Critical assertion is the intentional engagement of objects that asserts a definite character to them for the interpreter that is exclusive of other characters and that explicitly or implicitly affirms a case for the character involved. Its truth consists in whether what is important in the object is carried over into the interpretation. Whether it is known to be true depends on the cases that can be made for the assertion.

The making of cases introduces a secondary kind of theological truth, namely, the interpretive engagement of all the sorts of considerations that go into the cases that are not themselves engagements of ultimacy in some form or other. For instance, a case might consist in arguing from scripture. The engagement of scripture might take a philological form, a commentarial form, or literary, theological, historical, homiletical, anthropological, psychological, sociological, jurisprudential, or a host of other forms of inquiry. A case that involves a philological interpretation of some scripture itself rests on making cases in philology that might have little or nothing directly to do with ultimacy or even with theological interests. Such cases as would be made for a philological point are secondary theological interpretations only because they relate to making a case for a primary theological engagement of ultimacy of some sort.

In ordinary theological assertions, such as in doctrines, a host of cases involving presuppositions about the world and inquiries of various sorts are presupposed, perhaps without conscious attention. These form what might be called "plausibility contexts," and they constitute the cases made implicitly in critical assertion, say, of a doctrine. The plausibility contexts might be narrow and parochial, limited to a particular community that just assumes, for instance, a way of interpreting scripture. Or they might be broader, assumed by everyone with an interest in the case. The burden of argument in this book is that any parochialism in the context of plausibility that could be made vulnerable to correction by a broader context of plausibility should be. Theology becomes explicitly critical when some part of the assumed plausibility context needs to be appealed to in order to make a case, or when some interesting doubt arises about the plausibility context, or when the context itself is challenged from some external source.

As theology articulates awareness of its plausibility context and moves on to make cases to justify or amend that context, it becomes dialectical systematic theology. When a critical assertion with its implicit or explicit cases is employed to engage ultimate matters, it is making a primary theological truth claim. The claims made within the making of cases might not be theological except in the secondary sense specified.

Dialectical systematic theology is the deliberate building of an explicit plausibility context in which the maze of directions and topics of inquiry relevant to making cases for primary theological truth claims is analyzed and affirmed in responsible, critical ways. The constructive part of systematic theorizing has much to do with metaphysics. The reason for this is that metaphysics is the attempt to find conceptual language that is as literal as possible and explanatory of how different contexts relate to one another. Of course, metaphysics is also hypothetical, and has its own plausibility context and presuppositions. The dialectical part of systematic metaphysical theology aims to examine this critically as far as possible. The distinction between primary and secondary truth holds within dialectical systematic theology. The secondary truths are all those considerations that build the constructive parts of the system, that articulate relations between claims in apparently separate contexts, and all the rest. The primary truths are when the system as a whole is used to engage the points of ultimacy to which it might be referred.

The truth of practical reason is when the imaginative, critically assertive, and dialectical systematic true interpretations carry over what is ultimately important into the ritual patterns and crisis issues of life. Suppose there is a valid need to build a synagogue in a particular town. The enterprise of building the synagogue is the primary practical truth. Making sure that the foundation stones are well seated in order to hold up the building is a secondary practical truth. The sum of how people live in relation to the ultimate is their cumulative practical interpretation of ultimacy. How much of that is practically true depends on the truth of their imaginative, assertive, and systematic interpretations, and also on the effectiveness with which those interpretive guides are embodied in life.

"Ultimacy," "ultimate matters," "the ultimate," "ultimate concern," and related expressions have been used throughout this book as a kind of placeholder for the religious or theological objects. Just what ultimacy is would be the topic of books far longer than this one. The formal definition given here is that ultimacy has to do with finite/infinite contrasts and the bearing of these contrasts on dimensions and aspects of life. The sacred canopy, by which a religious community stitches together its sense of the boundaries and defining elements of its world, gathers and integrates many finite/infinite contrasts. Subsequent reflection on the ultimate elements in a tradition's sacred canopy, however, can reveal yet more finite/infinite contrasts. For instance, a theologian in a tradition that affirms in its sacred canopy, as expressed in its core texts and motifs, that God creates the world, can learn by studying physics that this takes place in a big bang. The ancient and modern scientific expression might refer to the same thing; nevertheless, they differ in their expressions of both the finite and infinite sides of each finite/infinite contrast. Theological systems themselves might articulate finite/infinite contrasts not found in the sacred canopy. Aquinas's conception of God as the Act of *Esse* has no parallels in the Bible, for instance, yet it is the articulation of a finite/infinite contrast. The sciences, arts, and practical experience might discover finite/infinite contrasts of which the extant religions know nothing. All of these are topics in theology.

Within a religious tradition and among all religious traditions brought under a comparative view, the vivid symbols expressed in core texts and motifs and arranged more or less harmoniously within sacred canopies constitute the primary imaginative world of the religious people. They shape liturgies and explicitly religious activities and also function as the main symbols that pattern the rituals of life and fund responses to crises. For most religious people, these symbols are not only passive background but are actively asserted and interpreted, often with a sense for at least some of the reasons for them. Perhaps only theologians go into detail about their interpretation and follow out the cases for them in the complicated ways discussed in the last several chapters. At the high end of the intellectual ladder is the metaphysics that attempts to say literally, and in a language that communicates across all religions, philosophies, sciences, arts, and the rest, what the reality is that the symbols carry across in those contexts in which they are true. Although the intellectual space between the immediate symbols of sacred canopies and a metaphysics that allows for a genuinely large public to articulate their truth conditions is wide, it is not a gulf. In fact, that space is filled, if not created by, the dialectic of case making about primary symbols and the communities of discourse brought into the secondary theological discussion making those cases.

Remembering that metaphysics is hypothetical, no matter how universalistic and cross-contextual its conceptions, the metaphysics relevant to theology (metaphysics is relevant to many other disciplines too) attempts to describe the basic ultimate realities that define ultimacy in human life, the finite/infinite contrasts. A properly pursued metaphysical project would work through all the sources of representations of finite/infinite contrasts, including the religions, sciences, arts, and normative practical disciplines, and attempt to describe and catalogue all the finite/infinite contrasts that bear ultimately and with orientation on human life. The earlier discussion lists, as finite/infinite contrasts, matters having to do with the contingency of the world and how people should respond, the source and nature of value and its defining of human worth and guilt, the human place in a cosmos conceived one way or another, how relating or becoming attuned to the ultimate is an ultimate defining goal of human life, and so on. These are only anecdotal, not a systematic list by any means.

In the long run, theology ought to be able to judge whether a given symbolic engagement, in the languages of primary witness, doctrine, system, or spiritual practices, truly allows given people in their particular contexts to engage ultimate matters with interpretations in which what is important in the ultimate objects is carried across into the interpreters in the relevant respects. This is not a private matter of theological judgment but one of examining the cases made, with the metaphysics as a stable model within which the indexical and iconic elements of symbolic reference as well as the different conventions of symbols from various traditions can be compared. Any theologian with sufficient interest and expertise ought to be able to make such assessments for any theological interpretive claim.

The pragmatism embodied in this theory of theology as symbolic engagement is often, easily and rightly, associated with the view that thinking is problem solving. John Dewey's *Logic: The Theory of Inquiry and Essays in Experimental Logic* argued that consciousness arises only when habitual modes of behavior meet some obstacle and thought has to be taken to inquire into new hypotheses for stabilizing behavior and accomplishing the purposes at hand (or altering the purposes). For Dewey, we are conscious only when solving problems of some sort. Peirce earlier had argued that inquiry begins because of the "irritation" of some real doubt. When it comes to testing theological interpretations as hypotheses, making cases for them, the pragmatic emphasis on problem solving is enormously important.

Dewey overstated the case that thinking is only problem solving, however. His motive in that rhetorical exaggeration was opposition to the Cartesian notion that consciousness is somehow the fundamental human reality. For Dewey, and for the truth of the matter, consciousness is a range of functions of interpretive attention that includes many other functions that are biological, subconscious, unconscious (in psychodynamic senses), and otherwise structured than by consciousness alone. If we do not pay attention to gravity and the placement of our body when we walk, we fall over; yet we are not conscious of paying such kinetic attention except when goaded by the irritation of stumbling or finding unaccustomed perilous ground.

A more serious error in Dewey's point is that it obscures the dimension of thinking that is rightly prized by the "Verstehen" tradition.[1] Aside from addressing specific problems, the purpose of thinking for this tradition is to understand things. To understand is to grasp things in their causal elements, in the richness of the meanings by which they are understood, in the nuances of their foreground and background elements, in the depths and their connections. To understand is to grasp how things fit into the big pictures of human civilization and experience. To understand is to grasp how the big pictures can be constructed with good warrants and correctible hypotheses. In the long run, thinking is for the sake of understanding in this broad sense. To be sure, practical problems of living need to be solved. Moreover, the work of gaining understanding requires the addressing of many problems in problem-solving modes. Testing the truth of hypotheses for understanding requires turning the hypotheses and their critical assumptions into problems for inquiry. Nevertheless, the result of high-level civilized inquiry, with all its problem solving, should be understanding: the grasp of the world in its richness and complexity of value and meaning. A truly knowledgeable person is one with deep understanding, wisdom.

The image of the instrumentalist (Dewey's term) problem solver is crass by comparison. Alfred North Whitehead captured this distinction in his contrast between the reason of Plato, which is shared with the gods, and the reason of Ulysses, which is shared with the foxes.[2] For Whitehead, the function of reason in general is "to promote the art of life," and both Plato's and Ulysses' kinds of reason are necessary for that; yet the appreciation in the art of life and the orientation of reason's promoting work is all on Plato's side. An irony about Dewey is that some of his books, for instance, *Experience and Nature*, are wonderful big-picture essays in understanding, providing whole new ways of grasping the world.

Theology as symbolic engagement stands squarely in the "understanding" tradition, with its insistence that signs, including whole theories, hypotheses with their cases implicit or explicit, are to be used to engage realities. The point about intentional as opposed to extensional interpretation is that the world is grasped by the complex of the sign in its networks and semiotic codes. The argument has said that imagination is a grasp of

---

1. In our time in Western philosophy, this is represented by "Continental philosophy," including hermeneutics, phenomenology, existentialism, and postmodern deconstruction.
2. See Whitehead's *The Function of Reason*, chap. 1.

the world, that critical assertions are grasps of the world, that dialectical systematic theories are grasps of the world, and so are practical ways of life and decision making.

The use of "grasp" in the previous paragraph to characterize understanding in contrast to problem solving was deliberate. As Dewey would say, when not in a problem-solving mood, we "enjoy" the world by grasping it with our complex theories and attuned tastes for what is important and valuable. To understand in this rich sense is to have the value of the world or, in the theological instance, of ultimate matters carried over into interpretive experience so that reality's complex value is registered experientially. Problem solving is necessary to acquire the signs, the understanding, for grasping the world this way. And such a grasp of the world might itself be helpful in solving some subsequent problems. Understanding as such, however, is the engagement of reality with interpretations that parse and deliver what is important to make the human his or her best. In all the modes of symbolic engagement, truth in theology is the *enjoyment* of ultimacy. Understanding in this sense is experience of ultimacy.

Having said this, however, the argument turns now for the moment to the question of problem solving in the making of cases for theological positions.

The Scope of Learning and Vulnerability

The "scope" of theology in this book means not only what theology is about—ultimate matters—but the kinds of considerations to be taken into account in assessing theological truth claims. There are considerations of considerations of considerations in assessing truth claims that are only secondarily about theological truth.

Another way of phrasing this part of the scope of theology is that it is that to which theology should be vulnerable. Even if a theological hypothesis is strongly believed to be true, it still might be mistaken and therefore should be vulnerable to being corrected. The scope of theology is the whole of what might correct theology, the range of things from which it might learn. Obviously, this is connected with the resources for theology discussed in chapter 5, now viewed as theology's teachers and correctors. To make a case for a theological image, assertion, theory, or practice, all of which are hypothetical in the ways of their respective modes, is to turn its truth into a problem: How can we see whether it is true rather than false?

Wesley J. Wildman has made the clearest case for the problem-solving character of pragmatic inquiry in his essay "The Resilience of Religion in Secular Social Environments." Developing a Peircean pragmatic theory of inquiry similar to the one in this book, he stresses the point that human inquiry evolved as an adaptive value. It is principally social in nature, although there are individual inquirers. In a given community, the shared assumptions of the culture need to include what above was called a "plausibility context," and within those shared assumptions are norms and procedures for good inquiry. "The inquiring community needs a stable identity," he writes, "focused around the practices and procedures for carrying out inquiry, and also around the norms for judgment applicable to resolving competing proposals for solving whatever problem inspires the cooperation in the first place." "On this view, then," Wildman goes on to say, "rationality is the joining of consensus and correctability, which in turn crucially depends upon the impressive yet uneven power of reality to correct hypotheses. The consensus part of this sacred union stabilizes group identity around norms and procedures for inquiry."

That the "power of reality to correct hypotheses" is uneven is a crucial point. Given the social framing of our signs and the variability of contexts in which they are used, when reality has quick "feedback," both the hypotheses in question and the norms and procedures of inquiry get ready confirmation or disconfirmation. So, the interpretive hypotheses involved in driving a car on a difficult road in heavy traffic receive very quick feedback, including the norms and procedures of what to watch out for. The natural sciences, says Wildman, have found many areas in which relatively quick and publicly appreciable feedback can be attained, although there are others where feedback cannot yet be found and scientific disagreements are left to matters of taste, tradition, or some other way of achieving limited consensus among the supporters of the competing hypotheses respectively. In theology, direct feedback is difficult to come by. The attempt in the West since the Enlightenment to articulate a conception of religious experience that would be fairly analogous to perceptive experience in experimental science has failed.[3] Religious experience is at least as complex as engaging ultimate matters with whole theologies as the interpretive signs.

In the face of little or slow direct feedback, theology tends to settle opinions, Wildman rightly notes, by falling back on local communities' shared assumptions regarding norms and procedures of inquiry. Each religious tradition, for instance, can say that its scriptures are proof-texts for its theological doctrines and need not share assumptions about the viability of other traditions' scriptures, because there is no recognized feedback that forces recognition of the others. As long as people are comfortable with the

---

3. Wayne Proudfoot's *Religious Experience* has been refuted a hundred times, yet its main point holds: the perceptual data for science do not find quick analogy in any experiential data for religion. The truth in the refutations is that religious experience is not at all like that of science, albeit the methods of inquiry in science and theology bear some similarity.

shared assumptions of their local community, they can ignore, or reject arbitrarily, the assumptions of other communities. Wildman uses this point to explain how religious communities with assumptions about the world entirely at variance with secular science can coexist and flourish in a secular social environment: they simply do not take the secular scientific assumptions about norms and procedures of inquiry to bear upon religious matters, which for them have different norms and procedures. This is compatible with their accepting the scientific norms for scientific and technological matters.

Wildman distinguishes three kinds of processes of inquiry. An efficient rational process is one in which consensus arises because proposals for norms and procedures can compete, creating agreement about winners and losers. An inefficient rational process is one in which competing proposals for norms and procedures of inquiry do not produce widely accepted winners and losers. An irrational process is one in which resources for the correction of hypotheses are arbitrarily neglected.

Theology at the present time is not an efficient rational process because there is little consensus among theologians in a given tradition, let alone across traditions, or with inquirers in other relevant fields of science, art, and practice about what constitutes good cases in theology. Our inefficient rational process in theology can be made more efficient by the creation of publics within which consensus can be sought. That is the topic of the next section.

The scope of theology has to do with overcoming irrationality in Wildman's sense. The scope consists in the resources that need to be engaged for the correction of hypotheses if such resources are not to be "arbitrarily neglected." "Arbitrary" neglect is when a process of theological inquiry has assumptions shared among those in the process that justify not attending to something that might correct its hypotheses. This does not seem arbitrary to those within that local community, because their own parochial norms and procedures, to continue to use Wildman's phrase, justify the neglect. Yet from the standpoint of actually correcting the hypotheses, the process is arbitrary if it does not consider all the cases that can be made against them, or in favor of modifying them, or indeed of confirming them, from the standpoints of other norms and procedures of inquiry. Moreover, the process is arbitrarily neglectful if it does not consider the strengths and weaknesses of the other norms and procedures of inquiry.

The reason for this is that feedback has a kick to it that is not entirely tamed by already given shared assumptions within a local group about norms and procedures of inquiry. A quick review of some of the points made in earlier chapters about "correction" of theological positions or hypotheses makes this point.

Suppose that a theological position is situated within a given religious tradition, complex with a history of internal divisions, accusations of heresy, and also dialogues with competing traditions. The position can receive feedback by interpreting itself as situated particularly within that tradition, needing to give reasons justifying its differences from other positions within the tradition, from heretical positions, and relative to how the tradition has engaged others. Most particularly, the theological position can contrast its assumptions about what constitutes a good case (the norms and procedures of inquiry) with the assumptions of those others. Its own assumptions should be amended to take into account all the good in the other assumptions, carefully leaving out what is implausible in those others (based on arguments as to why that is implausible).

In our situation where each religious tradition is confronted with others (a situation that occurred frequently in the past as well), those other traditions with their core texts and motifs, their sacred canopies, and their theological types and positions constitute an apparent challenge to any one tradition. The challenge might be only apparent. S. Mark Heim has argued that the major religious traditions are compatible because they define their goals, salvations, differently. In order to know that, however, the traditions need to be compared carefully.[4] They need to be compared to know whether they in fact challenge one another, where, and how. Moreover, the comparisons need to take into account differences in the assumptions about making good cases and to adjudicate among them in order to see what is true and false in each tradition, taking differences in context into account. Comparison in all these dimensions constitutes a rich array of feedback points.

The sciences also provide feedback, of two sorts and on several levels, as discussed earlier. One sort of feedback is direct criticism of theological positions based on the assumptions of inquiry in science that need to be adjudicated with those in the theological positions in consideration. The debate within conservative Christianity about scientific evolution versus the biblical account of creation is only in part about the admission of empirical evidence. It is in larger part about the assumptions about hypothesis assertion that distinguish the two groups. No matter how much each side stomps its foot and says its assumptions are the right ones for inquiry, the very disagreement is powerful feedback that the assumptions are arbitrary on both sides unless they take into account and adjudicate one another. In order to correct its positions as much as possible, theology needs to hunt up ways in which the sciences can challenge its hypotheses.

---

4. See Heim's influential *Salvations* and also *The Depth of the Riches*. These constitute a careful beginning for comparative theology of world religions, but from a very definite Christian point of view.

The other sort of feedback theology can gain from the sciences is new perspectives and information about ultimate matters. Astrophysics nowadays is as wild and speculative as the physical cosmology of the first century, far more interesting and non-commonsensical than the cosmological notions supported in the West by the long dominance of Aristotelian thinking. Insofar as theology is interested in ultimate questions about the contingency and existence of the cosmos, science can help define the parameters of that. Another of the important questions for theology is how human beings can be at home in the cosmos. The biological sciences provide all sorts of new ways of thinking about this that were simply not conceived in the ancient world when the core texts and motifs of the great world religions were first articulated. We have causal ways of understanding people as natural beings embedded in a wider environment that need to be taken into account for theology to have good ideas about what the "home" for humanity might be. Anthropology, sociology, psychology, and to some extent economics have provided important new ways of understanding religions. Although these tend to be external and reductive to explanatory principles that exclude religious ones, they still provide much insight into the nature and practice of religion from which theology can learn.

Art provides at least two kinds of feedback. As alternatives to verbal means of expressing religious ideas and guiding practice, the arts exhibit consequences of those ideas and practices that might otherwise be unnoticed. Worship in a Gothic cathedral is different from that (perhaps it would not be called worship) in a Japanese Zen monastery: What are the significances of that difference? More powerful feedback, however, comes from the imaginative productions of the arts that provide alternative ways of grasping religious realities. The images of creative art are explosive alternatives to the images of established religious communities. Even when they work within the traditions of those communities, they can produce novel perspectives. The very existence of a theologically relevant alternative is feedback that a position's case is not closed. Art is often the avenue of expression in religious matters for people who are not well tied in to the theological conversation, especially minorities and nonverbal people.[5]

Similarly, the experience of the practical normative disciplines provides feedback that can correct theological positions. The principal issues here often have to do with the assumptions in those disciplines, compared with those in theological communities, about what counts as a test of reality. Therefore, a principal part of theology's search for correction is the

---

5. See, for instance, the subtle analyses of art in Stephen Prothero's wonderful history of popular theology *American Jesus: How the Son of God Became a National Icon.*

articulation of the differences among those assumptions and the adjudication of them in matters having to do with engaging ultimacy.

Dialectical systematic thinking provides kinds of feedback that do not readily come to mind with the empiricistic rhetoric that Wildman employs, although such thinking here derives very directly from Peirce's notions that Wildman upholds. For a theological position to find itself situated in a system reveals implications the position itself might not express. These implications are not only those that follow for what might be found in experience if the position is true; those are very important and are thoroughly empirical; Wildman calls a system "hypothetico-corrective" rather than "hypothetico-deductive" to make Peirce's point that the experiential categories following from the system need to be checked independently.[6] The implications revealed within a system also include those concerning the connection of the position with all the other modes of inquiry and disciplines, evidence points, and perspectives that are involved in making relevant cases for and against the position. This is to say, the secondary theological truths can be corrective feedback for the primary theological truths when their connections are laid out within a system.

The dialectical search for and criticism of presuppositions in systematic thinking also provides crucial feedback. This is not feedback in the sense of finding a corrective empirical observation. Nor is it feedback concerning matters of consistency and unexpected connections. Rather, it is feedback concerning the grounds of rationality itself, as laid out in the problem of the one and the many. If the presuppositions of a system do not allow for an adequate solution to the problem of the one and the many, this is a strong message that the system cannot be wholly right.

In the long run, a theological system, with the various positions articulated within it plus all the cases made for and against them, is tested by being the guide by which a community lives. The problem with this feedback is that it is so slow in coming, quite the opposite of the feedback a driver gets about interpreting the road. If practical theology is nuanced in the ways it guides religious life, paying attention to particulars and understanding how religion is a very complex system whose parts can be tested in relation to one another, practical feedback can be speeded up some. The long run feedback, however, is the most decisive of all: as the complex sign by which to engage ultimate matters, a theologically guided practice of ritual and decision making will drop out of the evolution of society if it does not accomplish engagement and deliver what is important in ultimate matters. A religion might be maintained for a while as a matter of social

6. See Wildman's "The Resilience of Religion in Secular Social Environments."

organization. But it would cease to function as a religion if it did not fill people's ultimate concerns. Of course, defining those concerns, and the norms and procedures for defining fulfillment, is a theological matter. But the consensus about them, or lack of consensus, is determined in the long run by their delivering something of appropriate value.

The argument of this section has addressed Wildman's issue of relative lack of feedback for the correction of theological matters in comparison with that in much of the natural sciences. True, the feedback is not so direct. Nevertheless, with a carefully articulated theology of the sort described here as symbolic engagement, feedback can be found in many places to correct and stabilize theological hypotheses. In the long run, that means correcting and stabilizing theological understanding by which ultimacy is engaged and internalized to define human excellence. Theology will not likely ever gain the definiteness of feedback characteristic of the natural sciences. This is no argument for abandoning the attempt to get better feedback without sacrificing attention to the ultimate matters.

Creating Publics of Appropriate Scope

If attending to the appropriate scope of theology addresses the question of the rationality of theology, creating the publics within which the scope of theology can have intellectual life addresses the question of its efficiency. The notion of an intellectual public has two related sides, the institutions and habits of intellectual work on one side, and the language and conceptuality for that work and discourse on the other.

The first point to recognize about this is that the great civilizations of the world have different institutions for theological activity, and different languages and concepts. The primary institutional context for theology in the West is the academy, including religious schools for theological education that have some ties to the academy at large. This has long been true for theological thinking in Judaism and Christianity. It is becoming true for Buddhists, Hindus, Confucians, Daoists, and other smaller religious traditions that flourish in the West. The credentials for assuming positions of theological leadership and authority are academic degrees and, often, professorial positions. Even Islam is looking to thinkers who have been educated in Western-style academies. All over the world, educational institutions are being adapted to Western standards and habits of scholarship, and some in the former colonial countries have been Westernized for centuries. Although China was never a colony of a European imperial power, its Marxist government for the last half century imposed Western institutions on the country, including educational institutions. In Western-style academies, religion and theology are pursued alongside and sometimes in connection with the study of other subjects. The interdisciplinary character of theology as called for in this book rests easy with theology as practiced within the larger academy.

By contrast, the theological traditions in Buddhism and Daoism have lived mainly in monastic settings until very recently, with a current revival of monastic theology. Prior to the eighteenth-century establishment of Western academies in India, Hinduism in its many sects was organized mainly around families, with teachers creating households for theological learning, much the way Christian theology developed up through the time of Origen. Confucianism was much the same in its domestic setting. Confucian thinkers communicated with one another mainly through the institutions of public administration. Confucianism also has long had academies as well, a tradition going back to Confucius.[7] The contexts for Islamic theology have mainly been universities, a tradition Islam inherited and developed from Greek academic antecedents, in parallel and in some considerable communication with medieval European universities. Theology in Islam has been closely allied, if not simply identical, with jurisprudence; no special effort needs to be made to connect Islamic theology to practical normative discipline—it has always been so connected. Understanding the social, institutional contexts in which theology has been practiced is nearly as important as understanding the various core texts and motifs of different religious traditions for communication among theologians of those traditions.

Because of the increasing dominance of Western-style academies across the globe, however, the discussion here will focus on academic institutions as the base for theology. The first and most obvious public for theology is a practicing religious community, or collections of such communities. This is so because theology customarily arises out of traditions of religious practice, and also because theology has its practical expression in guiding religious practice. Many academic institutions were founded as religious institutions for the training of clergy and the education of religious people as well as the contexts for theology.

Yet the nature of the contemporary academy, especially in American and European education, creates a special problem for theology to maintain living religious practice as one of its publics. Ironically, the sophistication in

---

7. See Randall Collins's *The Sociology of Philosophies: A Global Theory of Intellectual Change,* chaps. 4–7.

academic theology, even in determinedly religious institutions, makes it extremely difficult for many theologians and theological students to enter into the public of what Rowan Williams calls "celebratory theology," as discussed in chapter 1. This is especially true when the celebratory theology is popular religion rather than the fairly esoteric high-liturgical theology Williams probably had in mind. Theology trained in the academy is often embarrassed by its popular celebratory roots.[8] It helps, however, for academic theology to recognize theology as symbolic engagement. Then the academic theologians could appreciate celebratory theology as highly indexical and non-iconic, if that is what it is, and inquire carefully into whether the celebratory theology in popular religion is true in the sense of carrying across what is religiously important into the popular interpretive context. Popular religion is in deep need of sophisticated theological analysis, embedded as it is in the values of ethnicity, economics, entertainment, and the like.[9] Perhaps what the core texts and other celebratory symbols carry across in their popular interpretive use is true, and perhaps not, perhaps they are even demonic. Careful theology can offer good guidance, although getting a hearing in popular religion requires special rhetorical skills as well as the capacity to get around entrenched interests. What academic theology needs from popular religion is a grasp of the power of the symbols when they are engaged truly. Without contexts of religious practice, theology can easily back away from intentional engagements of the religious realities to extensional analyses alone; that is, it can subtly turn from studying the ultimate to studying ideas instead.

A related public for theology is the study of the history of the religious traditions of which it is a part, including their scriptures and antecedents. Most religions have insider traditions for studying and representing their own history, traditions that are often as concerned about religious-identity formation through history as about the truth of the historical representations. Because the truth about the history is important for theology, even for the sake of identity formation, the disciplinary publics for this part of theology should be the disciplines of history, anthropology, sociology, and psychology, insofar as these are faithful to the norms and procedures of their own disciplines. Part of institutionalized theological education should

8. A careful study, far more nuanced than the quick remarks here, was undertaken by Ray L. Hart of the attitudes toward various kinds of study of religion and theology in American colleges and universities. See his "Religious and Theological Studies in American Higher Education."

9. For good examples, although from very different perspectives, see William Dean's *The American Spiritual Culture* and Stephen Prothero's *American Jesus*. The first is a kind of theology of culture controlled by a very liberal theology that cannot accept any literal supernaturalism, whereas the second is cultural history that scrupulously avoids normative judgments, although it likens the Americanization of images of Jesus as indigenization to St. Paul's Hellenization of Christianity (p. 298).

be sufficient expertise in these disciplines to engage specialists in theological conversation. Cases made for theological assertions and systems need to learn whatever might be relevant from these disciplines. Theology also needs to be accountable, according to professional standards, to these disciplines, insofar as it incorporates them. Theology needs to be able to function within the disciplinary publics of these historical and social scientific disciplines, and so includes their publics within its own.

The inclusion of comparative theologies (or comparative religions, in order to understand the concrete setting of theologies) in the scope of theology is an ideal that is difficult to realize at the present time because of both conceptual and institutional problems. Comparative theology has usually been done from the standpoint of one religion, usually Christianity in the West and Hinduism in South Asia, supplying the terms and motivations for comparing the others with itself. The obvious bias in this approach has led scholars either to reject comparison or to attempt to develop neutral comparative categories. The theory of comparison discussed earlier is one promising approach to the development of comparative categories.[10] Without a field of such categories more or less agreed upon by scholars, the public for comparative discourse has no defining language. Of course, the categories can continue to be developed, amended, and supplemented, but only when the field has enough steadiness to be able to assess good and bad arguments. Comparative theology is an emerging field. The institutions for supporting this emergence need to be collaborative projects in which experts in the various religions function to correct their colleagues' interpretations of their religions and also come to see their own specialties in terms of questions brought from the other religions and specialized disciplines. The first public for comparative theology will be those theologians (including religious historians, sociologists, etc.) who engage in the collaborative projects. This public will have as its language the language that emerges through the dialogue of collaboration, and it will have as its social habits those that grow out of the collaboration. Collaborative scholars are changed by working together, dealing with issues that they do not

---

10. For a careful study of the relation of the approach defended above to other comparative approaches, see chap. 9 of my *Ultimate Realities*, "How Our Approach to Comparison Relates to Others," by Wesley J. Wildman and me. For assessment of the approaches, see chap. 9 of my *Religious Truth*, "On the Nature of Religion: Lessons We Have Learned," also by Wildman and myself; Wildman was the lead author in both chapters. See also John Berthrong's "The Idea of Categories in Historical Comparative Perspective," which is chap. 10 of *Ultimate Realities*. Perhaps the most important story in the development of a comparative public among the participants in the Comparative Religious Ideas Project is told in the appendices by Wildman to each of the three volumes (including *The Human Condition* in addition to the two mentioned here); Wildman chronicles the social and emotional development of the group as well as the intellectual debates, showing what a real concrete public is in contrast to an idealized fantasy of cooperating scholars.

have to face within their own specialties of discipline and field. In effect, the development of a collaborative comparative public is the formation through intellectual work and socialization of a new intellectual discipline. The success of the cross-cultural Comparative Religious Ideas Project, to whose members this book is dedicated, consisted in the mutual transformations of the participants to create such a public. Collaborative scholars need to be expert in the discipline they bring to the collaboration and ready to learn from the disciplines of one another. But they do not need to be practicing or believing members of the religion or theological tradition they represent.

Interfaith dialogue, by contrast, is the institution in which committed representatives of the traditions engage one another, and is also a public required for theology. Interfaith dialogue has a long and honored history in the twentieth century, and is far more advanced in building concrete publics than collaborative comparative theology. Interfaith dialogue has as its base the project of each religion explaining itself to the others and learning what the others explain of themselves; the practical motivation for interfaith dialogue has often been the peace-promoting result that comes from mutual understanding. But the real and inevitable purpose of interfaith dialogue is to get to the truth of the theological issues that the religions share and also to those that are unique to some tradition or other. Not to raise the issue of truth in interfaith dialogue is to limit the dialogue to sociological or historical reports: this is what Daoists believe, that is what Muslims believe. What is important to religious people, however, is the truth of their beliefs. If the dialogue does not take the truth issues seriously, it is not taking the religious traditions seriously. So the various dialogues between religious traditions have to develop publics with personal and social habits that build sufficient trust, as well as intellectual conceptuality, that the truth issues can be raised in the comparative context. The work of collaborative comparative scholars is presupposed in the language needed for genuine dialogue about the truth of the issues. The public for interfaith dialogue requires a Janus face for its members. On the one hand, they look back to the traditions they represent, aiming to be faithful representatives. On the other hand, they look forward to what their traditions should become as a result of the dialogue. As with comparative theology, interfaith dialogue changes its members by asking questions their traditions had not addressed before and by discovering truths, and errors, that their traditions had not addressed. With respect to their traditions, participants in interfaith dialogue creatively and incrementally alter their traditions. To be full participants in a truth-seeking interfaith theological dialogue, the members recognize that their participation could lead to such changes in their own theological ideas that they go so far as to convert.

To the extent that the publics for comparative theology and interfaith theological dialogue develop successfully, theology itself may, but need not, identify itself as the theology of each of the traditions. Instead, theology would have a religiously global public consisting of those who seek the truth about ultimate matters in religion(s).

The discussion of publics for theology so far in this section has focused on various ways in which religion itself is the resource for theology. The sciences, natural and social, are also resources or components of theology's system required for making good cases, irrespective of whether they have anything to say directly about religion. The senses in which this is so were discussed in chapter 5. The institutional publics of the sciences are different from one another and often internally incoherent and conflictual. Theology needs to be able to enter into each of these publics and make them publics for theology within which theology is accountable. To do this requires a sea change in the education of theologians, because they need to know enough of each of the sciences to be accountable within the publics of those disciplines, at least in the areas in which those disciplines deal with ultimate matters.

Changing the education and expertise of theologians is not enough, however. The scientists themselves need to learn how to welcome theological conversation and allow their disciplines to participate as a theological public. This means developing language within the scientific disciplines to express theological interests in ultimacy. Sad to say, most scientists are as unschooled in sophisticated theology as theologians are in sophisticated science. Mostly, this is a result of the narrowness required for specialization in such complex professions. But partly scientific lack of sophistication about ultimate matters comes from hostility to theology itself (and sometimes hostility to religion in general). The key to overcoming this hostility is the representation of theology as a family of modes of inquiry about truth that consist in formulating and testing theological hypotheses. This is essentially the same method used in scientific inquiry. As Wildman pointed out, theology gets much slower feedback than most scientific experiments seek, but it gets feedback nevertheless. Theology as symbolic engagement is empirical, though in some ways not shared by sciences; insofar as theology as symbolic engagement is dialectically metaphysical, it examines its own suppositions perhaps even more thoroughly than philosophy of science. The "positive" character of primary witnesses might seem arbitrary in comparison to the sciences: religious commitment to those witnesses is not the same as the relatively arbitrary scientific choice of what to study; neverthe-less, the argument of this book has shown how even primary witnesses can be made vulnerable to correction and corrected. As argued, a theologi-cally shaped religious life is itself an hypothesis about how to live in light of ultimate matters and is tested in the living of it in the long run. The development of the sciences as publics within theology, to which theology can be accountable and from which theology can learn and be corrected, depends on coming to share a common conception of inquiry, no matter how differently shaped that is by different subject matters and instru-ments of investigation.[11]

The publics that incorporate the arts within theology's public are already rather well established. Art and religion have been intertwined since prehistoric times. The academic field in Western colleges and universities of "religion and the arts" is well established, though not always in the main-stream of most theological institutions in Judaism and Christianity. "Religion and the arts" includes engagement of both creative, practicing art making and art criticism. Although artists and critics are sometimes hostile to organized religion, they generally are very sympathetic to religious themes and interests. Many artists consider their "topic" to be the same as theology's: ultimate matters. Arts, both in their practice and their criticism, already are part of theology's public. Theologians merely need to pay rele-vant attention.

The Islamic model for bringing the normative practical disciplines into theology's public (or extending theology's public to include those publics) is not possible in a situation of genuine religious pluralism. It works only where a particular theology is established. In a pluralistic situation, the reli-gious public and the publics of the normative practical disciplines are somewhat separate spheres, however much they overlap in places and inter-act with one another. The advantage to the pluralistic situation is that the externality of the spheres allows the practical normative disciplines to be external critics to the theology that arises from mainly religious resources. That jurisprudence, politics, and economic activity have their own opera-tions, with their own kinds of feedback, makes them more valuable as con-tributors to the complementing and correcting of theology concerning ultimate matters.

Ethics is in a somewhat anomalous situation because of its close tradi-tional connection with theology within religions. Ethics is often construed as part of theology. The great religious traditions have been the places in

---

11. This is the crucial point of Wildman's "The Resilience of Religion in Secular Social Environments."

which ethical issues have been debated, and one value of those traditions is to carry the sophistication of those debates into present ethical conversation. Moreover, the religions have distinctive ways of patterning ethics, basic underlying values that have been represented as shaping the religious ways of life. There are distinctive Confucian ethics, Buddhist ethics, Hindu ethics, Jewish, Christian, and Islamic ethics, each with its core texts and motifs. With all the distinctiveness, great commonality exists across religious traditions in versions of the Golden Rule, advocacy of justice and peace, and those subtle elements that have given rise in recent decades to conceptions and global codes of human rights. Nevertheless, the great ethical issues of civilization usually have advocates on all sides in just about every religious tradition. Every tradition has pacifists and also just-war advocates; every tradition has divided views on beginning-of-life issues such as abortion and end-of-life issues such as suicide. Even when a tradition has an authoritative spokesperson, such as Roman Catholicism's pope with his magisterium, the tradition also has advocates for the opposite side. The practice of ethical reasoning and social leadership is not identical with religion. It does have its own engagements of ultimate matters and thus a public of its own somewhat separate from that of theology within religion. Moreover, many ethical leaders do not identify with a religion, even if they acknowledge the religious pedigree of many of their ideas.

The key to theology's developing a public that can learn effectively from the practical normative disciplines is theology's need to give practical guidance for public life. Insofar as ultimate matters bear on how to live in a civilization whose enterprises include the practical normative disciplines, theology needs to guide religious life in those bearings. As it does so, it inevitably interacts with the affairs guided by those disciplines, and that interaction is the joint that brings them into theology's public.

These remarks about developing publics within which theology should learn and to which it should be accountable in the cases it makes for truth claims at best can be anecdotal. The observations do serve to indicate, however, that academic theology needs both to be far more interdisciplinary than it usually is and to be far more engaged outside its customary professional practice. Theology's public needs to be genuinely global in that it can learn from and be vulnerable to correction by any mode of inquiry and critical practice that deals with ultimate matters.

The importance of developing global publics having been stated, it should be said at once that no guarantee exists that they will be developed in fact. Although this is the ideal of theology as symbolic engagement and is closely tied with the claim that theology should seek the truth, not all theologies will embrace this ideal. A steady theme of this book has been that practical reasons for firming up religious identity often lead theologians to refuse corrective publics, protecting their communities from what might undermine the faith at hand and girding their loins for active resistance to some social phenomenon. The theme in response has been that matters of religious identity and community solidarity should take only short-term priority over seeking the truth, for without truth-seeking, they lose their right to make claims for normative religious identity. They can also do great practical harm if protected from the feedback of correction. The result is that the development of a global public for theology is a highly contingent and uneven matter. It might never happen. But it would be good if it did.

By Their Fruits

Truth in theology should change people so that what is important in ultimate matters is incorporated into theological interpreters in such a way that they comport themselves appropriately to what is ultimate. This should happen to the theologians themselves, and their practical theological work should guide the larger community to incorporate what is ultimately important also. That larger community includes religious communities in the specific sense of religious traditions. It also includes communities of all those people whose ways of life, including lives of inquiry in other disciplines, have dimensions on which ultimate matters bear. In the larger sense, people are religious, whether they know it or not, in every instance in which something ultimate bears on their lives. Although religions attempt to pattern or ritualize ways of life that are particularly appropriate to living in ultimate perspective, such patterns are generally compromises that do not address everyone's needs for engaging the ultimate. Along with the current rising enthusiasm for traditional religious living patterns exists an opposite rising discontent with formal religion and enthusiasm for adventurous, free spirituality. People who are "spiritual but not religious" are those for whom the formal religious patterns they know are not engaging hypotheses about what they sense to be ultimate. The creative power of the spiritually adventurous, and the implied criticism of religious social forms, is itself an important religious phenomenon. Theology is civilization's tool for making that larger sense of religion subtle, deep, and true.

A profoundly important part of being human is how people comport themselves in ultimate matters. Ultimacy has ultimately important values, as expressed partially in the finite/infinite contrasts. When people incorporate those values, grasp them in understanding, and guide their lives by them, they take on as much ultimate value as human life can bear. One of the things that makes human beings unique in the cosmos as far as we know is that they have the capacity to respond to the ultimately orienting conditions for existence as such. Theology is the vocation to reflect on ultimate matters with imagination, clear assertion of truth claims, dialectical systematic theory, and practical application to guide human comportment in the face of ultimacy.

Another way of putting this point is that theology can cultivate a special kind of religious experience. Of course, many kinds of religious experiences are claimed and cultivated—mystical experiences, out-of-body experiences, siddhis of great virtuosity, prayer and meditative experiences, and the list could go on and on. Theology helps interpret these experiences and might give some clues for telling when they are authentic. On its own, however, a theology as complex as this approach to symbolic engagement provides a complex sign or symbol by which ultimacy can be experienced in the comprehensive complexity to which the theological sign refers. Theology is the way of handling the complexity of ultimate matters and knowledge of them. If we are ready with the signs, we can perceive the complexity of ultimate matters. Chapter 3 argued that imagination enables a kind of perceptive engagement of what is external to experience. In matters of ultimacy, "externality" is a tricky metaphorical affair. Most religious traditions hold that ultimacy is as much in the inner heart as in the outer world. Nevertheless, even that internal ultimate is not experienced until it is grasped interpretively. Chapter 4 argued that critical assertion allows the reality engaged to be carried over into the interpretation and interpreters. The causal language of carryover continues the theme of perceptive experience. Chapters 5 and 6 argued that the claims in critical theological interpretive assertions about ultimacy do not come by themselves, but suppose also at least implicit cases that justify them. The working out of those cases and the systematizing of the conditions for maximally efficient vulnerability to correction gives rise to dialectical systematic theology. The dialectical theological system in turn becomes the complex sign by which ultimacy, in the complexity of ultimate matters, is interpreted, and hence experienced. Practical reason in theology is the disciplined art of living out that experience, living lives informed by what is ultimately important.

The discussion here ends with a paradox. On the one hand, theology has the capacity to give rise to an extraordinary religious experience of kataphatic and apophatic moment. On the other hand, theology as described here is obviously a collaborative effort involving many different individuals with specialties that penetrate and integrate the scope and truth of theology. No one person can do what theology as symbolic engagement requires. Does this mean that only a genuine theological community can have the extraordinary religious experience? Or can individuals within that community prism the communal understanding to their own souls? What a good theological question!

Bibliography

Adams, William Howard. 1991. *Gardens Through History: Nature Perfected.* Principal photography by Everett Scott. New York: Abbeville Press.

Ahlers, Rolf. 1989. *The Community of Freedom: Barth and Presuppositionless Theology.* New York: Peter Lang.

Allan, George. 1986. *The Importances of the Past.* Albany: State University of New York Press.

———. 1990. *The Realizations of the Future: An Inquiry into the Authority of Praxis.* Albany: State University of New York Press.

———. 2001. *The Patterns of the Present: Interpreting the Authority of Form.* Albany: State University of New York Press.

Altizer, Thomas J. J. 1993. *The Genesis of God: A Theological Genealogy.* Louisville: Westminster/John Knox.

Anderson, Douglas R. 1987. *Creativity and the Philosophy of C. S. Peirce.* Dordrecht: Martinus Nijhoff.

———. 1995. *Strands of System: The Philosophy of Charles Peirce.* West Lafayette, IN: Purdue University Press.

Aquinas, Thomas. 1259–64. *On the Truth of the Catholic Faith: Summa Contra Gentiles: Book One: God.* Translated by Anton C. Pegis. Garden City, NY: Doubleday, 1955.

Aristotle. 1941. *The Basic Works of Aristotle.* Edited by Richard McKeon. New York: Random House. All quotations from Aristotle in the present volume are from this McKeon edition.

Asad, Talal. 1993. *Genealogies of Religion: Discipline and Reasons of Power in Christianity and Islam*. Baltimore: Johns Hopkins University Press.

Ashton, Loye. 2003. *An Exploration on the Idea of Rhythm in Metaphysics and Christian Theology*. Ph.D. diss., Boston University. UMI Microform #3083818.

Asvaghosa. First or second century. *The Awakening of Faith*. Falsely attributed to Asvaghosa. Translated by Paramartha about 550 CE (from Sanskrit into Chinese). Translated by Yoshito S. Hakeda, with commentary. New York: Columbia University Press, 1967.

Augustine. 398. *Confessions*. Translated by Albert C. Outler. Philadelphia: Westminster, 1955.

Barber, Ian G. 1997. *Religion and Science: Historical and Contemporary Issues*. Rev. ed. of *Religion in an Age of Science*. San Francisco: HarperCollins.

———. 2002. *Nature, Human Nature, and God*. Minneapolis: Fortress.

Barth, Karl. 1936. *The Doctrine of the Word of God: (Prolegomena to Church Dogmatics, being Vol. I, Part I)*. Translated by G. T. Thomson. Edinburgh: T & T Clark.

———. 1957. "An Introductory Essay" to Feuerbach's *The Essence of Christianity*. Translated by James Luther Adams. See Feuerbach.

———. 1958. *Anselm: Fides Quaerens Intellectum*. Translated by Ian W. Robertson. Zurich: Evangelischer Verlag; Cleveland: Meridian Books.

———. 1959. *Dogmatics in Outline*. Translated by G. T. Tomson. New York: Harper Torchbook. Original German edition: Zollikon-Zurich: Evangelischer Verlag, 1947. Original English translation: London: SCM, 1949.

Begbie, Jeremy S. 2000. *Theology, Music and Time*. Cambridge: Cambridge University Press.

Bell, Catherine. 1997. *Ritual: Perspectives and Dimensions*. New York: Oxford University Press.

Berger, Peter L. 1967. *The Sacred Canopy: Elements of a Sociological Theory of Religion*. Garden City, NY: Doubleday.

———, and Thomas Luckmann. 1966. *The Social Construction of Reality: A Treatise in the Sociology of Knowledge*. Garden City, NY: Doubleday.

———. 1992. *A Far Glory: The Quest for Faith in an Age of Credulity*. New York: Free Press.

———. 2004. *Questions of Faith: A Skeptical Affirmation of Christianity*. Oxford: Blackwell.

Berling, Judith. 1980. *The Syncretic Religion of Lin Chao-en*. New York: Columbia University Press.

Bernstein, Richard J. 1971. *Praxis and Action: Contemporary Philosophies of Human Activity*. Philadelphia: University of Pennsylvania Press.

Berthrong, John H. 1998. *Transformations of the Confucian Way.* Boulder CO: Westview.

———. 1999. *The Divine Deli: Religious Identity in the North American Cultural Mosaic.* Maryknoll, NY: Orbis.

———. 2001. "The Idea of Categories in Historical Comparative Perspective." Pages 237–59 in *Ultimate Realities,* edited by Robert Cummings Neville. Albany: State University of New York Press.

Bloesch, Donald G. 1978. *Essentials of Evangelical Theology: Volume One: God, Authority, and Salvation.* San Francisco: HarperSanFrancisco.

Braaten, Carl E. 1992. *No Other Gospel: Christianity among the World's Religions.* Minneapolis: Fortress.

———, and Robert W. Jenson, eds. 1995. *A Map of Twentieth Century Theology: Readings from Karl Barth to Radical Pluralism.* Minneapolis: Fortress.

Bracken, Joseph A., S.J. 1991. *Society and Spirit: A Trinitarian Cosmology.* Cranbury, NJ: Associated University Presses.

———. 1995. *The Divine Matrix: Creativity as Link between East and West.* Maryknoll, NY: Orbis.

———, and Marjorie Hewitt Suchocki, eds. 1997. *Trinity in Process: A Relational Theology of God.* New York: Continuum.

———. 2001. *The One in the Many: A Contemporary Reconstruction of the God-World Relationship.* Foreword by Philip Clayton. Grand Rapids, MI: Eerdmans.

Bradbury, Malcolm, and James McFarlane, eds. 1974. *Modernism: 1890–1930.* Middlesex, UK: Penguin.

Brakke, David. 1995. *Athanasius and Asceticism.* Baltimore: Johns Hopkins University Press.

Brown, Frank Burch. 1986. *Religious Aesthetics: A Theological Study of Making and Meaning.* Princeton, NJ: Princeton University Press.

———. 2000. *Good Taste, Bad Taste, and Christian Taste: Aesthetics in Religious Life.* New York: Oxford University Press.

Browning, Don S. 1991. *A Fundamental Practical Theology: Descriptive and Strategic Proposals.* Minneapolis: Augsburg/Fortress.

Brumbaugh, Robert S. 1961. *Plato on the One.* New Haven: Yale University Press.

———. 1989. *Platonic Studies of Greek Philosophy: Form, Arts, Gadgets, and Hemlock.* Albany: State University of New York Press.

Buchler, Justus. 1939. *Charles Peirce's Empiricism.* London: Kegan Paul, Trench, Trubner & Co.

———. 1951. *Toward a General Theory of Human Judgment.* New York: Columbia University Press.

————. 1955. *Nature and Judgment*. New York: Columbia University Press.

————. 1966. *Metaphysics of Natural Complexes*. Columbia University Press.

————. 1974. *The Main of Light: On the Concept of Poetry*. New York: Oxford University Press.

Bultmann, Rudolf. 1934. *Jesus and the Word*. Translated by Louise Pettibone Smith and Erminie Huntress Lantero. New York: Scribner's, 1958.

————. 1951, 1955. *Theology of the New Testament*. 2 vols. Translated by Kendrick Grobel. New York: Scribner's.

————. 1958. *Jesus Christ and Mythology*. New York: Scribner's.

————. 1960. *Existence and Faith: Shorter Writings of Rudolf Bultmann*. Edited and translated by Schubert M. Ogden. Cleveland: World Publishing Company.

Buri, Fritz. 1985. "American Philosophy of Religion from a European Perspective: The Problem of Meaning and Being in the Theologies of Imagination and Process." Translated by Harold H. Oliver. *Journal of the American Academy of Religion* 53 (4): 651–73.

Burrell, David B. 1986. *Knowing the Unknowable God: Ibn-Sina, Maimonides, Aquinas*. Notre Dame, IN: Notre Dame University Press.

Cahoone, Lawrence E. 1988. *The Dilemma of Modernity: Philosophy, Culture, and Anti-Culture*. Albany: State University of New York Press.

————, ed. 1996. *From Modernism to Postmodernism: An Anthology*. Oxford: Blackwell.

Capps, Walter H. 1995. *Religious Studies: The Making of a Discipline*. Minneapolis: Fortress.

Carlin, Laurence. 2000. "On the Very Concept of Harmony in Leibniz." *The Review of Metaphysics* 54 (1): 99–125.

Carse, James P. 1985. *The Silence of God: Meditations on Prayer*. New York: Macmillan.

Chan, Wing-tsit, ed. and trans. 1963. *A Source Book in Chinese Philosophy*. Princeton, NJ: Princeton University Press.

Clooney, Francis X., S.J., and Hugh Nicholson. 2001. "Vedanta Desika's *Isvarapariccheda* and the Hindu Argument about Ultimate Reality." In "Ultimate Realities," edited by Robert Cummings Neville. Albany: State University of New York Press.

————. 2001. *Hindu God, Christian God: How Reason Helps Break Down the Boundaries between Religions*. New York: Oxford University Press.

Cobb, John B., Jr. 1965. *A Christian Natural Theology: Based on the Thought of Alfred North Whitehead*. Philadelphia: Westminster.

————. 1967. *The Structure of Christian Existence*. Philadelphia: Westminster.

Colapietro, Vincent M. 1989. *Peirce's Approach to the Self: A Semiotic Perspective on Human Subjectivity.* Albany: State University of New York Press.

Collins, Randall. 1998. *The Sociology of Philosophies: A Global Theory of Intellectual Change.* Cambridge, MA: Harvard University Press.

Conze, Edward. 1951. *Buddhism: Its Essence and Development.* Preface by Arthur Waley. Oxford: Bruno Cassirer Limited; New York: Harper Torchbook, 1959.

———. 1962. *Buddhist Thought in India: Three Phases of Buddhist Philosophy.* London: Allen & Unwin; Ann Arbor: University of Michigan Press, 1967.

Corrington, Robert S. 1993. *An Introduction to C. S. Peirce: Philosopher, Semiotician, and Ecstatic Naturalist.* Lanham, MD: Rowman & Littlefield.

———. 1997. *Nature's Religion.* Lanham, MD: Rowman & Littlefield.

———. 2000. *A Semiotic Theory of Theology and Philosophy.* Cambridge: Cambridge University Press.

Coward, Harold, and Toby Foshay, eds. 1992. *Derrida and Negative Theology.* Albany: State University of New York Press.

Cox, Harvey. 1965. *The Secular City.* New York: Macmillan.

———. 1984. *Religion in the Secular City: Toward a Postmodern Theology.* New York: Simon & Schuster.

Crossan, John Dominic. 1994. *Jesus: A Revolutionary Biography.* San Francisco: HarperSanFrancisco.

Cupitt, Don. 1986. *Life Lines.* London: SCM.

———. 1987. *The Long Legged Fly.* London: SCM.

Davaney, Sheila Greeve. 2000. *Pragmatic Historicism: A Theology for the Twenty-First Century.* Albany: State University of New York Press.

Deacon, Terrence W. 1997. *The Symbolic Species: The Co-Evolution of Language and the Brain.* New York: Norton.

Dean, William. 1986. *American Religious Empiricism.* Albany: State University of New York Press.

———. 1988. *History Making History: The New Historicism in American Religious Thought.* Albany: State University of New York Press.

———. 2003. *The American Spiritual Culture: And the Invention of Jazz, Football, and the Movies.* New York: Continuum.

Delza, Sophia. 1985. *T'ai-Chi Ch'uan: Body and Mind in Harmony: The Integration of Meaning and Method.* Rev. ed. Foreword by Robert Cummings Neville. Albany: State University of New York Press.

Derrida, Jacques. 1976. *Of Grammatology.* Translated by Gayatri Chakravorty Spivak. Baltimore: Johns Hopkins Press.

Deuser, Hermann. 1993. *God: Geist und Natur: Theologische Konsequenzen aus Charles S. Peirce' Religionsphilosophie*. Berlin: De Gruyter.

———. 1995. *Charles Sanders Peirce: Religionsphilosophische Schriften*. Uebersetzt unter Mitarbeit von Helmut Maassen, eingeleitet, kommentiert and herausgegeben von Hermann Deuser. Hamburg: Felix Meiner Verlag.

Dewey, John. 1916. *Essays in Experimental Logic*. Chicago: University of Chicago Press.

———. 1920. *Reconstruction in Philosophy*. New York: Henry Holt.

———. 1922. *Human Nature and Conduct*. New York: Henry Holt.

———. 1925. *Experience and Nature*. LaSalle, IL: Open Court. Vol. 1 of *John Dewey: The Later Works*, edited by JoAnn Boydston. Carbondale: Southern Illinois University Press, 1981.

———. 1934. *Art as Experience*. New York: Minton, Balch, & Co.

———. 1938. *Logic: The Theory of Inquiry*. New York: Henry Holt.

Diamond, Jared. 1999. *Guns, Germs, and Steel*. New York: Norton.

Dilworth, David A. 1989. *Philosophy in World Perspective: A Comparative Hermeneutic of Major Theories*. New Haven: Yale University Press.

Dorrien, Gary. 1995. *Soul in Society: The Making and Renewal of Social Christianity*. Minneapolis: Fortress.

———. 1997. *The Word as True Myth: Interpreting Modern Theology*. Louisville: Westminster John Knox.

———. 1998. *The Remaking of Evangelical Theology*. Louisville: Westminster John Knox.

———. 2000. *The Barthian Revolt in Modern Theology: Theology without Weapons*. Louisville: Westminster John Knox.

———. 2001. *The Making of American Liberal Theology: Imagining Progressive Religion: 1805–1900*. Louisville: Westminster John Knox.

———. 2003. *The Making of American Liberal Theology: Idealism, Realism, and Modernity: 1900–1950*. Louisville: Westminster John Knox.

Doxiadis, Constantinos A. 1963. *Architecture in Transition*. New York: Oxford University Press.

Durkheim, Emile. 1915. *The Elementary Forms of the Religious Life*. Translated by Joseph Ward Swain. London: Allen & Unwin.

Eck, Diana L. 1993. *Encountering God: A Spiritual Journey from Bozeman to Banaras*. Boston: Beacon.

———. 2001. *A New Religious America: How a "Christian Country" Has Become the World's Most Religiously Diverse Nation*. San Francisco: HarperSanFrancisco.

Eckel, Malcolm David. 1992. *To See the Buddha: A Philosopher's Quest for the Meaning of Emptiness*. New York: HarperCollins.

————, and John J. Thatamanil. 2001. "Beginningless Ignorance: A Buddhist View of the Human Condition." Pages 49–71 in *The Human Condition*, edited by Robert Cummings Neville. Albany: State University of New York Press.

————, and John J. Thatamanil. 2001. "Cooking the Last Fruit of Nihilism: Buddhist Approaches to Ultimate Reality." Pages 125–50 in *Ultimate Realities*, edited by Robert Cummings Neville. Albany: State University of New York Press.

Eco, Umberto. 1976. *A Theory of Semiotics*. Bloomington: Indiana University Press.

Eliade, Mircea. 1959. *The Sacred and the Profane: The Nature of Religion*. Translated by Willard R. Trask. New York: Harper & Row.

————. 1978. *From the Stone Age to the Eleusinian Mysteries*. Vol. 1, *A History of Religious Ideas*. Translated by Willard R. Trask. Chicago: University of Chicago Press.

————. 1982. *From Gautama Buddha to the Triumph of Christianity*. Vol. 2, *A History of Religious Ideas*. Translated by Willard R. Trask. Chicago: University of Chicago Press.

————. 1985. *From Muhammed to the Age of Reforms*. Vol. 3, *A History of Religious Ideas*. Translated by Alf Hiltebeitel and Diane Apostolos-Cappadona. Chicago: University of Chicago Press.

Engell, James. 1981. *The Creative Imagination: Enlightenment to Romanticism*. Cambridge, MA: Harvard University Press.

Eno, Robert. 1990. *The Confucian Creation of Heaven: Philosophy and the Defense of Ritual Mastery*. Albany: State University of New York Press.

Evangeliou, Christos C. 1997. *The Hellenic Philosophy: Between Europe, Asia, and Africa*. Binghamton, NY: Institute of Global Cultural Studies Press.

Fauconnier, Gilles, and Mark Turner. 2002. *The Way We Think: Conceptual Blending and the Mind's Hidden Complexities*. New York: Basic Books.

Feuerbach, Ludwig. 1957. *The Essence of Christianity*. Translated by George Eliot. With an introduction by Karl Barth, translated by James Luther Adams. New York: Harper & Brothers.

Fingarette, Herbert. 1972. *Confucius—The Secular as Sacred*. New York: Harper & Row.

Ford, Lewis S. 1978. *The Lure of God: A Biblical Background for Process Theism*. Philadelphia: Fortress.

————. 1984. *The Emergence of Whitehead's Metaphysics: 1925–1929*. Albany: State University of New York Press.

Fredriksen, Paula. 1988. *From Jesus to Christ: Origins of the New Testament Images of Jesus*. New Haven: Yale University Press.

————. 1999. *Jesus of Nazareth, King of the Jews: A Jewish Life and the Emergence of Christianity*. New York: Knopf.

Frei, Hans W. 1974. *The Eclipse of Biblical Narrative: A Study in Eighteenth and Nineteenth Century Hermeneutics*. New Haven: Yale University Press.

————. 1992. *Types of Christian Theology*. Edited by George Hunsinger and William C. Placher. New Haven: Yale University Press.

Frisina, Warren G. 2002. *The Unity of Knowledge and Action: Toward a Nonrepresentational Theory of Knowledge*. Albany: State University of New York Press.

Gill, Robin, ed. 1995. *Readings in Modern Theology: Britain and America*. Nashville: Abingdon.

Girard, Rene. 1977. *Violence and the Sacred*. Translated by Patrick Gregory. Baltimore: Johns Hopkins University Press.

Green, Garrett. 1989. *Imagining God: Theology and the Religious Imagination*. Grand Rapids, MI: Eerdmans.

Grenz, Stanley J. 1994. *Theology for the Community of God*. Nashville: Broadman & Holman.

————, and Ed. L. Miller. 1998. *Fortress Introduction to Contemporary Theologies*. Minneapolis: Fortress.

Griffin, David R. 1973. *A Process Christology*. Philadelphia: Westminster.

————. 1991. *Evil Revisited: Responses and Reconsiderations*. Albany: State University of New York Press.

————. 2001. *Reenchantment without Supernaturalism: A Process Philosophy of Religion*. Ithaca, NY: Cornell University Press.

Gross, Rita M. 1993. *Buddhism after Patriarchy: A Feminist History, Analysis, and Reconstruction of Buddhism*. Albany: State University of New York Press.

————. 1998. *Soaring and Settling: Buddhist Perspectives on Contemporary Social and Religious Issues*. New York: Continuum.

Gruenler, Royce Gordon. 1983. *The Inexhaustible God: Biblical Faith and the Challenge of Process Theism*. Grand Rapids, MI: Baker.

Gunton, Colin E. 1993. *The One, the Three and the Many: God, Creation and the Culture of Modernity*. Cambridge: Cambridge University Press.

Hadot, Pierre. 1989/1993. *Plotinus, or The Simplicity of Vision*. Translated by Michael Chase. With an introduction by Arnold I. Davidson. Chicago: University of Chicago Press.

————. 1995. *Philosophy as a Way of Life: Spiritual Exercises from Socrates to Foucault*. Edited with an introduction by Arnold I. Davidson. Translated by Michael Chase. Oxford: Blackwell.

———. 1998. *The Inner Citidel: The Meditations of Marcus Aurelius*. Translated by Michael Chase. Cambridge, MA: Harvard University Press.

———. 2002. *What Is Ancient Philosophy?* Translated by Michael Chase. Cambridge, MA: Harvard University Press.

Hall, David L. 1973. *The Civilization of Experience: A Whiteheadian Theory of Culture*. New York: Fordham University Press.

Hallman, Joseph M. 1991. *The Descent of God*. Minneapolis: Fortress.

Hansen, Chad. 1983. *Language and Logic in Ancient China*. Ann Arbor: University of Michigan Press.

———. 1992. *A Daoist Theory of Chinese Thought*. New York: Oxford University Press.

———. 1993. "Term-Belief in Action: Sentences and Terms in Early Chinese Philosophy." In *Epistemological Issues in Classical Chinese Philosophy*, edited by Hans Lenk and Gregor Paul. Albany: State University of New York Press.

Hart, Ray L. 1968. *Unfinished Man and the Imagination: Toward an Ontology and a Rhetoric of Revelation*. New York: Herder & Herder.

———. 1991. "Religious and Theological Studies in American Higher Education: A Pilot Study." *Journal of the American Academy of Religion* 59, no. 4.

Hartshorne, Charles. 1948. *The Divine Relativity*. New Haven: Yale University Press.

———. 1962. *The Logic of Perfection and Other Essays in Neoclassical Metaphysics*. LaSalle, IL: Open Court.

Harvey, David. 1990. *The Condition of Postmodernity: An Enquiry into the Origins of Cultural Change*. Oxford: Blackwell.

Harvey, Van A. 1966. *The Historian and the Believer*. New York: Macmillan.

Hauerwas, Stanley. 1981. *A Community of Character*. Notre Dame, IN: Notre Dame University Press.

———. 1997. *Wilderness Wanderings: Probing Twentieth-Century Theology and Philosophy*. Boulder, CO: Westview.

———. 2001. *With the Grain of the Universe: The Church's Witness and Natural Theology*. Grand Rapids: Brazos.

Hawking, Stephen W. 1988. *A Brief History of Time*. New York: Bantam.

Heelan, Patrick. 1983. *Space Perception and the Philosophy of Science*. Berkeley: University of California Press.

Hegel, Georg W. F. 1830. *The Logic of Hegel*. Translated by William Wallace from Hegel's *Encyclopedia of the Philosophical Sciences*, 3rd ed. 1st ed., 1817. 2nd ed., London: Oxford University Press, 1892.

————. 1840. *Reason in History*. Translated by Robert S. Hartman from Hegel's *Lectures on the Philosophy of History*, 2nd ed., edited and published by Hegel's son, Karl, from classroom lecture notes.

Heidegger, Martin. 1962. *Kant and the Problem of Metaphysics*. Translated with an introduction by James S. Churchill. Bloomington: Indiana University Press.

Heim, S. Mark. 1995. *Salvations: Truth and Difference in Religion*. Maryknoll, NY: Orbis.

————. 2001. *The Depth of the Riches: A Trinitarian Theology of Religious Ends*. Grand Rapids, MI: Eerdmans.

Hopkins, Jeffrey, ed. and trans. 1977. *Tantra in Tibet*. Tsong-Ka-Pa's *The Great Exposition of Secret Mantra*, with an introduction by His Holiness Tenzin Gyatso, the 14th Dalai Lama, with an interpretive supplement by Hopkins. London: Allen & Unwin.

Janson, H. W., with Dora Jane Janson. 1977. *History of Art: A Survey of the Major Visual Arts from the Dawn of History to the Present Day*. 2nd ed. Englewood Cliffs, NJ: Prentice-Hall.

Jeffrey, David Lyle. 2003. *Houses of the Interpreter: Reading Scripture, Reading Culture*. Waco, TX: Baylor University Press.

Kant, Immanuel. 1763. *Observations on the Feeling of the Beautiful and Sublime*. Translated by John T. Goldthwait. Berkeley: University of California Press, 1960.

————. 1781, 1787. *Critique of Pure Reason*. 2nd ed. Riga: Hartknoch. Translated by Norman Kemp Smith. London: Macmillan, 1929.

————. 1790. *The Critique of Judgement*. Translated by James Creed Meredith. Oxford: Clarendon, 1928.

Kasulis, Thomas P., and Robert Cummings Neville, eds. 1997. *The Recovery of Philosophy in America: Essays in Honor of John Edwin Smith*. Albany: State University of New York Press.

Kaufman, Gordon. 1971. *God the Problem*. Cambridge, MA: Harvard University Press.

————. 1975. *An Essay on Theological Method*. 3rd. ed. New York: Oxford University Press, 1995.

————. 1981. *The Theological Imagination: Constructing the Concept of God*. Philadelphia: Westminster.

————. 1993. *In Face of Mystery: A Constructive Theology*. Cambridge, MA: Harvard University Press.

————. 2004. *In the beginning . . . Creativity*. Minneapolis: Fortress.

Kestenbaum, Victor. 2002. *The Grace and the Severity of the Ideal: John Dewey and the Transcendent*. Chicago: University of Chicago Press.

Kohn, Livia. 1989. *Taoist Meditation and Longevity Techniques*. Ann Arbor: Center for Chinese Studies at the University of Michigan.

—. 1991. *Taoist Mystical Philosophy: The Scripture of Western Ascension*. Albany: State University of New York Press.

—. 1992. *Early Chinese Mysticism: Philosophy and Soteriology in the Taoist Tradition*. Princeton, NJ: Princeton University Press.

—. 1993. *The Taoist Experience: An Anthology*. Albany: State University of New York Press.

Konstantine, Steven, with Ninian Smart. 1991. *Christian Systematic Theology in a World Context*. Minneapolis: Fortress.

Kuhn, Thomas S. 1962. *The Structure of Scientific Revolutions*. Chicago: University of Chicago Press.

LaCugna, Catherine Mowry. 1991. *God for Us: The Trinity and Christian Life*. New York: HarperCollins.

Lindbeck, George. 1984. *The Nature of Doctrine*. Philadelphia: Westminster.

Lints, Richard. 1993. "The Postpositivist Choice: Tracy or Lindbeck?" *Journal of the American Academy of Religion* 61 (4): 655–77.

Littell, Franklin H. 2001. *Historical Atlas of Christianity*. New York: Continuum. Rev. ed. of *The Macmillan Atlas History of Christianity*. New York: Macmillan, 1976.

Machle, Edward J. 1993. *Nature and Heaven in the Xunzi: A Study of the Tian Lun*. Albany: State University of New York Press.

MacIntyre, Alasdair. 1984. *After Virtue: A Study in Moral Theory*. 2nd ed. Notre Dame, IN: University of Notre Dame Press.

Magliola, Robert. 1984. *Derrida on the Mend*. West Lafayette, IN: Purdue University Press.

Marty, Martin E., and R. Scott Appleby, eds. 1991. *Fundamentalisms Observed*. Vol. 1, The Fundamentalism Project. Chicago: University of Chicago Press.

—, eds. 1993. *Fundamentalisms and the State: Remaking Politics, Economics, and Militance*. Vol. 3, The Fundamentalism Project. Chicago: University of Chicago Press.

—, eds. 1993. *Fundamentalisms and Society: Reclaiming the Sciences, the Family, and Education*. Vol. 2, The Fundamentalism Project. Chicago: University of Chicago Press.

Mason, John R. 1993. *Reading and Responding to Mircea Eliade's* History of Religious Ideas: *The Lure of the Late Eliade*. Lewiston, NY: Edwin Mellen Press.

McFague, Sally. 1982. *Metaphorical Theology: Models of God in Religious Language*. Philadelphia: Fortress.

————. 1987. *Models of God: Theology for an Ecological, Nuclear Age.* Philadelphia: Fortress.

————. 1993. *The Body of God: An Ecological Theology.* Minneapolis: Fortress.

McGrath, Alister E. 1997. *Christian Theology: An Introduction.* 2nd ed. Oxford: Blackwell.

McIntosh, Mark A. 1998. *Mystical Theology: The Integrity of Spirituality and Theology.* Oxford: Blackwell.

Mellert, Robert B. 1975. *What Is Process Theology?* New York: Paulist Press.

Milbank, John. 1990. *Theology and Social Theory: Beyond Secular Reason.* Oxford: Blackwell.

————. 1997. *The Word Made Strange: Theology, Language, Culture.* Oxford: Blackwell.

————, Catherine Pickstock, and Graham Ward, eds. 1999. *Radical Orthodoxy.* London: Routledge.

Miller, Ed. L., and Stanley J. Grenz. 1998. *Fortress Introduction to Contemporary Theologies.* Minneapolis: Fortress.

Miller, James. 2003. *Daoism: A Short Introduction.* Oxford: One World Publications.

Moffett, Samuel Hugh. 1992. *A History of Christianity in Asia.* Vol. 1, *Beginnings to 1500.* San Francisco: HarperSanFrancisco.

Mumford, Lewis. 1961. *The City in History: Its Origins, Its Transformations, and Its Prospects.* New York: Harcourt, Brace & World.

Neville, Robert Cummings. 1967. "Intuition." *International Philosophical Quarterly* 7 (4): 556–90.

————. 1968. *God the Creator.* Chicago: Chicago University Press. Rev. ed., Albany: State University of New York Press, 1992.

————. 1980. *Creativity and God.* New York: Seabury. Repr., Albany: State University of New York Press, 1995.

————. 1981. *Reconstruction of Thinking.* Vol. 1 of *Axiology of Thinking.* Albany: State University of New York Press.

————. 1982. *The Tao and the Daimon.* Albany: State University of New York Press.

————. 1989. *Recovery of the Measure.* Vol. 2 of *Axiology of Thinking.* Albany: State University of New York Press.

————. 1992. *The Highroad around Modernism.* Albany: State University of New York Press.

————. 1995. *Normative Cultures.* Vol. 3 of *Axiology of Thinking.* Albany: State University of New York Press.

————. 1996. *The Truth of Broken Symbols.* Albany: State University of New York Press.

———, and Thomas P. Kasulis, eds. 1997. *The Recovery of Philosophy in America: Essays in Honor of John Edwin Smith*. Albany: State University of New York Press.

———. 2000. *Boston Confucianism*. Albany: State University of New York Press.

———, ed. 2001. *Religious Truth*. Albany: State University of New York Press.

———. 2001. *Symbols of Jesus: A Christology of Symbolic Engagement*. Cambridge: Cambridge University Press.

———, ed. 2001. *The Human Condition*. Albany: State University of New York Press.

———, ed. 2001. *Ultimate Realities*. Albany: State University of New York Press.

———. 2002. "Contextualization and the Non-obvious Meaning of Religious Symbols: New Dimensions to the Problem of Truth." *Neue Zeitschrift Fuer Systematische Theologie und Religionsphilosophie* 44:71–88.

———. 2004. "David Hall as a Philosopher of Culture." *China Scholarship* 4 (4): 19–31. In Chinese, under Neville's Chinese name, Nan Loshan.

Niebuhr, H. Richard. 1951. *Christ and Culture*. New York: Harper.

Oberman, Heiko A. 1984. *The Roots of Anti-Semitism: In the Age of Renaissance and Reformation*. Translated by James I. Porter. Philadelphia: Fortress.

Ogden, Schubert M. 1986. *On Theology*. San Francisco: Harper & Row.

Otto, Rudolf. 1926. *The Idea of the Holy: An Inquiry into the Non-Rational Factor in the Idea of the Divine and Its Relation to the Rational*. Translated by John W. Harvey. London: Oxford University Press.

Panikkar, Raimundo. 1989. *The Silence of God: The Answer of the Buddha*. Translated by Robert R. Barr. Maryknoll, NY: Orbis.

Pannenberg, Wolfhart. 1990. *Metaphysics and the Idea of God*. Translated by Philip Clayton. Grand Rapids, MI: Eerdmans. Original edition, *Metaphysik und Gottesgedanke*. Goettingen: Vandenhoeck & Ruprecht, 1988.

———. 1991. *Systematic Theology*. Vol. 1. Translated by Geoffrey W. Bromiley. Grand Rapids, MI: Eerdmans. Original edition, *Systematische Theologie*, band 1. Goettingen: Vandenhoeck & Ruprecht, 1988.

———. 1994. *Systematic Theology*. Vol. 2. Translated by Geoffrey W. Bromiley. Grand Rapids, MI: Eerdmans. Original edition, *Systematische Theologie*, band 2. Goettingen: Vandenhoeck & Ruprecht, 1991.

———. 1998. *Systematic Theology*. Vol. 3. Translated by Geoffrey W. Bromiley. Grand Rapids, MI: Eerdmans. Original edition, *Systematische Theologie*, band 3. Goettingen: Vandenhoeck & Ruprecht, 1993.

Park, Sung-bae. 1983. *Buddhist Faith and Sudden Enlightenment.* Albany: State University of New York Press.

Parsons, Talcott. 1961. *The Structure of Social Action.* 2nd ed. New York: Free Press.

Peirce, Charles Sanders. 1931–58. *The Collected Papers of Charles Sanders Peirce,* edited by Charles Hartshorne and Paul Weiss. Cambridge, MA: Harvard University Press. Vol. 1, 1931. Vol. 2, 1932. Vol. 5, 1934. Vol. 6, 1935. Vol. 8, edited by Arthur Burks, 1958.

Petersen, Rodney L. 2002. *Theological Literacy for the Twenty-First Century.* Grand Rapids, MI: Eerdmans.

Plato. 1961. *The Collected Dialogues of Plato, including the Letters.* Edited by Edith Hamilton and Huntington Cairns. New York: Pantheon.

Prebish, Charles S. 1979. *American Buddhism.* Belmont, CA: Wadsworth.

Prothero, Stephen. 2003. *American Jesus: How the Son of God Became a National Icon.* New York: Farrar, Straus & Giroux.

Proudfoot, Wayne. 1985. *Religious Experience.* Berkeley: University of California Press.

Queen, Christopher S. 1996. *Engaged Buddhism: Buddhist Liberation Movements in Asia.* Albany: State University of New York Press.

———, and Duncan Ryuken Williams, eds. 1999. *American Buddhism: Methods and Findings in Recent Scholarship.* Richmond, UK: Curzon.

———, ed. 2000. *Engaged Buddhism in the West.* Boston: Wisdom Press.

Radhakrishnan, Sarvepalli. 1929. *Indian Philosophy.* 2 vols. 2nd ed. London: Allen & Unwin.

———, and Charles A. Moore, eds. 1957. *A Source Book in Indian Philosophy.* Princeton, NJ: Princeton University Press.

Rahner, Karl. 1989. *Foundations of Christian Faith: An Introduction to the Idea of Christianity.* Translated by William V. Dych. New York: Crossroad.

Raju, P. T. 1985. *The Structural Depths of Indian Thought.* Albany: State University of New York Press.

Raposa, Michael L. 1989. *Peirce's Philosophy of Religion.* Bloomington: Indiana University Press.

Robinson, John A. T. *Honest to God.* London: SCM.

Roof, Wade Clark, with Bruce Greer, Mar Johnson, Andrea Leibson, Karen Loeb, and Elizabeth Souza. 1993. *A Generation of Seekers: The Spiritual Journeys of the Baby Boom Generation.* San Francisco: HarperSanFrancisco.

Rorty, Richard. 1979. *Philosophy and the Mirror of Nature.* Princeton, NJ: Princeton University Press.

Rothenberg, David. 1993. *Hand's End: Technology and the Limits of Nature.* Berkeley: University of California Press.

Ruether, Rosemary Radford. 1983. *Sexism and God-Talk: Toward a Feminist Theology.* Boston: Beacon.

Rusch, William G., ed. and trans. 1980. *The Trinitarian Controversy.* Philadelphia: Fortress.

Russell, Robert John, Nancey Murphy, and C. J. Isham, eds. 1993. *Quantum Cosmology and the Laws of Nature: Scientific Perspectives on Divine Action.* Notre Dame, IN: Notre Dame University Press.

———, Nancey Murphy, and Arthur Peacocke, eds. 1995. *Chaos and Complexity: Scientific Perspectives on Divine Action.* Notre Dame, IN: Notre Dame University Press.

———, William R. Stroeger, and Francisco J. Ayala, eds. 1998. *Evolutionary and Molecular Biology: Scientific Perspectives on Divine Action.* Notre Dame, IN: Notre Dame University Press.

———, Nancey Murphy, Theo C. Meyering, and Michael A. Arbib, eds. 1999. *Neuroscience and the Person: Scientific Perspectives on Divine Action.* Notre Dame, IN: Notre Dame University Press.

———, Philip Clayton, Kirk Wegter-McNelly, and John Polkinghorne, eds. 2001. *Quantum Mechanics: Scientific Perspectives on Divine Action.* Notre Dame, IN: Notre Dame University Press.

Said, Edward W. 1978. *Orientalism.* New York: Random House.

———. 1993. *Culture and Imperialism.* New York: Knopf.

Sanders, E. P. 1993. *The Historical Figure of Jesus.* London: Penguin.

Schleiermacher, Friedrich. 1799. *On Religion: Speeches to Its Cultured Despisers.* Translated by John Oman. Introduction by Rudolf Otto. New York: Harper, 1958.

———. 1800. *Schleiermacher's Soliloquies (The Monologen).* Translated and with an introduction and appendix by Horace Leland Friess. LaSalle, IL: Open Court, 1926; Westport, CT: Hyperion Press, 1979.

———. 1811. *A Brief Outline on the Study of Theology.* Translated by Terrence N. Tice. Atlanta: John Knox, 1977.

———. 1826. *Christmas Eve Dialogue on the Incarnation.* Translated with introduction and notes by Terrence N. Tice. Richmond, VA: John Knox, 1967. 1st ed., 1806.

———. 1830. *The Christian Faith.* 2nd ed. Edited with various translators by H. R. Mackintosh and J. S. Stewart. Edinburgh: T & T Clark, 1928.

———. 1987. *Servant of the Word: Selected Sermons of Friedrich Schleiermacher.* Translated with an introduction by Dawn De Vries. Philadelphia: Fortress.

————. 1998. *Hermeneutics and Criticism, and Other Writings.* Translated and edited by Andrew Bowie. Cambridge: Cambridge University Press. Original posthumously published in 1838 in German.

Schulkin, Jay. 1992. *The Pursuit of Inquiry.* Albany: State University of New York Press.

————. 1996. *The Delicate Balance: Decision-making, Rights, and Nature.* Lanham, MD: University Press of America.

————, and Louis A. Schmidt, eds. 1999. *Extreme Fear, Shyness, and Social Phobia: Origins, Biological Mechanisms, and Clinical Outcomes.* New York: Oxford University Press.

————. 1999. *The Neuroendrocrine Regulation of Behavior.* Cambridge: Cambridge University Press.

————. 2000. *Roots of Social Sensibility and Neural Function.* Cambridge, MA: MIT Press.

Schweitzer, Albert. 1910. *The Quest for the Historical Jesus.* New York: MacMillan.

Smart, Ninian, and Steven Konstantine. 1991. *Christian Systematic Theology in a World Context.* Minneapolis: Fortress.

Smart, Ninian. 1996. *Dimensions of the Sacred: An Anatomy of the World's Beliefs.* Berkeley: University of California Press.

Smith, John E. 1961. *Reason and God.* New Haven: Yale University Press.

————. 1978. *Purpose and Thought: The Meaning of Pragmatism.* New Haven: Yale University Press.

Smith, Wilfrid Cantwell. 1979. *Faith and Belief.* Princeton, NJ: Princeton University Press.

————. 1981. *Towards a World Theology: Faith and the Comparative History of Religion.* Philadelphia: Westminster. Rev. ed., Maryknoll, NY: Orbis, 1989.

Spinoza, Benedict. 1670. *A Theologico-Political Treatise.* Translated by R. H. M. Elwes and published with *A Political Treatise.* New York: Dover, 1951. Original translation, 1883.

Stark, Werner. 1958. *The Sociology of Knowledge.* London: Routledge & Kegan Paul.

————. 1966–67. *The Sociology of Religion: A Study of Christendom.* London: Routledge & Kegan Paul. Vol. 1, *Established Religion*, 1966. Vol. 2, *Sectarian Religion*, 1967. Vol. 3, *The Universal Church*, 1967.

Stout, Jeffrey. 2004. *Democracy and Tradition.* Princeton, NJ: Princeton University Press.

Strong, David. 1995. *Crazy Mountains: Learning from Wilderness to Weigh Technology.* Albany: State University of New York Press.

Suchocki, Marjorie Hewett. 1982. *God–Christ–Church: A Practical Guide to Process Theology*. New York: Crossroad.

———. 1988. *The End of Evil: Process Eschatology in Historical Context*. Albany: State University of New York Press.

Sykes, Stephen. 1984. *The Identity of Christianity: Theologians and the Essence of Christianity from Schleiermacher to Barth*. Philadelphia: Fortress.

Thangaraj, M. Thomas. 1994. *The Crucified Guru: An Experiment in Cross-Cultural Christology*. With a foreword by Gordon D. Kaufman. Nashville: Abingdon.

Theissen, Gerd. 1999. *A Theory of Primitive Christian Religion*. Translated by John Bowden. London: SCM.

Tillich, Paul. 1932. *The Religious Situation*. Translated by H. Richard Niebuhr. New York: Henry Holt; New York: Meridian Books, 1957.

———. 1948. *The Protestant Era*. Translated by James Luther Adams. Chicago: University of Chicago Press. Abridged edition, 1957.

———. 1951. *Systematic Theology: Volume 1*. Chicago: University of Chicago Press.

———. 1952. *The Courage to Be*. New Haven: Yale University Press.

———. 1957. *Systematic Theology: Volume 2*. Chicago: University of Chicago Press.

———. 1959. *Theology of Culture*. Edited by Robert C. Kimball. New York: Oxford University Press.

———. 1963. *Systematic Theology: Volume 3*. Chicago: University of Chicago Press.

———. 1963. *Christianity and the Encounter of the World Religions*. New York: Columbia University Press.

Toulmin, Stephen. 1972. *Human Understanding: The Collective Use and Evolution of Concepts*. Princeton, NJ: Princeton University Press.

———. 1982. *The Return to Cosmology: Postmodern Science and the Theology of Nature*. Berkeley: University of California Press.

Tracy, David. 1981. *The Analogical Imagination: Christian Theology and the Culture of Pluralism*. New York: Crossroad.

———. 1987. *Plurality and Ambiguity: Hermeneutics, Religion, Hope*. San Francisco: Harper & Row.

Troeltsch, Ernst. 1902. *The Absoluteness of Christianity*.

Tu, Wei-ming. 1978. *Humanity and Self-Cultivation: Essays in Confucian Thought*. Berkeley, CA: Lancaster-Miller. Repr., Boston: Cheng & Tsui, 1998.

———. 1985. *Confucian Thought: Selfhood As Creative Transformation*. Albany: State University of New York Press.

Van Buren, Paul M. 1980. *Discerning the Way*. Part 1 of *A Theology of the Jewish-Christian Reality*. San Francisco: Harper & Row.

———. 1983. *A Christian Theology of the People Israel*. Part 2 of *A Theology of the Jewish-Christian Reality*. San Francisco: Harper & Row.

———. 1988. *Christ in Context*. Part 3 of *A Theology of the Jewish-Christian Reality*. San Francisco: Harper & Row.

Van Ness, Peter H., ed. 1996. *Spirituality and the Secular Quest*. Vol. 22, *World Spirituality: An Encyclopedic History of the Religious Quest*. New York: Crossroad Herder.

Vaught, Carl G. 1997. "Theft and Conversion: Two Augustinian Confessions." In *The Recovery of Philosophy in America: Essays in Honor of John Edwin Smith*, edited by Robert Cummings Neville and Thomas P. Kasulis. Albany: State University of New York Press.

———. 2003. *The Journey toward God in Augustine's Confessions: Books 1–6*. Albany: State University of New York Press.

———. 2004. *Encounters with God in Augustine's Confessions: Books 7–9*. Albany: State University of New York Press.

———. 2004. *Metaphor, Analogy, and the Place of Places: Where Religion and Philosophy Meet*. Waco, TX: Baylor University Press.

Watson, Walter. 1985. *The Architectonics of Meaning: Foundations of the New Pluralism*. Albany: State University of New York Press.

Weber, Max. 1946. *From Max Weber: Essays in Sociology*. Translated, edited, and with an introduction by H. H. Gerth and C. Wright Mills. New York: Oxford University Press.

———. 1951. *The Religion of China: Confucianism and Taoism*. Translated and edited by Hans H. Gerth. New York: Free Press. Introduction by C. K. Yang in the 1961 reprint.

———. 1951. *The Protestant Ethic and the Spirit of Capitalism*. Translated by Talcott Parsons. Foreword by R. H. Tawney. New York: Scribner's.

Weiss, Paul. 1961. *The World of Art*. Carbondale: Southern Illinois University Press.

———. 1961. *Nine Basic Arts*. Carbondale: Southern Illinois University Press.

———. 1969. *Sport: A Philosophic Inquiry*. Carbondale: Southern Illinois University Press.

———. 1975. *Cinematics*. Carbondale: Southern Illinois University Press.

———. 1995. *Being and Other Realities*. Chicago: Open Court.

———. 2000. *Emphatics*. Nashville: Vanderbilt University Press.

———. 2001. *Surrogates*. Nashville: Vanderbilt University Press.

Weissman, David. 1987. *Intuition and Ideality*. Albany: State University of New York Press.

———. 1989. *Hypothesis and the Spiral of Reflection*. Albany: State University of New York Press.

———. 1993. *Truth's Debt to Value*. New Haven: Yale University Press.

Whitehead, Alfred North. 1927. *Symbolism: Its Meaning and Effect*. New York: Macmillan. Repr., New York: Fordham University Press, 1985.

———. 1929. *Process and Reality*. New York: Macmillan. Corrected edition by Donald Sherburne and David Ray Griffin, New York: Free Press, 1978.

———. 1929. *The Function of Reason*. Princeton, NJ: Princeton University Press.

———. 1933. *Adventures of Ideas*. New York: Macmillan.

———. 1938. *Modes of Thought*. New York: Macmillan.

Wildman, Wesley J. 1998. *Fidelity with Plausibility: Modest Christologies in the Twentieth Century*. Albany: State University of New York Press.

———. 1999. "Natural Law Revisited: The Use and Abuse of Genetic Technologies." *American Journal of Theology and Philosophy* 20, no. 2.

———. 2002. "Theological Literacy: Problem and Promise." In *Theological Education*, edited by Rodney Petersen. Grand Rapids: Eerdmans.

———. 2004. "The Divine Action Project, 1988–2003." *Theology and Science* 2, no. 1.

———. 2005. "The Resilience of Religion in Secular Social Environments; A Pragmatic Analysis." *Religion in Dialogue with Science: Tradition and Plural Cultures*, edited by Thomas Schmidt. Frankfurt: Mohr-Siebeck.

Williams, Rowan. 1987. *Arius: Heresy and Tradition*. London: Darton, Longman, and Todd.

———. 2000. *On Christian Theology*. Oxford: Blackwell.

Wittgenstein, Ludwig. 1922. *Tractatus Logico-philosophicus*. London: Routledge & Kegan Paul.

Wyschogrod, Edith. 1985. *Spirit in Ashes: Hegel, Heidegger, and Man-Made Mass Death*. New Haven: Yale University Press.

Xunzi. Third century BCE. *Xunzi: A Translation and Study of the Complete Works*. 3 vols. Edited with translations by John Knoblock. Stanford: Stanford University Press. Vol. 1, books 1–6 (1988). Vol. 2, books 7–16 (1990). Vol. 3, books 17–32 (1994).

Yoder, John Howard. 1984. *The Priestly Kingdom: Social Ethics as Gospel*. Notre Dame, IN: University of Notre Dame.

Young, John D. 1983. *Confucianism and Christianity: The First Encounter*. Hong Kong: Hong Kong University Press.

Index

as hypothetical, x
identity, 19–20
imaginative mode of, 43
indexical reference in, 38–39, 132
kataphasis in, 176, 177–78
metaphysics in, 128
natural, 12
naturalistic philosophical, xvi, 56
nature of truth in, 35
neoplatonic theories in, 113
paradox/absurdity in, 16
philosophy vs., xii, 8
practical normative disciplines in,
    123–26, 192–93
Protestant biblicizing of, 110–11
role in shaping ritual patterns,
    168–69
science feedback in, 191–92
science relation to, 113
scope of, 2–4, 181–204
as specific traditions, 26–27
symbols in, 169
Tillich on, 7
truth in, 29, 35–40, 49, 181–204
ultimacy in, 5–7, 66–67, 176–77
vagueness in, 13
Yale School of, 16–18
theology, approaches to, 1–28
    history in, 7–13
    religious identity in, 13–20
    revelation in, 13–20
    theology publics in, 20–28
    ultimacy in, 5–7
theology, as symbolic engagement,
    29–53, 132, 199–200
    content meaning in, 84, 85
    context in, 49–53
    engagement in, 29, 31–35
    metaphysics in, 140–42
    modes of symbolic engagement,
        40–49
    network meaning in, 85
    reason for, 90
    religion as primary source for, 108–9
    semiotic theory in, 152
    truth in, 29, 35–40, 49–53
    in ultimate matters with symbols,
        169
theology, in history, 7–13

comparative/apologetic, 9–10
Deism, 11, 87
European Reformation, 9
modernism, 4, 10, 12
natural, 11
philosophy vs., 8–9
Protestant Reformation, 8
Roman Catholic Counter-
    Reformation, 9
Theology, Music and Time (Begbie),
    43n. 21, 115n. 18
Theology of the Community of God
    (Grenz), 8n. 9
theology, public
    assessment element in, 3
    audience element in, 2
    celebratory theology by Williams,
        22–23
    communicative by Williams, 23–24
    critical style of by Williams, 24–25
    dialogue element in, 3
    fundamental theology by Tracy,
        20–21
    practical element in, 3
    religious community in, 25–26
    systematic theology by Tracy, 20
    theology approaches to, 20–28
theoretical representation, in compari-
    son, 106, 146
theoria (theory), 128
theorizing, in theological systems, 1, 40,
    152
theory, 127–28
    dialectic systematic, 135–36
    to stabilize discussions, 138
Thomism, 112
Tillich, Paul, xvii, 6, 7, 12, 21, 25–26,
    117, 177
    "ultimate concern" by, 6
Toulmin, Stephen, xiin. 2
Toward a World Theology (Smith), 103n. 3
Tracy, David, 56
    on fundamental theology, 20–21
    on public theology, 20–21
    on systematic theology, 20
traditions, 185
    core text/motif in, 131, 140
    history of religious, 196–97